THE WINE ALMANAC

The WINE ALMANAC

Rosalind Cooper

MICHAEL JOSEPH LONDON

First published in Great Britain by Michael Joseph Ltd
27 Wrights Lane, London W8
1986

Typeset by Goodfellow & Egan, French's Road, Cambridge
Printed and bound by Hazell, Watson & Viney Ltd., Aylesbury

British Library Cataloguing in Publication Data
Cooper, Rosalind
The wine almanac.
1. Wine and wine making
I. Title
641.2'2   TP548
ISBN 0–7181–2735–8

CONTENTS

ACKNOWLEDGEMENTS

My gratitude goes to all the following writers on wine and food, who have inspired parts of this book, provided the basis for recipes or been reliable sources for hard facts: Burton Anderson (on Italian wines); Simone Beck, known as 'Simca', one of the best writers on French food; Clement Freud, for his immensely practical menus; the Gault-Millau guides on food and wine for their informative and witty analyses; Hugh Johnson; Alexis Lichine; Tony Lord (on Australia); Marc and Kim Millon (for their research on the wine and food of Europe); David Peppercorn (on Bordeaux); George Robertson (on port); George Saintsbury.

I should also like to thank Barbara and Tony Laithwaite, Tim Bleach and all the Wine Club staff for their assistance with both words and pictures, and especially for organising vineyard visits. Naturally I should also like to mention my husband Aldwyn, the patient Professor, and my rather less patient children Theodore, Zoe and the one as yet unborn.

The Author and Publishers would like to thank the following for permission to reproduce pictures on the following pages:

Australian Information Service, 65; Austrian Trade Commission, 67; Konrad Baeschlin, Camera Press, 109; Anthony Blake Photo Library, 122; Mike Busselle's Photo Library, 126; Camera di Commercio di Asti, 135; The Champagne Bureau, 3, 19, 51, 92, 113, 114, 166; Château Prieuré-Lichine, 127; Château Simone, 146; Château Vignelaure, 147; Raymond Charpentier, Dijon, 160; Hans Crusius and Son, 87; James Davis Photography, 108, 173, 177; José Luis Dias, 17; Patrick Eagar, 104, 151, 159, 174, 175 (left); Food and Wine from France, 89, 98, 125; French Government Tourist Office, 46, 53, 141, 158; German Wine Information Bureau, 83; Michael Guillard, Agence Scope, 124, 128 (top left); Robert Harding Picture Library, 30, 56; Denis Hughes-Gilbey, 2, 11, 21, 39, 47, 112, 121, 152; Leeds Castle Foundation, 72; Jorge Lewinski, 60; Moët et Chandon (London), 35, 37, 96; Tony Mott, 90; Bruno Paillard, 101; The Photo Source, 5, 118; Picture Index Ltd, 77, 79; Portuguese National Tourist Office, 13 (top right); Mr David Simmonds, Melbourne, 175 (top right); Tony Stone Associates, 13 (bottom left, bottom right), 23, 28, 69; Syndication International,

106; Venice Simplon-Orient-Express Photo Library, 62, 63 (top); Westbury Farm, 71; Micky White, 131; The Wine Club, 32, 33, 48, 63 (bottom right), 64, 73, 100, 101, 110, 129, 128 (bottom left), 149, 161.

The maps of the different areas are by Peter McClure. The line drawings are by Anne Ormerod.

JANUARY

The coming of a new year to the vineyards is not really a turning point for the winegrower because the 'wine year' rather begins with the vintage and the making of the new wine, all the excitement and agitation of creation during September, October and November. Then just before Christmas comes the time to start pruning the vines and this hard labour continues into February, through the iciest months of the year.

Of course the very first wines of any vintage are released even before the year turns. Beaujolais Nouveau, Vino Novello, Muscadet Nouveau and even New Zinfandel are all bottled and sold before Christmas as fresh and fruity young wines with the savour of an alcoholic fruit juice. But it is in January that the sampling of a full-blooded red or white wine may commence and the winemaker will invite friends and business associates to assess the young wines as they develop in cask, vat or giant steel tank.

On the basis of this sampling many fledgling wines will go forward for blending in the months to come. With the exception of certain areas such as Burgundy, the northern Rhône Valley and others which make 'varietal' wine, including Australia and California, a very high proportion of the world's wines are blends. Contrary to the popular view of a blend, some of the finest wines are the product of skilful blending; take fine claret, for example (see *September*). The art of the blender is forged over many years, even generations, and it may have to meet all types of different requirements. In certain areas such as Champagne, the purpose of the blend is to maintain a particular style from year to year. In others, the blend reflects the characteristics of an individual vintage: in Bordeaux, for example, an 'assemblage' of the recognised grape varieties is made according to tradition and to the weather conditions at the vintage. If the Cabernet Sauvignon has performed poorly in that particular year, then the blender might have to add more Merlot grapes within certain limits laid down by fine wine regulations.

For table wines, of course, there is more latitude and a blend is made according to consumer requirements. If the vintage has been poor, then

'This bread I break was once the oat,
This wine upon a foreign tree
Plunged in its fruit'
DYLAN THOMAS

wine from previous years may be added; alternatively the blend may be improved with small amounts of perfectly legal flavourings such as citric acid or concentrated grape juice.

It is convenient to blend wines when the weather is cool outside because low temperatures mean that the wine will be easy to handle, unlikely to begin a new fermentation or chemical change. A second fermentation is very common after the first which transforms the sugar to alcohol. This is often described as the malolactic fermentation as the malic (appley) acid is broken down into a softer lactic (milky) acid. (See *September* for a more detailed explanation.) The end result is a smoother wine and one more likely to behave itself once bottled. Secondary fermentation of this type may begin directly after the first, or may start up after the cold weather, after the blending of various vats. Most winemakers have no objection to this taking place as the wine is usually improved, but if it has been made with grapes grown in a hot climate then the adjustment in acidity may be too noticeable and mean the wine is soft-tasting – 'flabby' as it is known in the trade. In this case the winemaker will add sulphur dioxide (SO_2) to avoid secondary fermentation occurring.

So the month of January sees the start of activity in the cellar, the making of plans for the new wine. Some will be sold in the year to come, notably the white and rosé styles; the rest will be laid down in cask or bottle for a period of ageing which may be months or years. Wines which have gone through all these stages are now ready for bottling and labelling – the cold weather is an ideal time for these essential activities, although shipment has to be delayed if conditions are very icy. Wine can deteriorate while waiting on a frozen quayside, quickly negating all the effort which has gone into its production.

In the vineyard itself, pruning can be a very slow and laborious process. Each vine must be dealt with separately: most of the growth from the previous year is trimmed back leaving only one or two shoots to develop during the months to come. Such radical cutting back is essential to maintain quality in the grapes produced. If the wine is officially classified as a top-quality style – eg, Appellation Contrôlée or Denominazione di Origine Controllata – then pruning standards are also laid down.

Yet all this work does have some lighter moments. In France this is the season of the St Vincent festivities. After the overeating of the reveillon on New Year's Eve (St Sylvestre) comes the celebration of the patron saint of wine on 22 January (in certain districts the Saturday prior to this date is the important day).

In various districts in Bordeaux, including the Médoc and the Graves, in Burgundy and in Champagne as well as the Loire Valley,

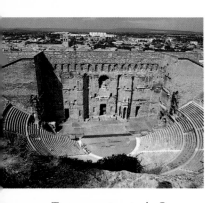

Taste new wines in the Roman surrounds of Orange

there are special masses organised in honour of the new wine, and after it has been blessed samples are carried in procession through the streets. Banquets are arranged and there is singing and folk dancing to end the day. In the little Loire village of Vouvray there is a wine festival held on 14–16 January and another in Angers at about the same time. The local châteaux are at their most impressive in this frozen season with the formal gardens a sculpture in frost. And moving further south to the warmer climes of Provence, the weekend closest to St Vincent is the occasion for a special tasting of new wines held in the grotto of the Roman amphitheatre at Orange.

St Vincent festivities

Other countries may have fewer formal celebrations but the new wine does not go unrecognised. In Austria the small wine bars called *Heurigen* are centres for sampling the fresh green-tasting young wine direct from the cask, and of course winegrowers everywhere enjoy any opportunity to show their wines to visitors with an educated interest.

WINE AS AN INVESTMENT

With the arrival of a New Year comes an inevitable look forward and perhaps a review of life in general. Relating this to wine, this is an appropriate moment to review your own cellar, if you have one, and to take stock of wines you may have bought as an investment. This concept may sound rather grand, yet investment in wine can be a very sensible and enjoyable way of using spare funds. And where once wine investment was seen as a game for the professional – with the possible exception of the odd case of port for a grandchild's birthday – today any amateur can go to auction or to a wine merchant and buy wines which are bound to increase in value.

There are two ways of playing the investment game. You may choose to keep the wines you buy until they are fully mature and ready to drink, by which time you will be able to realise a good price for them at auction or in a private sale to another collector or perhaps a restaurant. With this profit in mind you can gain in two directions – sell some of the wine and drink the rest – but of course all this involves considerable patience.

Alternatively, you may go into wine 'futures' – buying very young wines direct from the cellar and keeping them for no more than three years, then exchanging them for younger bottles and making a tidy profit in the process. This is a strategy for the purist as you may never even see the wine you own, yet any profit can go towards the purchase of wine to drink at home every day.

So, which wines are you to choose? Obviously your purse will dictate your choice to some extent, but it is worth buying the most famous name you can manage, providing the vintage is a reliable one. Take advice on all sides, using your wine merchant and the major auction houses (see Appendix 00). Attend tastings and listen to wine gossip, ask about release dates for fine wines and how to buy 'en primeur'.

The safest styles to go for are the top clarets. Any fine red Bordeaux which is classified in the 1855 listing will prove its worth over the years, but try to acquire a name you have seen on wine lists and auction tables rather than a wine from one of the more obscure châteaux, some of which are not absolutely consistent in quality. If you subscribe to an auctioneer's mailing list you will soon learn which wines are most popular.

Beyond claret there is vintage port, a fairly long-term investment as ten years must elapse before it even begins to realise a good price at auction. But it is relatively inexpensive to buy when young, and demand is steady thanks to all those traditional clubs and restaurants in this country. Notable shippers include Cockburn, Croft, Dow, Quinta da Noval, Sandeman, Taylor and Warre. Those with a Portuguese name may be excellent in quality yet somehow never realise as much over the years as the familiar English names. And remember it is only *vintage* port you should buy, not tawny or late-bottled; those are for home consumption only.

Beyond this tried and trusted wine selection you should tread warily. Burgundy is now so pricey to buy *en primeur* that it makes subsequent profits look uncertain, and many buyers are now suspicious of quality. Also you need specialist knowledge of shippers to be sure of success. Other French wine regions have very little investment potential, with

The traditional cellar – Berry Bros & Rudd in London

certain exceptions such as fine red Rhône wines (eg, Côte Rôtie, Châteauneuf-du-Pape) and the rare white wines of this area (eg, Château-Grillet, white Hermitage).

White wines in general are to be avoided, unless your budget runs to the very finest and sweetest such as Château d'Yquem or Schloss Johannisberg Trockenbeerenauslese. German wines represent marvellous value relative to quality at auction; a Kabinett or Spätlese wine is often underpriced. But do not make the mistake of thinking that you might resell these wines at a profit – fairly few people appreciate the difference between an ordinary German Qualitätswein and a QmP (Qualitätswein mit Prädikat), and fewer still are willing to pay the true market value of the latter.

Buying Ahead
If you plan to purchase some wine at source and keep it there until it can be resold, consult a reliable wine merchant. If the wine is mainly for personal drinking then go for the bargain, such as a *cru bourgeois* claret, as opposed to one of the big names. But if you are looking for a cash return on your investment, stick to familiar names. Even the most notable wines have to be better value when first released than later in the day, although the great problem for the amateur is to obtain wines like these. Production from a great château or estate is never substantial, due to the immense attention to detail given to a great wine, so rationing has had to be introduced – sharing the wine between Britain, the USA, Japan and all the other collectors, investors and drinkers all over the world! Befriend your wine merchant and make sure he realises you are serious about forward buying.

In the first instance you will commit yourself to a certain number of cases and pay a deposit of between twenty and fifty per cent. The balance will be due when the wine is shipped to you, plus duty and VAT charges. If you plan to resell and reinvest this can be done in Bordeaux after two years have elapsed, but you must ensure your wine is not accidentally despatched to you, otherwise you will be liable for customs duties when it arrives in the country.

All of this may sound intimidating, and it can be complex. Forward buying in particular can pose problems. You must be very careful to deal only with a reputable broker and you will have to calculate all your extra expenses at the time of shipment, as well as delivery to your home when it arrives or payment of storage charges. One answer is to hand over responsibility to your wine merchant; the other is to start on a very small scale, committing yourself to just one or two cases of a well-known wine you have *tasted*. Keep both for a year or two, then sell one and drink the other.

ENTERTAINING

WINTER FORTIFICATIONS: FORTIFIED WINES

Chill winter weather often means a retreat indoors and a search for something warming to drink by the fire. After spending time out in the snow and ice the thought of, say, a cool crisp white Muscadet somehow lacks charm. Even a good sturdy red wine might seem lacking in body at such moments. The best answer has to be wine with something extra – fortified wine to be precise.

The concept of a fortified wine has overtones of the medicinal; these are the wines our ancestors sipped or swigged in days before central heating and fitted carpets. Many an English cold has been warded off with the aid of a good glass of port or sherry. But make no mistake – these are not simply tonic wines concocted from grape juices, sugar and spirit; the making of a true fortified wine requires at least as much art as any fine table wine. Sadly, the glory days of Madeira, Málaga and Marsala are now history. But this is all to the good: such fortified wines as still exist are remarkable value.

In the days of long sea voyages wines used to spend long periods on board ship before the eventual consumer sampled them. This often meant that while the wine was perfectly palatable when it set out, it was remarkably unappealing on arrival. Those days or months of varying temperatures and constant movement led to oxidation and chemical change in the wine resulting in a sour taste.

Most wine was shipped in wooden casks and the sailors noted how some of it took on a 'burnt' taste. This is the origin of the word brandy – *brandewijn* or burnt wine. The 'burnt wine' was found to keep well, although the taste still left something to be desired. One solution was to heat wine to the point where it began to evaporate. Once condensed, it became a primitive brandy. This raw product of distillation benefited from keeping in wooden casks and even from sea voyages.

But this did not solve the problem of transporting table wine whose alcohol level was too low for it to survive a long journey. The British came up with an answer early in the eighteenth century when the signing of an important trade treaty with the Portuguese (the Methuen Treaty, 1703) meant that French wines would in future be challenged by newcomers from Portugal. This was considered quite acceptable as French-British relations were uneasy at the time, but the problem was the quality of the alternative. It was decided to experiment by adding grape brandy to ordinary Portuguese *consumo* wine so that it would have improved keeping qualities. This new idea also brought other benefits. The addition of brandy during fermentation curbed the action of the yeast so that the wine tasted quite sweet and was naturally also higher in alcohol. This style of rich wine was soon to become a British favourite.

Styles of Fortified Wine

PORT Today port is available in many versions, ranging from the humble pub ruby, aged briefly in wood then blended and bottled, to the subtle tawny, which has seen quite a long period in wood and hence has a pale golden colour and a genteel, faded flavour, to the hefty, mouth-filling vintage ports which are not made every year and need at least ten years in the cellar once they are bottled (two years after the vintage). Finally there are hybrids developed to please certain tastes such as the late-bottled vintage (LBV), sounding like part of a cricket commentary, which all dates from one year but can be sold sooner than the vintage varieties; and crusted port, a blend that throws an impressive sediment once decanted.

MADEIRA Madeira is also made under the Portuguese flag and also derives from the days of sailing vessels. On long voyages to the East Indies it was discovered that the casks of Madeira wine were much improved by being exposed to the sun, so they were often used as ballast on ships heading off to fetch cargoes of spices and other exotica. This effect of natural heat was then artificially created in Madeira using a specially heated room called an *estufa*. The resulting 'baked' wine was also fortified with grape brandy and sometimes aged in bottle for many decades before drinking. Madeira was the great favourite of the early American gentry in the eighteenth century and of course became the excuse for that famous phrase in Britain, 'I must have one by eleven, else I'll have eleven by one', referring to the practice of offering a glass of Madeira and some plain (or Madeira) cake at around eleven in the morning. A very civilised custom that might bear revival.

SHERRY Sherry has its place in the sun too. The so-called *solera* system uses the very word (in Spanish) to remind the drinker that this full-flavoured wine has been stored in barrels which have been warmed by the sun. Sherry is only drawn off from the bottom layer; the other layers are subsequently and regularly topped up with a subtle blend of wines (already fortified) so that some of the sherry which is drawn from the bottom may well be quite old. The Tio Pepe *solera* for instance was started about a century ago and traces of that ancient wine will still remain in the barrels.

   The flavour of sherry comes not only from sun, wine, brandy and wood but also from a curious floating yeast which forms daisy-like patterns on the surface of certain barrels during fermentation; this is called *flor* (flower). It gives a sharp pungency to sherry and is most noticeable in fino, which is not actually fortified when consumed in Spain. The sweeter varieties, which mask the taste of the *flor*, are fortified to suit the demands of the export market.

Rest assured that the sherries sold in Britain are normally fortified (just check the alcohol content if you are not certain – it will be around 18–20°). Fino is the lightest style, very dry on the palate and pale in colour. Amontillado is a fino which has been aged in wood for some time and also has added sweetness. An oloroso has not developed *flor* so has less sharpness and is full and round, although not always very sweet. In fact the flavour of a dry oloroso (quite a rare creature) has a curious hint of burnt rubber. Sweeter olorosos may be referred to as amorosos or, if very rich, they are cream sherries, the most popular commercial style in the world.

New variations of sherry include a pale cream which has had its colour quite literally 'bleached' away by a special process designed to give it a light appearance yet at the same time retaining its rich taste, and the latest cocktail sherries which are low in alcohol and intended as mixers. Finally there are two extremes of character: the bone-dry, salty manzanilla which is a fino made by the sea, and the nutty dark sweet brown sherry which is now quite rare but once graced many a vicarage table.

MARSALA This is a relation of sherry in style, although it has a shorter history; sherry was the 'sack' of Shakespeare's plays. ('If sack and sugar be a fault, God help the wicked!' *King Henry IV, Part II.*) An Englishman named John Woodhouse, who lived in Sicily for a while, was responsible for turning the production of Marsala into a commercial venture and this sweet, rich wine was stocked by Nelson and contributed to his victories in the following decades. There are various grades of Marsala named *fine* (very sweet); *superiore* (caramel in taste); *vergine* (something like a dry oloroso); and several *speciali* including Marsala flavoured with eggs, coffee or bitter almond extract. This last smells like cyanide and seems a rather appropriate creation from the home of the Mafia. A great deal of Marsala is used in cooking, for *sauce Madère* and for the light dessert made with egg yolks called zabaglione. The Germans love it and import a great deal.

OTHER FORTIFIEDS There are quite a few wines made with the Muscat grape which have brandy added to them. These may be called Moscato in Italy or California. In France such sweet Muscat wines are often known as *vins doux naturels*, though they are not entirely natural as the brandy is added to give a richer flavour and more sweetness. Examples are Banyuls, Muscat de Beaumes de Venise (which tastes of fresh apricots) and Muscat de Frontignan. The French sip these southern wines as apéritifs, well-chilled.

The Portuguese version of this wine is Moscatel de Setúbal, named for its grape variety. This rich dark concentrate has been aged in wood for at least four years.

In Spain there is Malaga, another historic old wine made in a range of styles, strangely at odds with its area of production which is only a short drive from the garish delights of the Costa del Sol.

It is important to note that not every rich sweet wine is necessarily fortified and not every Muscat is sweet. In Alsace, for example, they make a bone-dry light white Muscat which is delicious with fish or the local onion tart. It may even remind you of Muscadet – but that confusion is another story (see the section on Wine Blurb in *May* for further help with confusing names). And be careful not to imagine that a wine like Sauternes is fortified – all that full flavour comes from the sweetness of the grapes alone.

FOOD OF SUBSTANCE

The rich fortified wines of winter have a role in entertaining too. Mention has been made of how Madeira and Marsala are used for sauces and puddings, but maybe you have not considered serving wines like this with a meal.

It is possible to plan a menu which includes a different fortified wine with every course. The range of styles available for sherry, Madeira and port means that you can choose to stay with just one type of fortified wine from hors d'œuvre to dessert. For instance, when visiting Portugal you may be offered white port with ice or tonic water as an apéritif; then more white port with a fish course and tawny port with pudding. Alternatively, the meal might end in classic gentlemen's club fashion with a glass or two of vintage port accompanied by cheese and walnuts.

If you are serving sherry, the evening could begin with a glass of fino or manzanilla as an apéritif, followed by a light dry oloroso with clear soup and a game main course such as pheasant; the conclusion would be a cream or brown sherry with nuts and fruit.

Madeira is available in light versions such as the attractively-named Rainwater which you might offer as an apéritif; then another light wine such as Verdelho could appropriately accompany a pâté; next might come a veal dish with more Verdelho or Sercial; finally a choice of cheese or fruit with sweet Bual. Malmsey is so rich that only nuts or very plain Madeira cake should be served with it.

Insulating Menus Without going so far as basing a meal on fortified wine, here are some suggestions using it both in the kitchen and on the table:

MENU

Apéritif: Fino sherry served with smoked almonds/olives.

*

Crème à la Vierge (turnip soup) with more fino or a light white wine such as Mâcon Blanc or Soave.

*

Jambon d'York braisé au Madère (York ham braised in sweet Madeira such as Bual or Malmsey) with a choice of Madeira or a full red wine such as a Burgundy or a Rioja.

*

Cheese with more of the red wine.

*

Zabaglione served with a glass of Marsala or a festive glass of sparkling wine such as Asti Spumante.

Apéritif: White port with tonic or soda water, ice and lemon, served with *tapas*, delicate Spanish appetisers such as fried squid rings, stuffed eggs and marinated mushrooms.

*

Cassoulet (a dish made with haricot beans and various meats including goose) or Alubias (a Spanish version including spiced sausage, *chorizo*) accompanied by a dry oloroso sherry or red Rioja wine.

*

Winter Salad (eg, coleslaw or waldorf salad) served without wine to cleanse the palate.

*

Mont Blanc (a mound of chestnut purée with cream and brandy) with a fortified Muscat wine or a medium Madeira such as Sercial.

Cassoulet – warming and spicy

The Ultimate Winter Diet
This is not recommended by the medical profession but no doubt your wine merchant would approve – and followed for a short period (no more than 7 days) it really does guarantee weight loss.

Breakfast: Porridge (made with skimmed milk to reduce calories), fruit juice and coffee or tea.
Lunch: A winter salad with hard-boiled egg(s) or a warm goat cheese (*salade tiède* in the French style) or braised chicken livers, plus one glass of red wine and mineral water.
Supper: One medium glass of good vintage or tawny port, a few nuts of your choice, a good book and a roaring fire – nothing else. Savour this combination slowly an hour or two before bed and you will feel quite full; almost as good as eating three courses.

The Cold Cure
Try this extraordinary proposal from Noël Cossart of the well-known Madeira family – add a glass of Malmsey to a cup of hot Bovril. This is said to prevent influenza and depression, and certainly sounds more agreeable than soluble aspirin or hot milk.

The Beauty Treatment
Malmsey has yet another use which may be apocryphal; it is said to turn a drinker's red nose blue. Of course this solution may not suit every sufferer . . .

MADEIRA

If your budget does not extend to a Caribbean cruise and you like the idea of a little wine-tasting in January, where should you go? Madeira, a volcanic island with close links to Portugal, has been a winter haunt of the wealthy for many years and with good reason. It is quite extraordinarily beautiful, very green and lush with crops as varied as sugar cane, cabbages and pineapples flourishing amid the vines. The vineyards are terraced to fit the vertiginous slopes.

To the seasoned traveller Reid's Hotel is synonymous with a high standard of service and elegance. Of course there are other fine hotels on Madeira but none other that is quite so intriguing. Reid's is probably one of the few European hotels which retains something of the stately atmosphere of pre-war days. As the clientèle tends to be elderly the wearing of dinner jackets in the evening, for example, may not seem too extraordinary. With its warm swimming pools and gorgeous views over the coastline it makes a perfect refuge from the British winter.

Though the island looks lush even in January, naturally the vines are not yet in growth but this does not prevent the visitor from tasting a full range of the wines. Originally each of them was named for a particular grape but today the names are mainly associated with degrees of sweetness.

The wine trade on Madeira is based at Funchal where all the 'lodges' of the various shippers are situated. Here wines are stored until ready for shipment and the blends assembled from at least ten different wines which may be of varying ages. There are very few vintage Madeiras as the tradition is firmly set with blended wines to a particular style. A visit to a lodge is very worthwhile and can easily be arranged (see Appendix 00).

The period charm and luxury of Reid's Hotel, Madeira

Flowers and fruit grow amid the vines on Madeira

Luxuriant vegetation on Madeira

PORTUGAL

The landscape which forms the backdrop for port production is wild and stark, like the Yorkshire Moors, but with a warm climate and terraces laid to vines. So even in winter it is beautiful, even if it is a bleak beauty. Northern Portugal in general may be a shock for anyone who knows only the lazy style of the south, perhaps the Algarve. The coast near Oporto has the rugged glamour of Cornwall and even the people seem different – tough and hard-working small farmers for the most part. Houses are tiled in the Portuguese manner and lace and embroidery may be found for the souvenir hunter. But the finest souvenir has to be the product of the harsh soil – port.

The story of port is a curious monument to the enterprise of the British merchant. As long ago as the seventeenth century dauntless souls were making their way to Oporto and thence on up to the Douro to supervise the hacking of vineyards from bare rock and slate. The sheer effort of making an industry from this unpromising terrain is impressive, and especially so when one looks at the prosperity of the descendants of those men still living in Oporto today.

The 'port barons' enjoy a lifestyle which bears some relationship to that of their eighteenth- and nineteenth-century forebears and it certainly recalls the Indian Raj with its insistence on the British cricket club and even the British preparatory school. Yet these families are Portuguese-born and speak both English and Portuguese to perfection.

The homes of these fortunate few are not grand châteaux as in France but comfortable country houses with a residence in town as well for business purposes. They track the progress of their wine from the grape grown in the Upper Douro to the lodge in Oporto.

To complete the picture of British upper-class existence amid the socialist people of Portugal, there is the gentlemen's club, known as the Factory House. It was constructed as long ago as 1789 for the sole benefit of the British port merchants. No Portuguese was or is permitted to be a member and ladies may dine there by invitation only. Mrs Thatcher was a special guest in 1984.

Humbler mortals may dine there as guests of a port shipper on classic British fare with slight French overtones, accompanied by various ports and Dão wines from a little to the south of Oporto but with a full dry flavour reminiscent of unfortified port. A typical menu might consist of a beef fillet, preceded by a seafood soufflé and followed by raspberry mousse and walnuts. A dry white port might be served as an apéritif, then white and red Dão wines with the first and second courses, a chilled ten-year-old tawny port with the mousse and finally a vintage port with the walnuts.

Even after toasts to the Queen and the President of Portugal, the feast is not over. At this point all the action switches from one perfectly arranged mahogany table resplendent with Royal Worcester and silver to another identical table in the adjoining chamber. Vintage port, it is explained, must never be consumed in any room where food has been served, hence the move and the strict diet of vintage port and walnuts to close the evening. True port lovers such as the members of these old families – Robertsons, Guimaraens, Sandemans and others – sip their own vintage port very slowly and with great reverence for its age.

And even though the Georgian elegance and refinement of the Factory House with its elite membership of only some thirty or so seems an anachronism, perhaps it needs to exist as the perfect environment for a true appreciation of its own finest product.

In Portugal, the labour involved in producing any wine at all is intense, with the terraces so steep that they must be hand cultivated and each bunch of grapes carried away by human effort, not machine. And the Douro is one of the few areas left in the wine world where you may still see grapes being crushed in the time-honoured fashion – by human foot. Indeed, at some of the *quintas* the grape-treading is the occasion for quite a party, with all the locals and their English employers co-opted to join in. Sons and daughters of the port barons arrive fresh from Eton or Oxford ready to help out with this legendary and highly enjoyable aspect of the family business. Music is played on drums and pipes as the Portuguese love to dance and indeed they will entice many a vineyard visitor to join them. If you are British you are sure of a friendly welcome as ties are very strong.

So base your visit in Oporto which has a good deal to offer: views over the wide Douro with its romantic white-sailed *barcos*, once the vessels which transported the casks of port to the lodges and beyond; steep-sided streets with overhanging ancient dwellings; dark churches with gold glinting in corners; simple street markets with no aggressive 'hard sell' to the tourist; and of course the port lodges, many of which may be visited without any appointment.

To visit the lodges and perhaps gain access to one of the *quintas* (estates) found high up the twisting Douro valley, ask for an introduction from your wine merchant or contact one of the following shippers: *Cockburn Smithes & Cia Lda* (a company which still has its own cooperage making the traditional barrels known as 'pipes'); *A. Ferreira Succrs* (who organise motorboat trips on the river from May–October); *Quinta da Noval-Vinhos SARL, Sandeman & Ca Lda, Taylor, Fladgate & Yeatman-Vinhos* or *Warre & Ca Lda*.

Most of the visits arranged by Quinta da Noval-Vinhos SARL take place upriver, north of Pinhão – try the train service to get there as it makes a memorable scenic journey. And Taylor, Fladgate & Yeatman-Vinhos own some of the loveliest *quintas* in the hills including Quinta de Vargellas, but note that most of these companies offer tours on weekdays only.

If visiting Oporto be sure to look at some of the other vineyards as well.

COCKBURN SMITHES & CIA LDA,
rua D. Leonor de Freitas,
Oporto.

A. FERREIRA SUCCRS,
rua da Carvalhosa, 19,
Oporto.

QUINTA DA NOVAL-VINHOS SARL,
rua Candido dos Reis, 575,
Oporto.

SANDEMAN & CA LDA,
Largo Miguel Bombarda, 3,
Oporto.

TAYLOR, FLADGATE & YEATMAN-VINHOS,
PO Box 24,
Oporto.

WARRE & CA LDA,
Travessa do Barao de Forrester, 10,
Oporto.

Sogrape-Vinhos de
  Portugal, sarl,
rua Sa da Bandeira,
819-2-DTO,
4000 Oporto.

Most famous of all is Mateus Rosé, a multi-million industry fascinating in its combination of palaces and factories, with unparalleled working conditions for its employees. Whatever your opinion of the wines (and they do a rather good Vinho Verde called Casal Garcia) a visit is instructive.

Sociedade Agricola e
  Commercial da Quinta
  da Aveleda,
PO Box No 121,
4002 Oporto.

The palace is at Mateus itself, near Vila Real, and the winery and glass factory at Avintes. Write for an appointment to SOGRAPE-Vinhos de Portugal, SARL.

The most attractive estate making light dry Vinho Verde has to be the Quinta da Aveleda, with its eccentric English eighteenth-century garden stuffed with follies and flowering shrubs. And the wine is excellent. Contact Sociedade Agricola e Comercial da Quinta da Aveleda.

A THOROUGHLY BRITISH WINE:
Smith, Woodhouse port

'Be sometimes to your Country true,
Have once the public good in view:
Bravely despise Champagne at Court
And choose to dine at home with Port.'
      JONATHAN SWIFT

Dean Swift penned this not-very-stylish poem in the first decade of the eighteenth century, when port was first being shipped on a grand scale to Britain. At that date it was often an unfortified table wine, white or red, and quite undistinguished, as Swift admitted in a letter of similar date: 'I love white Portuguese Wine better than Claret, Champagne or Burgundy; I have a sad, vulgar appetite.'

The French certainly had a monopoly on quality at that time. The only problem was that the British were at war with them, hence the call to be patriotic and find an alternative to the enemy beverage. But relatively few English drinkers complied at first and it took a while for the fledgling port trade to establish itself. Despite heavy levies on French wine and preferential treatment for those from Portugal it was not until later in the century that these 'new' wines gained acceptance.

Of course, Portuguese wine from the Douro region was hardly new: there are records of a wine being made there with the French Pinot Noir grape as early as the eleventh century and there was a trade treaty concluded between Portugal and Britain in 1353 when Edward III agreed with Alfonso IV that the Portuguese could fish cod off the English coast in exchange for cargoes of wine, shipped in small casks and goatskins from Viana do Castelo.

The alliance with England gradually strengthened over the centuries. John of Gaunt, brother of Edward the Black Prince (who was Prince of

Aquitaine in France), in spite of his marriage to Blanche of Castile lent support to nearby Portugal when it was in danger. During the tense years of the Armada threat in the late sixteenth century there was an English consul in Portugal to protect our trading interests and the first English wine shippers became established in the region at around the same time. Trade between the two countries suddenly increased, with the Portuguese buying cured cod from the English and the English importing larger quantities of the Douro wines which were renowned for their power and ability to travel, even if not for their finesse.

There were years of unrest in Portugal during Spanish rule, until independence was agreed in 1668. This period was known as 'the captivity' and the English took advantage of Portugal's problems to seize some of her foreign colonies. Eventually, in 1662 a treaty was signed with Charles II at the time of the Restoration and on the occasion of his marriage to Catherine of Braganza, sister of the Portuguese monarch. British merchants in Portugal were given special privileges and they soon grew powerful and prosperous with dealings in wine, fish, cotton and wheat. The war between Britain and France enhanced British-Portuguese relations even further, as did the signing of the Methuen Treaty in 1703: this officially gave preferential treatment to Portuguese wines in Britain and to British textiles in Portugal.

But as Swift suggested, the wines were not inspiring and it was not long before the shippers decided to try fortifying them by adding

A timeless scene – port ageing in the Smith, Woodhouse cellars

SMITH, WOODHOUSE & CO
 LDA,
Travessa do Barao de
 Forrester,
Apartado 26,
4401 Vila Nova de Gaia
 Codex.

brandy. (It was around 1730 that port took on the style we know today.) These fortified wines needed time to mature (unlike the table wines which had preceded them) and the British merchants took over this important aspect of the trade, investing heavily in stocks to be 'laid down'.

Famous names in the port trade like Warre and Croft date back to the seventeenth century and many more were established in the decades to follow. The house of Smith for example (not yet Woodhouse) was founded in 1784 when a certain Christopher Smith, already prominent in the London wine trade and a Member of Parliament, set up offices in Oporto and London to trade in 'Douro' as port was often described then. He later became Lord Mayor of London and the company thrived: it was inherited by his sons who were joined by the brothers Woodhouse and in 1828 the firm of Smith, Woodhouse Bros & Co was born. It has made excellent port ever since.

Although the company offers a full range of ports it is especially renowned for the quality of its vintage bottlings. Their vintage wines are still made by traditional methods including the stone *lagares*, troughs used for treading the grapes. Their major estate is the Quinta de Vale Dona Maria on the north bank of the Rio Torto Valley, facing south and rated 'A' in the classification of quintas. Professor George Saintsbury's now-famous cellar book makes this reference to Smith, Woodhouse port, praise indeed – 'I don't think I ever drank – I certainly never had – a better '87 than some Smith, Woodhouse.'

To visit the Smith, Woodhouse port lodge in Vila Nova de Gaia (close to Oporto) write to Miss Bridget Bull at Smith, Woodhouse & Co Lda.

FEBRUARY

February is a month when wines may well be treated. After all, they have now been in existence for some four months and as wine is subject to all sorts of chemical change it does need a little help to stay agreeable on the palate. Our ancestors knew only too well how appalling table wines could taste when left to age 'naturally', hence the fashion in preceding centuries for either very sweet wines high in alcohol or spirits which were unlikely to alter once bottled.

In the vineyards, pruning may continue as the weather is normally still very wintry. And grafted vines are planted out to make new areas.

'Look not upon the wine when it is yellow, when the colour thereof shineth in the glass. It goeth in pleasantly; But in the end, it will bite like a snake, and will spread abroad poison . . .'
PROVERBS, 31–2

'The Germans are exceedingly fond of Rhine wines; they are put up in tall, slender bottles, and are considered a pleasant beverage. One tells them from vinegar by the label.'
MARK TWAIN,
A Tramp Abroad

'Gentlemen, do not invest your money in diarrhoea!'
THOMAS COOK

The pruner's lonely toil

As a rule, vines are at their most fruitful about eight to fifteen years after planting; they subsequently deteriorate gradually until they are between thirty and fifty years old, at which point they are unceremoniously uprooted. The vineyard is fumigated and allowed to rest for at least a year before new vines are planted. There are famous exceptions to this rule of thumb; some vines are over a hundred years old and these are often referred to as 'pre-phylloxera' vines. Perhaps the most celebrated example comes from a small area in Champagne which is the source of the rare blend, 'Vieilles Vignes', made by Bollinger.

Legends surround the flavour of wines made before the phylloxera scourge of the 1880s in Europe. Many of the vines from this time survived until the Second World War but not beyond because the sulphur-based chemicals used to treat them became in short supply. One vineyard which falls into this category is Romanée-Conti, most sought-after of all the Côtes de Nuits wines of Burgundy. It covers less than five acres and produces a wine with exceptional finesse, said to taste of violets and cherries. Like all the red Burgundy *appellations*, the variety planted is Pinot Noir.

THE HEALTH OF A VINE

When a vine is in 'good heart' it grows vigorously, responds to pruning by flowering abundantly and producing plenty of fruit and not too many leaves, and stays lush and healthy during its annual cycle.

During the year, various treatments are carried out to prevent damage by various moulds and insects and to improve the quality of the fruit. In February or March many vineyards are fertilised either with artificial compounds or with stable manure, although in some areas such as Provence and the Napa Valley of California there are 'organic' winemakers who only use grapes treated with naturally-occurring compounds. For instance, one way of nourishing the roots of the vines naturally is to grow high-nitrogen plants, such as mustard, between the rows and then plough these into the soil. And mustard flowers are much prettier than the fertiliser they use in Champagne; this curious mixture is processed from all the Paris garbage and tends to retain mysterious fragments of blue plastic which look very out of place on the Montagne de Reims.

Of course a grapegrower can rarely afford to indulge such aesthetic considerations. When an entire livelihood may be wiped out by sudden frosts or disease of the vines every precaution must be taken, and economy practised. Phylloxera is a particular hazard. This tiny louse preys on the roots and leaves of vines, forming nodules which can lead to the death of the plant. Certain vine varieties are resistant to the bug, notably the native American vines such as *Vitis labrusca*, but the European species, *Vitis vinifera*, tends to be susceptible.

Since the end of the last century every vine planted in a vineyard which has experienced phylloxera must be grafted. An American rootstock is cultivated and then the tender *vinifera* cutting is grafted on, either in a greenhouse (bench grafting) or in the vineyard. The process is similar to that used for certain modern roses, as anyone who has tried to remove a stubborn rose rootstock from a flower-bed would quickly discover – the parent is sturdier than its offspring.

After grafting, the young vines are generally planted out in the spring. Naturally this is an expensive process and places that have escaped phylloxera to date may well not opt for this course of action but this can be a mistake. Many regions in England have experienced outbreaks of phylloxera for the first time in the 1980s and this means ungrafted vines will have to be torn out. To date, no one has found a cure for the bug and there is still a substantial reward (in gold *louis d'or*) available, offered by the French authorities at the time of the first outbreak.

Phylloxera is not the only plague of vines. They have to be sprayed regularly from May onwards to avoid downy mildew (peronospora), powdery mildew (oidium) and grey mildew (*Botrytis cinerea*). All three are forms of mould but the third has the distinction of causing the so-called noble rot which gives Sauternes and Beerenauslese sweet wines their distinctive qualities. (For more details on these rare wines see *April*.)

Spraying takes place before the flowering of the vine in June, and then again as the flowers are replaced by embryonic grapes. July and August are also important months for this unromantic task carried out by men with packs on their backs, by tractor, or even by crop-spraying plane or helicopter. Copper sulphate, that blue compound familiar from school chemistry lessons, was the cause of many a blue-stained wall around a vineyard in years past, but now newer formulae have largely replaced the old 'Bordeaux Mixture'.

Sulphur is another vital ingredient, both in the battle against plant infection (particularly oidium) and in the finished wine. One interesting way of telling when a row of vines is about to succumb to one of these fungus attacks is to plant a few roses at the end: if their leaves show telltale signs of rot then the grower can act fast, as vines take longer to fall prey to moulds.

Apart from these problems, growers are on the watch for red spider mites (most insects are a problem but none as harmful as these) and larger predators such as deer which nibble the young vine shoots, rabbits which feast on leaves and grapes, and all types of birds. In

Vines noble and humble must all be sprayed against disease. At Clos de Vougeot in Burgundy they avoid too much technology

France and other countries where the Sunday huntsman with his shotgun is a familiar sight, very few of these animals are allowed to escape. The French have their own characteristic fashion of taking revenge: one prized dish in grape-growing areas is Grives aux Raisins – thrush stuffed with grapes.

English *vignerons* have softer hearts but eventually they too are forced either to spend a fortune on special fencing or to invest in the services of a hunter. In the USA they have less familiar vine enthusiasts such as gophers (burrowing rodents) and it is not unknown for a small-scale grapegrower to sit on his veranda, glass in hand, and binoculars and gun at the ready to ward off these Walt Disney-like pests.

It may be a comfort to learn that all these treatments of the vine must be completed well before the vintage so that not a trace of chemical remains on the grape skins when the fruit is picked. However, once the wine has been made it must be monitored regularly for signs of ill health.

On grape skins there are naturally occurring bacteria called acetobacter; these are the 'germs' of vinegar and they will spring into action if the wine is neglected during fermentation and subsequent storage. The resultant faint fizz and smell of vinegar is known as volatile acidity. Sulphur dioxide is the way to prevent this disaster: in small amounts it acts against these bacteria and without flavouring the wine, although if too much is added it gives the wine a sharply chemical nose, makes your eyes sting and taints the flavour. So sulphur is handled with caution, especially where a 'fine wine' is concerned. Apart from preventing bacterial spoilage it also slows down oxidation.

Oxidation really means contact with air, and this is essential for any wine which has aging potential. The contact is made through the cork or the barrel for a gradual alteration and improvement in flavour (see *October*), but the process must be regulated: if it goes too far the wine is said to have 'died', and if too fast then it is 'maderised' and a case of premature senility. The wine takes on a brownish tinge and a caramel taste – in fact, this is often the reason for a bottle being sent back in a restaurant.

Other assorted additions to certain wines include sugar, which is added *before* fermentation to increase the subsequent alcohol level; acids such as tartaric acid to preserve the wine or to raise its acidity and give a sharper taste; potassium bicarbonate to *reduce* acidity; dried blood, egg white or kaolin among other substances used to *fine* or clarify the wine; and even carbon dioxide (CO_2) to add that fizz to certain famous rosés among other popular wines.

Of course, not all of these ingredients will appear in a single wine and there is nothing particularly alarming about any of them. As 'additives' all we need to consider is whether they are overused and thus take away the individuality of a wine. Certainly very little is added to the finest wines but in these cases the *vignerons* enjoy the luxury of employing plenty of labour and devoting considerable time to the winemaking, an impossibility for the makers of everyday table wine.

CARNIVAL AND MARDI GRAS

Although there are few official wine festivals in February, this is a month for the wine lover to experience some marvellous fun in various regions of Europe. In Venice, there is the unforgettable Carnevale with masked revellers roaming the canal bridges and even purloining the gondolas, with an abundance of Soave and Valpolicella from nearby vineyards on hand. In German-speaking countries, the equivalent is Fasching, another Lenten festival featuring balls and processions, culminating in a riotous celebration on Shrove Tuesday. Then there is the Carnival in summertime Rio de Janeiro, or Mardi Gras in New Orleans . . . although neither is strictly speaking at the heart of a wine region . . .

Fasching brings warmth and wine to chill February

Nearer home, the Loire Valley has several wine festivals, including a celebration of Bourgueil (an excellent red wine) during the first week of February, the Saumur festival in the second week, and at Azay-le-Rideau in the final week of the month. So you might consider taking a winter break and combining visits to some Loire châteaux, still beautiful and romantic in winter, with a local wine festival or two (see *March* for more ideas on visiting the Loire).

ENTERTAINING

'There is no love sincerer than the love of food.'
GEORGE BERNARD SHAW, *Man and Superman*

February is a wicked month. Well, it may not be quite as amoral as August but given the double stimuli of St Valentine's Day and the cold weather outside, perhaps we are bound to seek romantic diversions. And given the prevailing temperatures, wine and food are vital ingredients in the wooing and the winning.

Is wine an aphrodisiac? Many a lover has quoted the words of Omar Khayyám about bottles of wine and thou to many an intended, but of course the number of bottles needs to be calculated with care, so that the beloved is not fast asleep at the vital moment. Who could forget the diatribe uttered by the drunken porter at the gates of the castle in *Macbeth*, full of wit and realism?

'Drink, sir, is a great provoker of three things . . . Marry, sir, nose-painting, sleep and urine. Lechery, sir, it provokes and unprovokes; it provokes the desire, but it takes away the performance.'

It seems to be agreed even by serious scientists that Champagne and other sparkling wines do act a little faster on the nervous system as the bubbles irritate the stomach lining and stimulate rapid absorption. Similarly, spirits deliver a blow to the senses far more powerful than that packed by wine, particularly when served without food and in a cocktail, which may contain up to three measures. Try a Negroni or a Stinger sometime if you want to test the effect . . .

So a combination of wine and food would seem the best approach. Certain foods such as oysters, caviare and raw steak have quite a reputation as aphrodisiacs, so the would-be lover might try a combination like this:

MENU

Apéritif: Vintage Champagne (or the best equivalent within the budget)

*

Oysters with tabasco and more Champagne.

*

Steak Tartare with a mixed salad including truffles, served with a heart-warming bottle of red Burgundy or Italian Barolo.

*

Cheese: Optional for the greedier lover, served with more red wine. Perhaps goat cheese and garlic varieties might be avoided unless you are quite sure about your partner's tastes.

*

Fresh figs, served with *fromage blanc* if you omitted the cheese course. Sip a glass of Muscat de Beaumes de Venise or more Champagne, even a dessert style if the budget extends thus far.

*

Coffee: At the discretion of the host but it could serve as an excuse for a (small) sip of cognac or fine old Calvados.

For rather obvious reasons many of the foods said to be aphrodisiacs cost a fortune. Either it's a case of supply and demand, or simply the association of expense with glamour, but it is unlikely that oysters enjoyed quite the reputation they have now in the days when they were sold on every market stall in Victoria's England.

Other ingredients for romantic success have hot spicy overtones and are obviously meant to bring a flush to the cheek – ginger, curry spices and pepper to name a few possibilities. For a second tongue-in-cheek menu, try this:

MENU

Apéritif: Vodka flavoured with pepper (the real Russian variety) or ginger wine, served over ice.

*

Mussels baked in the oven with a mixture of breadcrumbs, parsley and curry spices to taste. Serve with a pungent white wine such as Alsace Tokay, Gewürztraminer, Australian Sémillon or Bulgarian Chardonnay.

*

Salade Gourmande, based on as exotic a selection of salad ingredients as possible (radicchio and other bitter varieties if obtainable, plus nasturtium leaves and dandelion, picked very young). Mix with this some sliced pâté de foie gras from a tin or sauté fresh chicken or duck livers if you can find them. Add grilled scampi or lobster tails and very

lightly poached or fried quail's eggs. Top it all with a dressing made with wine vinegar and hazelnut or walnut oil plus a hint of thyme, fresh or dried. Go easy on the vinegar because you could serve more of the white wine. Alternatively substitute a very fruity young Beaujolais or a rosé from Provence or California.

*

Cheese: Look for a small bright orange cheese called Boulette d'Avesnes or perhaps a ripe Boursault or even some mature Stilton. Serve with a glass of late vintage port.

*

Peaches drenched in Armagnac (optional depending on the amount of port consumed).

SHERRY AND SUNSHINE: Spain

The thought of a visit to Spain in February may not perhaps seem wildly original. After all, many Britons actually buy villas there to escape the British winter, although they tend to cluster around the traditional holiday areas of the Costa Brava and Costa del Sol, some distance from Spain's finer wine regions. For a contrast, venture towards the Rioja and Jerez, where the climate is still mild and the wines marvellous.

Rioja
The old province of Spain which is home to Rioja is called Old Castile, a more romantic name than would be suggested by the landscape which is quite bleak and dramatic. The name Rioja comes from the small river, Rio Oja, which runs along the ancient pilgrims' route towards Santiago de Compostela; and wines have been made here for as long as pilgrims have travelled the roads. The pride of Rioja is the full rich red wine but the white versions are also interesting and nowadays increasingly light and delicate where once they were heavy and wood-scented.

Approach the area by crossing from Plymouth to Santander with a car, then head towards Bilbao and Haro; they are excellent roads (for a small price). The true centre of the wine region is Logroño on the river Ebro, a mixture of old and new with elegant shops as well as older dwelling quarters and the ancient city walls. Its cathedral, Santa Maria de la Redonda, is typically Spanish with an atmosphere of Gothic drama lifted by the occasional small friendly side chapel lit by candles.

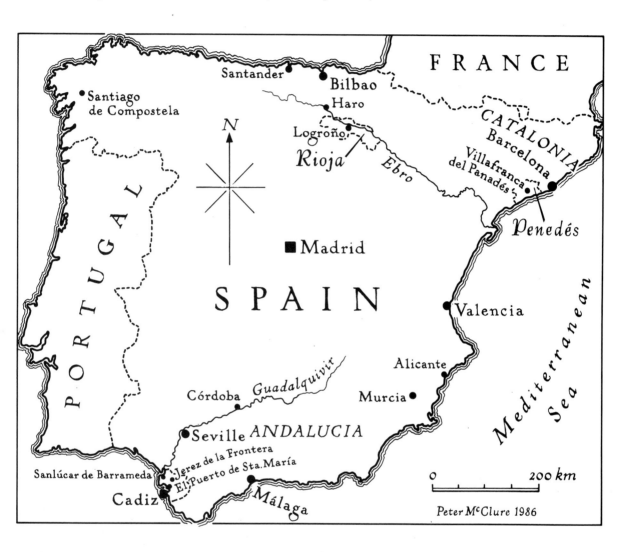

Peter McClure 1986

The food served to accompany the local wine is quite simple, based on regional produce; vegetables flourish here and the locals are inordinately proud of their asparagus. A typical lunch with a wine producer might feature asparagus to begin with, tinned or fresh, served with the dried ham which is pungent in flavour and tastes like the French jambon de Bayonne or German Schinken. These hams give a particular musky aroma to the small grocery shops to be found all over Logroño and neighbouring towns. Lovers of spicy food will discover marvellous peppers and preserved meats in these enchanting emporia where all the goods are suspended from the ceiling or stacked in barrels, even in the most elegant of shopping districts. Look out for bottles labelled 'Cointreau' or other well-known liqueur names; these are passable copies of the original made illicitly (or even legally) in Spain and sold at a fraction of their price abroad. But beware of other spirits which have a tendency to be on the primitive side; Spanish gin can produce a hangover like no other . . .

Following the asparagus and ham there will probably be a barbecue of young kid or lamb, served whole at the table. Finicky table manners have to be set aside as diners attack the animal with knives and forks! Haricot beans are another popular food, made into a type of casserole with spiced sausage (chorizo), well flavoured with peppers and garlic.

The cheese in this area is not very interesting although the Manchegan cheese from Don Quixote territory is strong and good with Rioja reds. Desserts tend to be simple, chocolate mousse being a particular favourite.

The wineries themselves often have an appearance of great age from a distance as they rise above the plains, but on approaching closer you see that they are actually concrete versions of ancient castles. Most of the hard work goes on below the main building in deep cellars which may occupy several floors underground.

As a rule, you will be welcomed warmly and without formality, but do make contact beforehand to arrange a time for the visit. If you would like to go to a Rioja *bodega*, contact Vinos de España who can send you a list of names and addresses, or ask your wine merchant for advice. If you do not make arrangements before arriving in the area, then your hotel or the Logroño tourist office may well be able to organise a tasting or two.

What to look for when you take a tour? Try to contrast the old and new approaches to Rioja by seeing a vast establishment such as Compania

The modern sherry cellar is like a cathedral consecrated to the vine; vast and impressive

Vinicole del Norte de España (CVNE) and a small family firm such as Bodegas Muga. It is a revelation to compare giant steel vats and aging cathedral-like vaults with the tiny cramped cellars of a smaller producer who may still be using egg whites beaten by hand to clear the wine. Standards are generally very high and the particular charm of Rioja is its warm vanilla-like pungency which is derived from the American oak barrels traditionally used. Even the largest producers make wines with plenty of character and you will be able to taste wines made perhaps a decade before – a rarity in French cellars! Keep an open mind when trying the white wines as they are still at the experimental stage. And even in Britain none of these interesting wines will be expensive.

Jerez

If the Rioja region seems a little unfamiliar, try these names for a contrast – Seville, Córdoba, Cadiz. Jerez de la Frontera is in Andalucia, situated by a coastline which has been fought for by Romans, Moors and Christians and was a trading area in the days of the Phoenicians. Apart from Jerez itself, which is the derivation of the name 'sherry', two neighbouring towns are major centres of production, Puerto de Santa Maria and Sanlúcar de Barrameda. The latter is so close to the Atlantic that experts claim to detect a salty tang in the wine made there, mainly the very light, dry Manzanilla. The whole coastline is known as the Costa de la Luz, the Coast of Light. And the white Moorish buildings and sandy beaches indeed befit the name, as do the beautiful white-walled *bodegas* where sherry is stored to age and improve before bottling.

This is the area to watch bullfighters, flamenco dancers and the performance of the venenciador – not, as his name suggests, one of the performers who appears prior to the matador at a bullfight, but a highly theatrical sommelier who will pour sherry from way above his head into the traditional tulip-shaped copita glasses using a tiny scoop called the venencia. In essence, then, this is a region offering plenty of glamour and fun. And it is not far from the tourist traps of the Costa del Sol, certainly within driving distance.

Sherry sold on the spot is often unfortified and a much tarter, lighter and fruitier version of the cream varieties so popular in Britain. It tastes good with seafood and other local fish dishes. Tapas is the name for a very agreeable type of 'fast food', including many fishy elements such as morsels of fried squid, grilled sardines and anchovies or baby sole fried in oil. Or try the Spanish equivalent of the British fish shop – an open-air stall selling freshly-fried fish wrapped in paper.

Some fish and meat dishes are cooked with sherry, such as mussels steamed in sherry and kidneys with a fino sauce. Fino sherry is also a perfect accompaniment to some dishes which overwhelm lighter wines, such as the omelette or its Spanish version, the tortilla. Finally, try a chilled fino with cool gazpacho, a spicy soup made with tomatoes, peppers, onions and garlic, as well as a touch of vinegar.

Some sherry *bodegas* may be visited without an appointment but most like you to contact them at least a couple of days before your planned visit. In Jerez itself notable names include Gonzalez Byass, Sandeman, Pedro Domecq, Williams and Humbert, Garvey, Croft and John Harvey. For more information write to the Sherry Institute of Spain.

Visit a sherry *bodega* to admire the vats as well as the wine. Some still employ coopers who are fascinating to watch at work

Civilised Catalonia
Rioja has incomparable velvet-smooth red wines and an atmosphere of aristocratic hauteur (most of the producers seem to buy their suits in

Savile Row and wear English tweed caps); Jerez hints at sensuality and languor; but Catalonia is faster moving and very much of the modern world. The wines, too, have made great strides of late and now represent quality in many styles, ranging from 'champagne' to fine red and white table wines.

The stylish Catalan may be seen on the streets of Barcelona, a marvellous city which is ideal for a winter weekend, combining as it does the delights of art, architecture, food and drink with the comforts of some fine old-fashioned hotels. It is a fairly compact city and walking is recommended. Indeed, walking is really essential if you are to explore the Ramblas, the old Gothic quarter, and discover all the sights and sensations of a medieval city. Yet the adjoining avenues feature buildings of the grander civic style and elegant boutiques patronised by smart locals. The only problem you are likely to have is understanding the language, because even though it bears a strong resemblance to old French and even middle English, it is extraordinarily hard to grasp when spoken.

The Catalans love to dance and sing and their religious holidays feature dance contests in the city streets with local costumes and songs. Their exuberance is reflected in the designs of Gaudi, a modern 'Renaissance man' who dreamt up the bizarre church of the Sacred Family, a vast and fantastic structure like a city from some distant planet; it has been under construction for a hundred years. His other work is secular and features amazing tile patterns with gold tints, not entirely dissimilar from the style of the Brighton Pavilion.

Artists who loved Barcelona included Miro, who was born there, Picasso, who has a museum dedicated to his work and Dali – all eccentrics like the city itself. The cellist Pablo Casals was also a Catalan and expressed their love of music at its most refined.

The wine producer most associated with Catalonia is Miguel Torres, who grows a vast array of grape varieties and makes fine wine of every style. The production region is generally referred to as Penedés or Panadés and is centred on the town of Villafranca del Panadés. Torres use Chardonnay grapes in some of their white wine to give a rich fullness, while others are very light and 'clean', Viña Sol for example. The red wines include both local and French varieties such as Cabernet Sauvignon. Coronas is the full dry red and Gran Coronas an older blend with a full bouquet obtained from maturing the wines in oak for twenty months or more.

The Torres have immense energy and have, almost singlehanded, made Penedés a well-known region. Miguel's daughter Marimar has spent many years in the US and marketed the family wines there; she also writes about Spanish food. The family is at the forefront of a move to make Spanish wines more acceptable to palates attuned to Beaujolais

Nouveau and Muscadet. To achieve a lighter style and greater delicacy in their wines, they use a range of grape varieties but also believe in spending money on new equipment such as gentler presses and controlled fermentation vats both of which mean more fruit in the wine. Similarly, wood casks are used judiciously so that the flavour of the wood is subtle rather than pungent, requiring years to 'smooth out'.

Torres is not the only famous name in Penedés. The sparkling wines made not far from Barcelona by the correct Champagne method and aged in vast limestone caves just as in the Champagne region are considered some of the closest rivals to the 'real thing' in the wine world, and they are very much cheaper. Production is substantial and naturally quality can vary, although both Codorniu and Freixenet are reliable. Either of these cellars may be visited by the tourist and deserve attention for their sheer size if nothing else.

To arrange visits in the Barcelona area contact Vinos de España or ask for information at your hotel in the city – many *cava* sparkling wine producers take visitors without an appointment.

HIGH TECH AND TRADITION:
BODEGAS MARTÍNEZ BUJANDA RIOJA

This company has a lovely label of white cartridge paper, delicately embossed with grapes and leaves in a *vignette* shape. There is a discreet crest and the lettering is in gold and a deep wine colour. The effect is very elegant indeed.

Despite its classical lines this label is very much the product of modern marketing techniques and the combination of the old and the very new is typical of the enterprise. If you visit the winery you will see the most intimidating array of modern stainless steel hardware dedicated to making the 'cleanest' wine imaginable, yet equally the company stands by many of the old principles.

The Martínez family have grown vines since 1889 and now the fourth generation are in charge, with some 550 acres to be tended. This emphasis on ownership of the vineyard is unusual in Rioja where buying in from various sources is commonplace. The Martínez Bujandas aim to make all their wine from their own grapes and they grow an interesting assortment of varieties, again traditional and innovative at the same time.

The traditional Rioja varieties, Tempranillo (red) and Viura (white), are widely grown, as well as older grapes such as the Mazuelo (red) and Malvasía (white) which are now rarely cultivated. The family feel these old varieties add smoothness to their wines. To add a quality factor they have also planted Cabernet Sauvignon and Riesling.

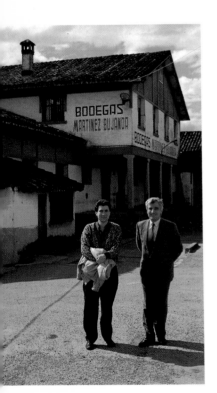
Members of the Martínez Bujanda family 'at home'

In the cellar hygiene is paramount and there is minimum handling of the grapes. These are carefully sorted as they arrive, only the whole bunches being acceptable. The winemaking 'pavilion' (as they describe it) is a vast concrete box set apart from the ageing and bottling areas which have their own 'pavilion'. Everything in the winemaking area is of gleaming steel.

Many of the wines are made by the carbonic maceration process (see *September*) to give a very light fruity style. The vintage red wines are fermented traditionally but also in steel. There is rigorous temperature control throughout to keep the fermentation stable and continuous.

Those wines intended to be sold at their peak of fruity charm are bottled direct from the vat – white, rosé and red. Those destined for a longer life as their *reservas* are aged in immaculate small oak barrels arranged in a vast hall which can house up to eight thousand barrels at any one time. The ageing cellar is not subject to the vagaries of the climate but fully air-conditioned and even humidified as required. After about two years of barrel age the wines are bottled and stored for another period in the 'bottle chamber' which holds a million bottles.

The scrupulous attention to detail is supervised by the family's winemaker who is the son of a man known locally as 'The Professor' – Gonzalo Ortiz, the winemaker at Berberana Rioja. There is no doubt that the result of all this effort and expense is a selection of wines which embody the best Rioja has to offer today. Gone are the over-oaked heavy white wines of the past and their companion red wines which often tasted of wood at the expense of fruit. Now the fruit is evident yet balanced by the attractive 'vanilla' bouquet of wood age. Overall these are seductive wines which belie their high-tech origins.

Rioja *reserva* ages in oak for at least two years before bottling

Bodegas Martínez
   Bujanda SA,
Camino Viejo de Logroño,
Oyon,
Rioja Alavesa.

MARCH

In March the seasons begin to turn and the vines show the first signs of growth, the sap rising with any hint of warmth. In the cellars a secondary fermentation will begin (see *February*). In the southern hemisphere the vineyards of Australia, South Africa and South America are in full flood of vintage and their new wines will come to market as the vines of Europe flower in early summer.

Pruning is more or less complete now and the vines are firmly attached to wires or stakes to support the coming shoots. In some countries they are trained high above other crops for economic reasons (Italy and Portugal, for instance), while in others they squat low to the ground (southern France). The relationship between vine and soil is one reason for this. If there are stones storing heat on the ground the vines can gather warmth from them at night. If, on the other hand, the earth is damp and cool, then raising the vines prevents damage by mould and wet. Many vines in chilly climates such as Germany and Britain benefit from so-called 'high-training'.

Tradition is another reason for maintaining certain methods of pruning and staking. And tradition plays a vital role in another important facet of wine production – the choice of grape varieties. Here the European vineyards have an immense advantage over the more recent cultivations. The vine types cultivated in Bordeaux or Burgundy have been there for a thousand years or more, since Roman times or even earlier, and no one questions the value of any particular variety for any particular wine. Younger winemakers must start from scratch and test out as many varieties as possible in order to find the best combination of soil, climate and grape type. Mistakes are bound to occur along the way and much time is wasted as it takes four years for a vine to bear grapes which may be made into wine and then more time has to elapse between removing one variety from the soil and planting another.

THE CHOICE OF GRAPE VARIETIES

Roughly speaking, grape varieties fall into two categories, aristocrat and peasant. This may sound rather sociological, but as a rule certain varieties are acknowledged as being finer than others, *regardless* of exactly where they are planted or of the wine they produce. These include the Cabernet Sauvignon, Pinot Noir and Chardonnay from France; the Riesling of Germany and even the Furmint of Hungary, which makes ageless Tokay.

These grapes and certain others like them tend to yield frugally but they command high prices on the market and produce wines with potential for keeping and improving rather than for immediate consumption. Today they are grown all over the winemaking world, from Canada to New York to Santiago to Sussex, and every winemaker who uses them has a certain minimum standard of excellence in mind. The names imply quality.

By contrast, certain grapes have little reputation except as 'work orses': for example, the Carignan, Chasselas and Ugni Blanc of France, the Müller-Thurgau of Germany and England, and the Zinfandel of California. When a fine wine is produced from any of these varieties it tends to be regarded as an exception to the general rule and the producer rarely features the grape type on a label so prominently as he might an 'aristocratic' variety. The ultimate example of a workhorse grape has to be the Thompson Seedless of California, grown in vast areas for raisins and for use as a table grape; it also serves as a bland neutral 'base' for millions of gallons of blended California 'Chablis' and 'Burgundy'. Winemakers have been known to put this name on a label as a featured variety, but it was meant as a joke. Wine made with Thompson Seedless has no style at all.

The yellowish tinge of ripe Chardonnay grapes is echoed in the wine and the bottles used for white Burgundy

In France, the finest of grapes are known as *cépages nobles*. For white wines these include the spicy Gewürztraminer of Alsace, the elegant 'buttery' Chardonnay of Champagne and Burgundy, the creamy-flavoured Sémillon used in making Sauternes, the honey-scented Chenin Blanc of the Loire Valley, the distinctive 'green' aromatic Sauvignon Blanc and the sultry, spicy Muscat of the south.

Red wines may be made with Cabernet Sauvignon, the grape which imbues Bordeaux wines with all their legendary austerity and power; Pinot Noir, with its aromas of violets, raspberries and old velvet; Gamay, a deliciously fruity creation at its best in the Beaujolais; Syrah, the black pepper pungency of fine Rhône wines; and Muscat again, in its red incarnation.

Of course, other countries would offer different lists. In Italy, for instance, the Nebbiolo of Piedmont and the Sangiovese of Tuscany are undoubtedly the superior varieties for red wine; in Spain, the relatively humble Grenache of southern France is the Garnacha of Rioja's finest reds. For certain climates may affect the ultimate quality of a wine made from a particular grape: in California or South Africa wines made with Chenin Blanc are agreeable but not exciting, while in the Loire Valley this variety yields wines of fine quality both still and sparkling, dry and sweet.

With few exceptions, wines are not labelled simply according to grape type. In newer wine regions such as South America, Australia, South Africa and the USA, grape varieties are mentioned on the label to help the consumer, but most of the world's more famous wines do not specify the variety, usually because there are many varieties involved and the combination is the key to the wine's identity. It is in cases where the wine does not really have a familiar 'image' that reference to the grape type will help both buyer and seller. Take Bulgaria as an example. Although Bulgarian Cabernet Sauvignon and Chardonnay do not closely resemble French claret and white Burgundy, at least the potential consumer can get some idea of the wine's style from the grape type indicated on the label.

Sometimes the buyer may not even be aware that he is looking at a grape type. Did you know that Muscadet is the name of a grape variety as well as a wine? This is a rare instance of so-called 'varietal' labelling in France. The Muscadet grape yields light dry white wine that makes an ideal accompaniment for seafood. It is also known as the Melon de Bourgogne and was first planted near the coast of Brittany after a disastrous winter when the vines died and even the bays froze. Vines were brought in from Burgundy and adapted perfectly, and since then the wine has been known by its varietal title.

It is worth memorising a few grape types and their wines. Pouilly Fumé from the Loire is made with Sauvignon Blanc whereas Pouilly sur Loire is a far less interesting wine made with Chasselas. In California, the word 'fumé' associated with the style of wine made with Sauvignon Blanc has actually been appropriated as a kind of 'varietal' – hence Blanc Fumé, a wine made with Sauvignon Blanc and first popularised by Robert Mondavi.

It is easy to panic at the thought of committing all the grape types and their wines to memory, but of course this is not essential. Concentrate on the finer 'noble' varieties at first, then add any others which take your fancy. You may have a liking for very crisp clean Swiss wine, so you can look for a reference to Fendant on a label; you may prefer the more pungent orange-tinted rosé of the south to the pinker style of the Loire Valley, in which case you would ask about Grenache rather than Gamay. Today many wine companies are realising that their basic 'house' wines often benefit from a mention of the grape varieties involved, so your education may move ahead rapidly, simply by tasting a selection of 'varietal' wines.

In Bordeaux, the Cabernet Sauvignon is probably the best known grape variety, yet no claret would be made using only this grape. The blend is created with Merlot, which adds fruit and fullness; Cabernet Franc, which has a 'nutty' sharp quality; and Petit Verdot, an old-fashioned variety used in small amounts to add a certain earthiness to the wine. Each vineyard has a formula which is used to obtain a particular character in the wine, but this may obviously vary according to the vintage. In 1984, for example, the Merlot, which is an early ripener, was badly affected by harsh weather and so the other varieties were used in higher proportions. This was hard for the producers of St-Emilion and Pomerol within the Bordeaux *appellation* as they rely heavily on Merlot for their style of rich, 'meaty' wine.

So the greater is mixed with the lesser to yield the right wine, much as a fine blended Scotch is made up of magnificent single malts and some blander grain whiskies as well. A wine made solely from one famous variety can be overpowering viz. certain California examples (such as the Cabernet Sauvignon wines from the Napa Valley) which are very expensive and have a significant shortcoming: their flavour is so intense that they are unsuitable as an accompaniment for food.

Some very famous wines are made with more than a dozen grape varieties including Châteauneuf-du-Pape which normally includes thirteen. And a red wine may not be made only with red varieties. Chianti has traditionally included some Malvasia Bianca, a white relation of the Muscat.

Pinot Noir – the glory of Burgundy and Champagne

Champagne is a fascinating example of the way varieties are blended. It is important to note here that although the skin of the grape is red, the juice is almost always white, so if the skins are not used in making the wine, you have a white wine made with black grapes. Champagne employs two noble varieties, red and white, and another red grape called the Pinot Meunier. The stars are Pinot Noir and Chardonnay and the way they are used determines much of a Champagne's style. The very lightest Champagnes are made with Chardonnay only and are known as 'Blanc de Blancs' (a white from white grapes). The fullest use a fair proportion of Pinot Noir and have a noticeable richness of flavour unconnected with age or producer. Pink Champagne is made in the usual way (see *July*), then a dash of red wine made with Pinot Noir is blended in to give a hint of colour and taste.

FESTIVALS

In certain years this is the month for the celebration of Holy Week and Easter, a joyous time for churchgoer and wine lover alike, especially in Catholic countries such as Spain and Italy with their traditions of processions and street festivities. The risen Christ will be saluted with such earthly delights as banquets, often very musical occasions with singing and dancing, and naturally plenty of local wine in evidence. Even countries behind the Iron Curtain show a more relaxed countenance at this time of year.

Apart from Easter, there are some wine events in France which are celebrated to mark the arrival of the new wines. In Eguisheim, Alsace, the new wines are presented on the second Sunday in March, while in Burgundy, the last Saturday in March is the occasion for a *tastevinage*, a special offering of new wines at the famous Clos de Vougeot. This lovely château is open to visitors all year long and visits are well-organised both for individuals and groups; it even has its own wine museum. It may seem a little commercialised but is worth a visit as an introduction to the fine wines of Burgundy (see *November*).

The most publicised wine auction in the world must be at the Hospices de Beaune, held each November, but there is another Burgundian auction in March, this time in Nuits St-Georges, heart of the Côte de Nuits. Buyers and sellers gather at the Hospice de Nuits on the last Sunday of the month. Finally, the Loire Valley has much to offer in March: the various local festivals include one held in praise of the red wines of Chinon, on the first Saturday. This pretty medieval town is the birthplace of François Rabelais, the lusty poet and philosopher who declared, '*Buvez toujours, ne mourez jamais*' ('Always drink, never die').

If Easter falls in March, then Easter Day is the occasion for feasting and festival in Amboise, Bourgueil, St-Nicolas de Bourgueil and St Georges-sur-Cher. Lovers of Muscadet might visit Vallet, not far from Nantes, for their festival on the second Saturday of the month.

The mediaeval town of Chinon seen across the broad Loire

ENTERTAINING

It seems that doctors, magazine editors and television pundits are all continually conspiring to tell us that our diet is wrong, that we must eat lighter food and drink lighter drinks. The combined influence of nouvelle cuisine, health food and a scare about additives has meant that fruit, vegetables and fish have assumed new importance in menus both at home and in restaurants. We are urged to take pity on our poor bodies and not subject them to lots of sugar, alcohol and carbohydrates. Exercise has become mandatory. In part, this is no more than fashion but it is sometimes taken to such extremes that the eventual response may be an attitude like that of one of the characters in Woody Allen's

'70s film *Sleeper* – a Rip Van Winkle who awakes in the next century and is offered masses of cream cakes, sweets and cigarettes, favoured foods for the beautiful people of the future!

For the food and wine lover there are two important points at issue: one is simply to learn how to adapt menus at home to new tastes and styles, and which wines to serve with unfamiliar dishes or very delicate flavours. The second is the question of determining how much wine is good for you, or is wine to be considered a vice, no better and no worse than smoking?

WINE YOUR WAY TO HEALTH

'God, in his goodness, sent the grape
To cheer both great and small;
Little fools will drink too much
And great fools none at all.'
ANON

If the current trend is to return to a simpler diet, with meals involving organically-grown foods and many raw ingredients, then the health food 'buff' should regard wine as the perfect accompaniment. It is one of the oldest drinks in the world and also one of the oldest medicines. The alcohol in wine is certainly a mild drug but the effects of this are negligible when you drink and eat at the same time. After all, the Italians are copious wine drinkers but the incidence of alcoholism in Italy is not high when compared with that in northern countries such as Sweden or the USSR. The Russians are trying to solve their drink problem by introducing their citizens to Pepsi-Cola but wine is far more agreeable and almost certainly healthier.

There is one certain fact about drinking wine with a meal; it makes everything seem more relaxed! Even if the food is not quite perfect or the company less than compatible, wine helps to smooth out these difficulties. And wine can enhance and make memorable even the plainest fare. Witness the title of one of Elizabeth David's books, *An Omelette and a Glass of Wine*, evoking the simplest of snacks but a delicious combination of tastes.

Can wine do you any positive good? Opinions divide here, but certain research has shown that moderate amounts of wine can ease glaucoma (abnormal pressure in the eyeball), certain heart ailments (again by reducing pressure, this time in small arteries), and nosebleeds (sit down, hold the nose and sip a glass of red wine slowly). It has even been claimed that wine can slow down the effects of a high cholesterol diet by helping to break up fatty substances in the blood. And the development of arteriosclerosis (hardening of the arteries) may well be hindered by a regular moderate intake of wine.

Wine is perhaps the ideal tonic for old age. Cynics may say it simply makes life rose-tinted, offering an escape from reality, but it has been shown that elderly people are far happier when given wine than sleeping pills. The social aspect of wine drinking is important and many an old people's home has become a more congenial place since wine drinking has been authorised anew.

In 1972 a certain Andrew Hastings of Louisville, Kentucky, celebrated his centenary. For his birthday feast he ate his way through two fried eggs, several rolls spread with peanut butter and a large helping of sauerkraut. He washed this down with beer and finished with a shot of hard liquor. His explanation for the choice of drink was simple: 'Water will rust your insides.' So much for the mineral water lobby . . .

The moral of Mr Hastings's tale seems to be that everyone needs to find a diet which suits them, though it may be sensible to go easy on the very richest foods. There are certain culinary tricks designed to keep menus light. Instead of frying with oil or butter, use a non-stick frying-pan and then 'blot' the food on kitchen paper. Instead of roasting and basting with fat, cook in a roasting bag made of plastic or an earthenware 'brick', both of which seal in the juices and prevent shrinkage. Wrap fish or chicken fillets in greaseproof paper or aluminium foil and bake in the oven using lemon juice or wine instead of fats for moisture. Vegetables may be steamed or stir-fried with just a trace of oil in a wok, Chinese style. Or serve them raw but cut very fine (use a food processor to help with slicing and shredding). Although it is hard to achieve the artistry of, say, Michel Guérard (famous for Cuisine Minceur and owner of one of the rare three-rosette restaurants in France), it is possible to give your own meals an appealing 'look' by paying attention to garnishes and using colour cleverly on a very plain white plate.

During Lent it used to be the custom to give up meat and even wine, making the diet austere and simple in keeping with the religious season. Today fewer people follow the tradition but in this hedonistic age we start thinking about summer holidays and getting into shape for the beach. So with whatever motive, perhaps a little restraint in early spring may be worthwhile.

How do wines tie in with this desire to eat simply? First of all, it is easy to identify wines which are not recommended. The rich fortified wines of mid-winter and sweet dessert wines are out: any wine of over 15° would certainly not fit with a diet. Many wine lovers make the mistake of thinking that only white wine is light but in fact many red wines are very low in 'residual sugar' (sugar which naturally remains in the wine after fermentation is complete) and make perfect light drinks. Serve both white and red wines cool, and don't forget that a rosé can also be very light and refreshing.

If you are dieting seriously and really trying to lose weight rather than simply resting the liver, then consider mixing your wine with either sparkling mineral water or soda water to make a spritzer. The health-

'Wine works the heart up, wakes the wit;
There is no cure 'gainst age but it:
It helps the headache, cough and tisic,
And is for all diseases physic.'
JOHN FLETCHER

conscious rather than the dieters might blend a fruity white wine such as a German Riesling or Loire Vouvray with orange juice to taste. Try mixing a Soave or Australian Sémillon with apricot juice, or be more daring yet and blend a fruity rosé from the Loire with cranberry juice.

MENU

Moules marinière with French bread

*

Salad with chives

*

Baked bananas

*

Wines: Muscadet or Chablis with the moules, or choose a Sauvignon de Touraine for economy. A Gewürztraminer goes well with the baked bananas, or try a Pinot Grigio from Italy.

Instructions

Moules marinière: Clean mussels well and remove 'beards'. Put chopped shallots or small onions into a large pan with some dry white wine (about 4 tablespoons white wine to 4 pints mussels, enough for 8). Toss in the mussels and heat fiercely for a few minutes until all have opened. Reject those which remain closed. Add more wine, a knob of butter and chopped parsley – reheat and serve with warm French bread.

Salad with chives: Slice segments of grapefruit, apples and raw mushrooms. Arrange on a bed of lettuce and top with cooked French beans and chopped chives. Offer a light dressing made with lemon juice on the side.

Baked bananas: The bananas are baked in foil with a piece of vanilla pod and a dessertspoonful of white wine mixed with orange juice; dot with honey if your sweet tooth is aching!

MENU

March Hare casserole

*

Fromage blanc with fruit compote

*

Wines: Serve with a light red wine, such as a Loire Chinon or Bourgueil, a red Bergerac, a young Chianti or a Valpolicella.

Instructions

March Hare casserole: Marinate the hare pieces with sliced carrots, garlic, shallots, a bay leaf, some thyme and parsley stalks and black pepper to taste, mixed with plenty of olive oil. After 24 hours remove meat and dry on kitchen paper. Sauté lightly with oil in a flameproof casserole, then pour over a bottle of light red wine. Add peeled whole small onions and mushrooms and heat on top of the stove for 15 minutes. Thicken with a little potato flour if necessary, then cook in a slow oven (150°C/300°F/Gas Mark 2) for 2 hours or more. Serve with steamed potatoes and braised celery.

Fruit compote: This may be made with dried apricots and figs mixed with white wine or with fresh fruits, a spoonful of honey and some wine to taste. The fromage blanc is sold in supermarkets under trade names such as Jockey – look for the variety labelled 0% fat.

A STATELY PROGRESS: THE LOIRE IN SPRING

In summer, the châteaux of the Loire Valley are crowded with tourists; in winter the flat landscape seems too bleak and chill; but in spring and autumn this glamorous region is at its best. Travelling along near-deserted roads between lines of poplars towards the mirage of a turreted château is certainly romantic and there are local wines aplenty to add to the attraction. A car is probably essential for your visit although it is perfectly possible to fly to Paris and hire one at the airport. In fact, a combination of the Loire Valley and Paris makes an ideal break.

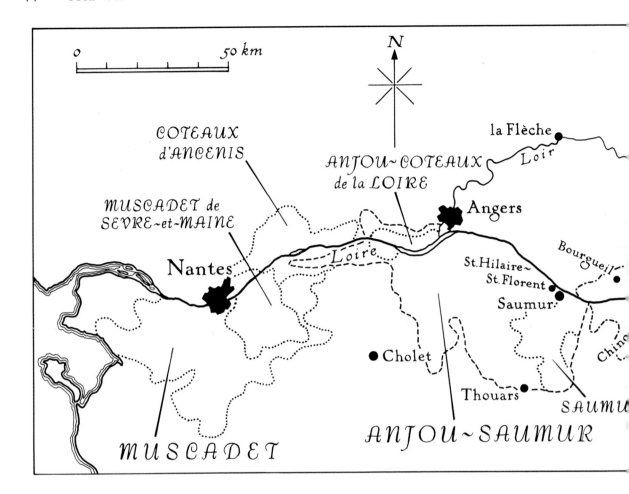

LOUIS MÉTAIREAU
La Févrie
Maisdon-sur-Sèvre
44690 la Haye-Foussière

One of the most fascinating aspects of this wine region is its diversity, hardly surprising when you consider that the river is some 400 miles long with wines both white and red, sweet and dry all the way from the Atlantic to the tiny area around Pouilly sur Loire, not far from Bourges. If you begin your progress at the coast there are no fairytale châteaux but you will find good honest white wines made either with Muscadet or Gros Plant, and a few red wines from the Gamay grape. The uncrowned king of Muscadet has to be Louis Métaireau, a wine showman who makes wine as if he were staging an opera. Write to him to arrange a visit to his immaculate cellars.

Ranging eastward, the next area to visit has a remarkable selection of sweeter white wines including Quarts de Chaumes, Bonnezeaux and Coteaux du Layon, which are all made using grapes affected by 'noble rot' (see *April* for more about sweet wines). These luscious wines are long-lived and an appealing alternative to the better-known Sauternes and Barsac of Bordeaux.

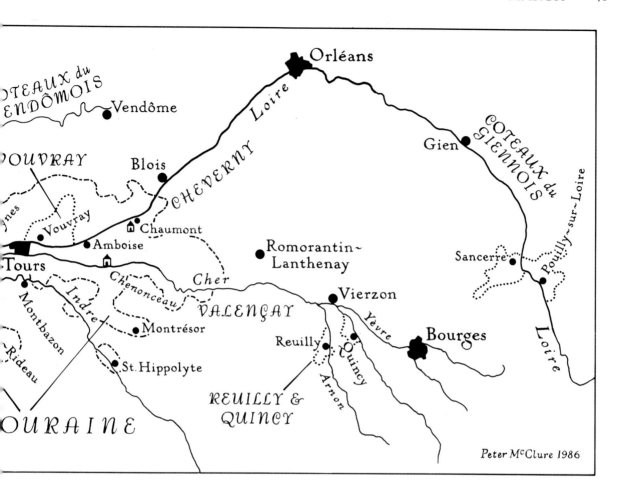

Peter McClure 1986

The major grape variety for white wines in this part of the Loire is Chenin Blanc, also known as the Pineau de la Loire. It is an adaptable grape, with its honey scent discernible in sweet wines, light dry table wines such as Anjou Blanc and even sparkling wines. The most notable of these is probably sparkling Saumur, which has had a controversial history in Britain since one supermarket unwisely described it as being identical to real Champagne. Of course it is made by the proper Champagne method but has a quite distinct character, very clean and easy to drink. To sample the wine, visit Bouvet-Ladubay close to Saumur itself, but note that prior to the summer season you will need an appointment.

While in the area look out for mushroom caves which are interesting to visit, as well as the so-called troglodyte dwelling, actual homes hacked into the rock, some with elegant town house façades. These are to be seen alongside the river. And the château of Saumur is very striking and especially alluring for horse lovers as it houses an exhibition on all things

BOUVET-LADUBAY,
rue Ackerman,
St-Hilaire-St-Florent,
49416 Saumur.

equestrian. There is also a famous riding school, the Cadre Noir, in the town and the French cavalry were stationed here until 1969.

Closer to Paris, you will pass through the much-touted 'Rabelais country', the French equivalent of Stratford although mercifully far less commercial. This lusty poet and philosopher was born in Chinon, home of a particularly fragrant red wine. Both this town and Bourgueil across the river grow many vines on rich alluvial river soil, contrary to all the so-called rules of viticulture, the result being a fruity yet rather austere and long-lived wine, much underrated. One of the prophets of Bourgueil is a young winemaker called Pierre-Jacques Druet who has devoted his time and notable wine qualifications to improving the status of this wine, with much success so far. He is giving Cabernet Franc a position with Cabernet Sauvignon among the *cépages nobles* and it would be worth paying a visit to his cellars.

PIERRE-JACQUES DRUET,
'La Croix Rouge',
Benais,
37140 Bourgueil.

Chenonçeau – a romantic château associated with Diane de Poitiers and Catherine de Medici

Vouvray has been a standby of the British wine list for many years and was perhaps the best-known of all Loire wines before the ascendancy of Muscadet with the new passion for 'light' wines. In good years it may be made in a rich semi-sweet style and a full dry version, both of which are examples of Chenin Blanc at its best, with a hint of apple blossom on the nose. In ordinary vintages a fair quantity of sparkling wine is made and this is very drinkable and ideal for 'mixed drinks'. Visit the Château de Vaudenuits while in the town: it is not one of the prettiest of the Loire castles but is a working co-operative, the Cave des Viticulteurs de Vouvray, making a full range of Vouvray wines to a good standard.

CAVE DES VITICULTEURS DE VOUVRAY,
route de Vernou,
37210 Vouvray.

Follow the river along past the imposing château of Amboise and the forbidding walls of Blois towards Orléans, where you will find a restaurant worth 'le détour' as they say in Michelin guides. This is La Crémaillère which has at least one reasonably priced menu and a balanced selection of local wines. The food is delicate and yet sustaining and the service typical of the relaxed formality of the best French restaurants.

With renewed energy you could then press on to the outer reaches of the Loire *appellation* at Sancerre, Pouilly sur Loire and the lesser known Quincy and Reuilly. The two most famous names, Sancerre and Pouilly, face one another across the river and produce memorable wines from the Sauvignon Blanc grape. There are also much smaller quantities of rosé and red wine which are best served chilled, though they may perhaps be too sharp for palates used to a richer red wine.

The everyday wines of the Loire are really Sauvignon de Touraine, a very light and agreeable wine which mixes well with Cassis liqueur (blackcurrants) to make the apéritif called Kir, and Gamay de la Loire, a light yet fruity red like a less assertive Beaujolais, served cool.

If you want to sample some of the grander local wines in glorious surrounds, visit one of the Relais et Châteaux hotels in the area or, better still, spend a night there in luxury. The three notable names are the Prieuré at Chênehutte-les-Tuffeaux near Saumur, which boasts a fantastic cheese board for fromage fanciers; the Château d'Artigny at Montbazon, not far from Tours, with a renowned cellar; and the Domaine de Beauvois, situated high on a hill above the small town of Luynes with its ruined château.

Finally, make sure you pay a visit to two of the most exquisite Loire châteaux – Azay-le-Rideau and Chenonceau. There has been a vineyard at Chenonceau since the days of Catherine de Médici and wine is still made there today. The grape varieties grown are very much those traditional in the area including the *cot* grapes for red wine, now rarely seen. Other varieties include Cabernet Franc and Chenin Blanc.

The wines themselves are very well made and certainly not just a tourist attraction. Apart from a fine dry white wine and a rounded red, there is a rosé with more colour than the standard pale pink of most Loire wines and some excellent sparkling wine. The rosé sparkler seems most appropriate to the château and its history, especially if you are ever fortunate enough to eat a meal there in the Orangery.

To visit the vineyard or to book a group meal at the Orangery, write to SC Chenonceau-Rentilly, 37150 Bléré; single bottles of the wines are available at the castle gates. If you decide to stay at Chenonceaux for another day (note the village has an 'x' but not the château itself), then try the hotel and restaurant nearby.

LA CRÉMAILLÈRE,
34, rue Notre Dame de
    Recouvrance,
Orléans.

Amboise – both château and fortress

Azay-le-Rideau appears to float in its watery setting

LE BON LABOUREUR
ET CHÂTEAU
6 rue Dr Bretonneau,
Chenonceaux,
37150 Bléré.

For further general information about visiting the Loire Valley, contact the French tourist office or Food and Wine from France.

APPELLATION MÉTAIREAU: THE GOURMET'S MUSCADET

Louis Métaireau is a man who defies conventional description, both as a winegrower and as a mere individual. In fact, there is nothing 'mere' about him; his every attitude is passionately expressed, and even his clothes have a theatrical extravagance. He has the look of an ageing French film producer, perhaps one of the 'jet set' who annually grace the beaches at Cannes. Yet beneath this flamboyance is a man who knows almost all there is to know about making his particular wine – Muscadet.

Louis Métaireau displays the fruits of his labours with the Vignerons d'Art

'Appellation Métaireau' is a wine trade joke: it is said that there are two *appellations* in his region – AC Muscadet and AC Métaireau. This is a mark of affection and acknowledges his very successful efforts to make wines far removed from the simplicity of many bearing the Muscadet name. Sadly they are not inexpensive.

On the face of it, Louis Métaireau's enterprise is another in the long list of French wine co-operatives. Since 1957 he has been working with other local growers to combine their vineyards and make economic sense of the business of producing wine. Today there are nine growers in the group and they have a total of 170 acres of grapes under cultivation, some their own land, some belonging to absentee owners.

Where Métaireau's arrangement differs radically from a co-operative is in the production of individual wines. Each one is sold under a Métaireau label but they are not blended at a central cellar. The wines are made by the growers themselves then tasted and selected 'blind'. The initials of the particular grower are stamped on the cork. The tasting panel (composed of the growers) quite frequently rejects about half of the wines submitted and this is accepted by the group – an extraordinary display of humility by the French winegrowing fraternity.

In 1971 the fraternity became a legal 'Groupement d'Intérêt Economique', called Louis Métaireau et ses Vignerons d'Art, indicating Metaireau's role as the guiding personality in the group. Quite apart from his evident flair as a showman and marketing entrepreneur, he also takes care of the finances and sales.

This unusual co-operative is now into its second generation as two of the original members have retired and their sons have taken over their responsibilities. And M. Métaireau's children are likewise involved in the business, notably the charming Marie-Luce, who deals with public relations with all her father's aplomb and dedication.

The wines themselves are very much a natural product, treated as little as possible, as befits wines as delicate as Muscadet. Muscadet may not exceed 12% alcohol by volume and the Vignerons d'Art aim for a lower level, closer to 11%. They are not wines made with very ripe, sugar-rich grapes, but with those still high in acidity: 'The best Muscadet is made in a year with little sun,' says Métaireau.

Another significant feature of the winemaking process is the use of a technique known as *mise sur lie* – allowing the wine to rest on its lees in a barrel. The barrel is placed in such a position that the bung (stopper) is wet and hence very little air can enter. The result is a tendency to re-ferment and an agreeable faint fizz in the wine, as well as a richness of flavour drawn from the lees. This procedure is carried out at the individual growers' cellars and kept fully legal by special certificates, proving it is a separate, not a collective operation. Such attention to strict detail is typical of Métaireau and his organisation.

Today the wines sell worldwide and there is a move towards even higher quality with named Domaines such as *Grand Mouton*. Such acquisitions certainly raise the image of Muscadet from that of a poor relation of Chablis, to a château-bottled fine wine in its own right – a destiny Louis Métaireau has done much to bring about.

APRIL

April can be a very tricky time of the year for a grapegrower. As the sap starts to rise in the vine, so lingering frosts may wipe out all hope for a healthy vintage in the autumn. Vigilance is vital and it is not unknown for growers to sleep out amid the vines ready to take action against frost.

If a frost is really severe it may be impossible to prevent the worst fear of a grower – damage to the roots of the vine – but this is very rare as the roots go deep in their search for water. Temperatures of $-30°C$ or lower spell disaster during the winter but in spring only $-5°C$ may be serious. Certain grape varieties such as the Müller-Thurgau are more resistant to low temperatures and wine research institutes are working on the creation of hybrids which will not be affected by frost or disease. The only snag is that vines produced by crossing an American species such as *Vitis labrusca* with the European *Vitis vinifera* are not usually legal in the EEC. Curiously enough, to date the English vineyards have counted as 'experimental' so have been able to plant tough hybrids such as Seyve-Villard and Seibel.

For a vine to thrive the average temperature during the year needs to be about $10°C$ and preferably higher, and if winter temperatures average less than $3°C$ it is not a good area for winegrowing unless the grower is experiencing a particularly unlucky year! Later in the season the vine flowers need a minimum average of $15°C$ day and night to 'set' the microscopic grapes, then there are the crucial hundred days leading up to the harvest. During the summer temperatures ought to hover around the $22°C$ mark to ensure the grapes will ripen fully. Ideally the grapes receive around fourteen hundred hours of sunshine over the course of a growing season, which sadly rules out a good deal of Britain north of Watford. Germany and northern France also struggle to reach this target in a dull year like 1985, but all may be redeemed by a glorious September and October.

Winegrowers frequently refer to 'microclimates', meaning climatic variations within an area, and it is in fact remarkable how conditions can vary even within a confined area such as, say, the Côte d'Or in Burgundy or the Napa Valley of California. The contributing factors are the proximity of the vines to water (a lake, perhaps, or a river) and to trees, which add moisture to the atmosphere; the amount of shelter available and whether this is offered by a towering mountain or a sloping hillside; and of course the aspect of the vineyard. The most successful vines generally grow on a south or south-west facing hillside with good drainage and shelter from wind and frost. Altitudes of more than 800ft. may be too harsh for vines although in Switzerland you will encounter vines amid the edelweiss up at 4000ft.

A nearby *plan d'eau*, as the French would say, has a beneficial effect on a vineyard, whether it is a small lake, a river, or even a sheltered sea cove as for some plantings in the South of France. The effect of the water is to store up the day's heat and release it overnight, helping to moderate the effects of extreme temperature change. Growers with sufficient financial resources have been known to dig a lake or even a large swimming pool to improve conditions for their vines.

The water may also come into its own for irrigation, if this is permitted, and for frost protection. Special sprinklers can be installed for action when the temperature falls, coating each budding vine with water. Within its ice sheath the young shoot or grape is more likely to survive than if left exposed.

Smudge pots in action against frost in Champagne

If not water, then fire. Bizarre-looking metal canisters are to be found in some vineyards, a cross between the Tin Man and a chestnut brazier. These 'smudge pots' are stoked up when frost threatens and they heat up the air around the vines. This air may be circulated with fans, and in California or Australia it is not unusual to see an ancient prop engine from some defunct aircraft pressed into service for this job.

Once the frosts have passed, there is no time to relax. The flowering vine may be subjected to a hailstorm which can literally tear off every fledgling bunch in a matter of minutes. It may seem that little can be done to avert this disaster, but there are ways and means. If a storm is forecast then rockets may be fired to disperse the clouds and growers with private planes or access to cropsprayers will take up those rockets themselves.

In summer, once the young bunches are established, growers must either expose them to all available sun or shelter them from excess heat depending on the region. Foliage is trimmed back to let the grapes bask in sun when a hot summer is not anticipated but in more southern climes this may be risky as an overripe grape quickly turns to a near-raisin and is spoiled for fine winemaking. So in areas like southern Italy, Greece and the Central Valley of California growers allow leaves to flourish and hide the bunches, and grapes are picked as early as possible to avoid scorching.

WINE AND THE SOIL

Authorities divide over the question of the most suitable soil types. For the French, the earth is all; the wine is a product of the soil. For the Germans, skill and technology are as important as natural gifts. Ancient regions like Greece have never needed to give the matter any thought. Italy, for instance, was called 'Enotria' (meaning land of vines) by the Greeks as it seemed the vine grew there without any assistance from man. But in newer regions, decisions must be made about what to plant where and whether or not the soil is suitable.

What soil best suits a vine? Obviously, it must offer drainage and yet at the same time enough body to ensure the roots retain moisture. Clay, lime and organic matter are all necessary in varying quantities and as vines benefit from the absorption of many trace elements like potassium, magnesium, iron and zinc, these are an advantage. A very rich soil full of nitrogen which would be perfect for many crops is not good for vines as the plant tends to produce too many leaves and the grapes yielded are not very flavoursome. Soil with very little nitrogen may yield a small crop of grapes but these would be of a very subtle flavour indeed if various minerals were present. The different quantities of minerals are in all probability one of the major causes of the variation in flavour between grapes grown in neighbouring vineyards.

Gardeners among you may be interested to learn that the pH of soil ideal for a vine is around 6.8–7.0. Many of the world's vineyards are found in river valleys, not too close to the water but on soils made up of gravel, sand and weathered rocks but other very fine wines are produced on the poor soil which overlays a limestone outcrop (as in Champagne and Burgundy).

FESTIVALS

If April is the month for Easter, then wine will flow as part of the celebrations (see *March*). Otherwise, if you find yourself in the neighbourhood of Avignon on 25 April, join the festival for St Mark, patron saint of the village of Châteauneuf-du-Pape. While in Avignon be sure to visit the Papal Palace, a monument to long-gone grandeur well-maintained for the visitor today.

Not far away, rosé wine has its moment when the festival of St Vincent is celebrated in Tavel (rather later than in other parts of France), an excellent excuse for some feasting and drinking of the local orangey dry rosé wines.

In Beaujolais, the village of Chiroubles has a fête on 24 April. The fruity red wines made here are delicate and live for only a few years as a rule, so enjoy them while you may. This is one of the nine villages entitled to be named on a Beaujolais bottle, or to contribute wine to the variety labelled 'Beaujolais Villages' (see *November* for more about Beaujolais).

On a larger scale, April is normally the time for Vinitaly, a vast trade fair which is open to the public. All the wines of Italy, in their dizzying variety are on view at Verona, with plenty of opportunity to taste. And then there is the enticing food pavilion with pungent scents of garlic, tomato sauce, olive oil, fresh bread . . . certainly one of the more appealing of the world's wine fairs. Spend a day here while you are visiting the Veneto (see the section on Venice and the Orient Express at the end of this chapter) and look out for the stand run by the helpful Istituto Enologico Italiano who can give guidance on every area and offer selected tastings.

Palais des Papes; an inner courtyard

ENTERTAINING

Wine is a wonderful temptation. The variety of flavour, colour and scent combined with style differences between regions means that there is a wine to suit every moment of a day, every month of the year. Some wines have very specific characters – a young Cabernet Sauvignon, for instance, is rather severe and demands care in serving and matching

'This wine should be eaten; it is much too good to drink.'
Jonathan Swift

with food. But there are also wines which represent sheer self-indulgence and are meant to be consumed with the type of furtive relish associated with chocolate-eating.

Rich wines are mouth-filling and sumptuous like perfect patisserie. The flavour is so full that alcohol seems almost incidental, a bonus for the sinner. Many sweet wines are quite high in alcohol as they are made with very ripe grapes bursting with sugar. Even after fermentation has ceased there is still plenty of residual sugar as well as alcohol, as high as 16% in some cases. Alternatively, a sweet wine may be fortified (see *January*).

Dean Swift's remark has a lot of truth; some wines are as substantial and satisfying as food. Indeed any wine is more like a food than other alcoholic drinks. Tasters often refer to wines as 'chewy' or 'flabby', 'mouth-filling' or 'velvety', as if they were referring to dishes on the menu at a dinner party.

Wine is alive. It changes in the bottle or glass in a matter of hours or even minutes. An old wine may literally fall apart during the course of a meal and become undrinkable, while a young wine may improve and smooth in the same time, thanks to the contact with air. 'Wine is a chemical symphony,' said one Californian authority.

There is a lot of talk these days about minerals and vitamins, with conflicting advice as to whether we need to supplement our modern diet with extra pills and potions to stay healthy. Wine actually contains many of the ingredients we are told we require, including all four elements of medieval medicine: earth, air, fire and water. It is obviously a product of the earth and absorbs many of the trace elements found in the soil; it needs to ferment and to mature; its alcohol is its 'fire'; and like every other living organism it contains plenty of water.

Before it is fermented the fresh grape juice contains some 250 chemical agents. The finished product contains phosphorus and calcium, essential for the formation of bones and maintenance of the blood; sulphur, which actually assists the liver in its 'purifying' process; and magnesium, which acts in conjunction with other elements to build bones and soft tissues as well as defending the body against infection. Magnesium also helps to break down sugars in the body, as does zinc, a 'fashionable' compound apparently lacking in a typical modern diet. Dentists would certainly approve of the mineral content of wine.

There is another interesting feature of wine: a high-alcohol variety also contains a good deal of glycerine, an excellent sugar substitute. If you have ever tasted pure alcohol then you will know that once the fire wears off the overall impression is of sweetness. This is the glycerine. It can be seen in a wine as it runs down the sides of the glass in rivulets, known as 'legs' in American wine circles.

More good news for the health buff – the sugars naturally present in wine are monosaccharides (such as glucose and fructose) which are handled quite easily by the liver. And vegetarians who are urged to take iron supplements because of the absence of red meat from their diet now have an answer. The French homeopathic doctor E.A. Maury describes red wine as 'vegetable blood' and reminds patients that a litre of good Bordeaux or Burgundy may contain up to 6 milligrams of iron. Hence the concept of wine as a tonic.

COOK'S CHEER

With all these nutrients in its makeup, it is hardly surprising that wine acts as a stimulant on the taste buds and tends to inspire any activity, although admittedly for a short time only . . . In the kitchen there is nothing like a glass of wine to urge the cook to action. And the best possible wine for this purpose is probably something sweet and lush, kept very cool in the fridge. The combination of sugar and alcohol gives a lift and of course a sweet wine keeps better than most, so a glass for the cook is not a waste of a bottle. If your budget does not run to Sauternes or Barsac, try Monbazillac from the Bergerac region or Muscat de Beaumes de Venise.

The vast majority of sweet wines tend to be white. The occasional rare red 'late harvest' sweet wine may be treated in the same way as white and served with dessert or viewed as an alternative to port and served after a meal with nuts or dried fruit. Italy and California are the major producers of really sweet red unfortified wines, some of which are made with the scented Muscat grapes. Others may even be made with a 'noble' variety like a Cabernet Sauvignon which happens to be very ripe in a certain vintage and yielding a very full style of wine.

Where does the natural sweetness in a wine come from? Once fermentation has begun, the sugar in grape juice (must) is gradually transformed into alcohol and would automatically continue until a maximum of about 16° is reached. At this point the yeasts die off and the process halts of its own accord. If the grapes contained a very high level of sugar on picking, then some of this would be retained in the ensuing wine as residual sugar, even at this high level of alcohol.

Assuming the winemaker takes a hand in the procedure, however, it is possible to determine just how sweet a wine is to be by stopping the fermentation with the addition of sulphur. In this way a wine of normal alcohol content (say 12–13°) may still be quite sweet, although it will not have the richness of a higher alcohol version. Another alternative is to add brandy to the fermenting juice, but this then makes a fortified wine which is really another story (see *January*).

Noble rot is unattractive yet is the source of such exquisite wine

The greatest sweet wines in the world share a particular feature known as *Edelfäule, pourriture noble* or noble rot, depending on the country of origin. Sauternes, Barsac and Coteaux du Layon in France, Beerenauslese and Trockenbeerenauslese in Germany, and various wines of the so-called New World, all make use of a natural phenomenon called *Botrytis cinerea*. This is the very fungus which may make greenhouse tomatoes wither and shrink to the horror of gardeners, but a winemaker will gather each shrunken grape with care and press them to make a very particular nectar.

Normal climatic conditions for *Botrytis* are sunny days and misty evenings which stimulate the mould growth. The mould pierces the grape and so some of the juice evaporates through the skin. As it evaporates so it becomes concentrated and the sweetness more noticeable, and the mould itself lends a subtle aroma of fresh mushrooms and honey to the finished wine which is irresistible once you learn to like it.

SWEET SERVICE

In Britain we have a fondness for sticky puddings and heavy cream desserts, neither of which really balances well with a fine-quality sweet wine. If you really want to offer a dessert wine with an English 'pud' then consider a semi-sweet Italian wine such as Orvieto, a Premières Côtes de Bordeaux or Entre-Deux-Mers which is labelled 'demi-sec' (semi-sweet); 'doux' (sweet); or 'liquoreux' (richly sweet).

Apart from very heavy sweet fortified wines, there are really three other categories. The first and noblest is the fine wine made with so-called botrytised grapes. Second are unusual sweet or semi-sweet wines made by drying grapes in the sun or indoors on racks to obtain a greater concentration. Examples of these are the Vin Santo of Italy and the Recioto variants of such familiar wines as Valpolicella and Soave. In France these wines are sometimes called *vins de paille* as the grapes were traditionally dried on straw (*paille*) mats. The South of France yields up many versions, often unavailable elsewhere. The third category is the very varied remainder, including all levels of quality from the delicacy of a demi-sec Vouvray (not always a *Botrytis* wine) to Yugoslav Tiger's Milk, very much an acquired taste. Austria and Germany have many delightful Spätlese or Auslese wines which are sweet yet not too rich, while newer wine regions feature all types of 'dessert' wine. As the climate of California's Central Valley and much of the Australian wine zone is very hot in summer, they started as sweet winemakers par excellence and there are still many good Muscats and late-harvest wines to be had.

Incidentally, late harvest on a label normally means that extra ripe grapes have been used and the wine is sweet. However, a winemaker may choose to 'ferment out' the sugar and create a dry alcoholic wine. If residual sugar is mentioned, then the wine will be sweet. Study the label before deciding to buy: a wine made with late-picked grapes is not necessarily a 'noble rot' wine either, but it may be. You can determine this from the price – noble rot comes expensive.

And do not overlook the possibilities of sweeter sparkling wine (see *July* for more detailed information). Sweet Champagne with cake or Asti Spumante with a rich dessert are both quite acceptable in their countries of origin.

Serving Sweet Wines

The Smart Set: Botrytis wines. Serve these well-chilled as an apéritif, extraordinary as this may seem. They also make an interesting accompaniment for rich delicacies such as pâté de foie gras; oddly a glass of Monbazillac or Sauternes with goose liver is not as heavy as it sounds. Similarly, the pungency of Roquefort cheese (made with ewe's milk and aged in caves like fine wine) is best set against a full sweet wine. The saltiness of the blue cheese is modified by the depth of the wine's flavour. And if all of this advice sounds a little far-fetched, consider taking a glass after the meal with some ripe fruit, such as apricots, peaches or melon.

Plain cakes also taste good with a full rich wine. In St Emilion they make little (overpriced) macaroons to nibble with Sauternes and Barsac. At home make or buy your own version or offer a very plain cake, made without too much fat. The Americans call this a pound cake, and they also make some fine cookies called vanilla wafers which team well with sweet wines like late-harvest Gewürztraminer.

Sultry Southerners: Wines made from dried grapes have a rich taste reminiscent of dry sherry. In Italy, these would be served with sweetmeats like nougat made with chopped nuts, cocoa, spices, lemon rind and sugar. Alternatively try one of these unusual wines with Monte Bianco (Mont Blanc in France): take 1½ lb fresh chestnuts and boil them in water for about 20 minutes, then peel off the outer shells and inner skins. Combine with 1½ pints milk and heat gently for about 30 minutes until the nuts are quite tender. Drain and blend or mash, then beat in ½ lb sugar (caster is best). Force this mixture through a food mill and allow it to fall into a mound or 'monte'. Chill in the fridge for at least an hour. When ready to serve whip some double cream (a small carton is enough) and add 1 or 2 tablespoons of *grappa* (Italian spirit like French *marc*) or three-star brandy. Spread this like a snow peak over the chestnut mixture.

In both Italy and Portugal, another favourite with a sweet rich wine is almond tart. Make the Portuguese version by boiling ½ lb sugar with ¼ pint water for five minutes. Add ½ lb ground almonds, 4 egg yolks and 2 stiffly-beaten egg whites to this liquid; return the pan to the stove and add 2 oz butter, 2 oz plain flour and ground cinnamon to taste. Stir until you have a paste which looks like caramel. Put this into a greased 7-inch flan tin and decorate with whole peeled almonds; bake in a moderate oven (150°C/300°F/Gas Mark 2) for 20–30 minutes until browned. Serve chilled. The toasted almonds complement any dark sweet wine perfectly.

Sweet Scents: This mid-range of sweet wines, such as the Spätlese, may be made with a touch of noble rot or none at all. They are quite light yet rich in flavour with a dry finish, and are not expensive. If the wine is made with the Muscat grape, try converting it to a fragrant jelly by mixing with four sachets of powdered gelatine per bottle. Pour into a wetted charlotte mould or similar. Then make a jelly with diluted red grenadine (pomegranate syrup). When set, chop the red jelly and serve the muscat jelly in the centre. It is light yet really delicious.

In Germany they use mid-priced sweeter wines to make a *Weincreme* (wine cream): mix together ¾ pint wine with 5 tablespoons of sugar, ¼ pint water, 5 eggs, the juice of half a lemon and its grated rind in a double boiler. Stir over low heat until you have a thick frothy 'milkshake'. Serve in chilled glasses; sprinkle with cinnamon. This goes well with plain cake and more of the wine used to make it.

Other possibilities for sweet wine accompaniments are pancakes stuffed with chestnut or hazelnut purée or apple, or the more sophisticated crêpes suzettes. These go well with sweet Loire wines like Coteaux du Layon or with Hungarian Tokay (not the finest and rarest, which should be sipped with reverence and without food!). Medium-sweet Italian wines are often served with a light cheesecake made with subtle Ricotta cheese (like cottage cheese, and obtainable in delicatessens). Take 1 lb sieved cheese and add to it 4 beaten egg yolks, 4 oz sugar, some candied peel to taste, the juice and grated rind of a lemon and 3 oz ground almonds. Beat all these well together, then transfer to a buttered flan tin and bake in a medium oven (180°C/350°F/Gas Mark 4) for 40 minutes until set. Serve warm or cold and sprinkle with caster sugar, accompanied by an *abboccato* Italian white wine such as a Soave or Orvieto.

THE VENETO REGION

The Veneto region is not perhaps the best known by name, but its wines and cities are certainly among Italy's more popular attractions. Take Soave, Valpolicella and Bardolino; add Verona, Vicenza, Padua and of course Venice itself and you can begin to appreciate the riches of the region both vinous and cultural. The wines are not the rarest or most expensive in Italy – that honour goes to the produce of Piedmont and Tuscany – but they have great charm and are made in a variety of styles from very light and delicate whites to the richest and even sweetest of reds. There is also a thriving output of good-quality sparkling wine, with Ferrari the most notable producer; this is not the fragrant fizz of Asti but a dry and sophisticated bubbly quite appropriate for owners of designer cars.

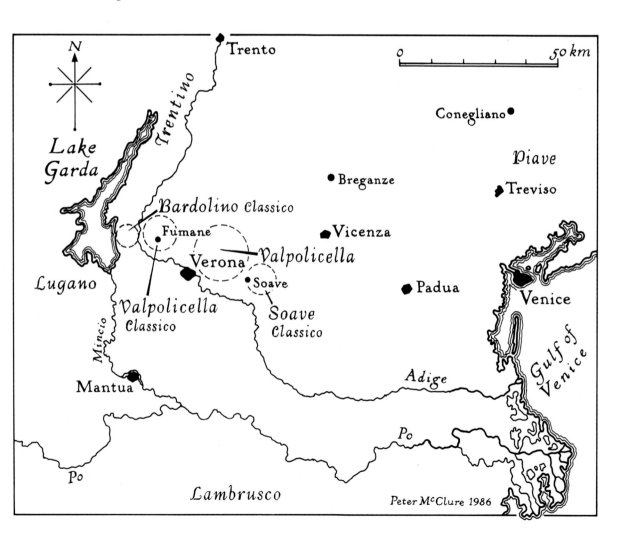

Peter McClure 1986

Italy is a most stylish place to visit. On the city streets you will see even office clerks dressed to kill with impossibly narrow shoes and gleaming leather jackets. It is easy to imagine how some of the ancient cities must have looked in Renaissance times. If you spend a day or two in Verona you will come across hidden alleys, squares and fountains reminiscent of every production of *Romeo and Juliet* ever staged, with inhabitants who glance from windows, doorways and balconies with the sharp brown features of a Caravaggio painting.

To reach the Veneto region, travel either to Milan or Venice by air – or arrive in style on the Orient Express. From Milan head first for Lake Garda and visit not only the lake itself with its river steamers and spectacular tunnels built to accommodate lakeside roads, but also neighbouring vineyards. One of the most delicate wines of the area is Lugana, made on the south shore of the lake and technically in the Lombardy region. It is made with the Trebbiano grape, a popular variety throughout Italy, and goes very well with the lake fish and with *polenta*, a cornmeal dish often served in the area.

Another fine white wine to try is Bianco di Custoza, made in vineyards extending from the south-east corner of the lake to Verona. Again Trebbiano is an important component, with some Garganega and Tocai. Its smooth flavour is similar to Soave. The red counterpart is Bardolino, not a modest wine. It can be very bright pink and have an almost 'mouthwash' quality, but at its best and tried on the spot it is fresh, clean and fruity. Drink it very young and with the glorious view of Lake Garda below the terraced vineyards it will taste just right.

Classic Venetian scene viewed from San Marco

For those more famous names, Valpolicella and Soave, you must travel beyond Verona into the hills but you can readily explore this area from a base in Venice. Soave is made mainly with the Garganega grape, with some Trebbiano di Soave in the blend, and has a straw-like colour and faint aroma of almonds which makes it very drinkable alone or with food, especially freshwater fish or classic risotto. Like Chianti it has a Classico defined area (a traditional, not a legal concept) which is known to yield the top wines. Co-operatives make a good deal of the Soave we see in shops in Britain and it is normally of good quality, but small family producers like Pieropan (see page 63) show how very fine this wine can be. They also make a Recioto version, drying the ripe grapes on special racks to give a deep yellow wine, high in alcohol and sugar.

Like Soave, Valpolicella exists on two levels: the very drinkable mass-produced version, and the more complex style made by family-owned concerns. One of these is Allegrini at Fumane di Valpolicella (see page 64) where you may taste not only Valpolicella Classico but also a Recioto and a full, faintly bitter Amarone style made by fermenting out the dried grapes so they give depth of flavour and alcohol with great ageing potential – an acquired taste.

North of Venice near Treviso there are some intriguing wines being made with the Cabernet Sauvignon grape, not normally thought of as typically Italian. The best-known producer here is Venegazzù, between Breganze and Conegliano. The blended wines are only categorised as table wines (Vino da Tavola) as they are something rather different. Like Bordeaux red wines, they include Cabernet Sauvignon, Cabernet Franc and Merlot. Part of the harvest is dried on mats and fermented separately to be added to the blend, and some of the wine is deliberately re-fermented in bottle (like a Champagne) and then blended in to give a 'prickle' on the tongue and fascinating flavour.

So the Veneto offers not only scenic beauty but a wide range of wines in all categories of price and quality. It is Italy's second largest production region (the Emilia-Romagna is the largest) and has numerous treasures to offer the wine lover. For more information on visiting vineyards here write to the Italian Trade Centre.

THE ORIENT EXPRESS

If glamour and nostalgia are alluring, you will find both on the Orient Express. It is like travelling back in time – the service alone is a lost art, with uniformed flunkeys bowing you from carriage to decorated carriage and stokers crouching in narrow corridors to keep the radiators ablaze in each compartment. Yet somehow the restoration has preserved a sense of realism and it is not too Disneyland perfect: the curtains are just slightly faded and the upholstery is just the moquette of just the shade of pink beloved of our mothers and grandmothers in the '30s.

Elegant dining on the Orient Express

Lovers of food and wine will likewise be gratified, for the cooking is truly first-class, even though produced in the most cramped of conditions. Rows of immaculate young chefs chop and stir in stainless steel galleys and the result is nearly three-star. The wines on offer are high-quality French, with plenty of opportunity for extravagance in your cabin. The 'room service' features the stuff of American soap opera with caviare and Krug top of the list, yet such frivolity is not a requisite for enjoyment. Just watch the view and relax as you roar through the Vorarlberg tunnel in mild spring sunshine and suddenly emerge into the blazing glare of snow.

Of course sitting in a bar car listening to a pianist play at ten in the morning may seem strange – but what could be more fun? Especially if you have just seen Paris and are en route for Calais and then Dover where you join the exquisite cream-coloured Pullman cars of the British part of the train for that most English of treats – afternoon tea with antimacassars. Quite the perfect way to adjust from a wine holiday back to realities of life at home . . .

Crossing the Alps on the Orient Express

THE RED AND THE WHITE: Allegrini
Valpolicella and Pieropan Soave

These two wines of the Veneto are known for their reliability. As Cyril Ray has said, 'I have never had a bad Soave.' Many is the Italian restaurant where they feature as house wine, many the large-size bottle purchased at a supermarket for parties and picnics. Soave in particular has become a favourite of the Americans with consequent increases in demand and production; it is outsold only by that curious semi-sparkling red, Lambrusco. But most drinkers see it as a light, inoffensive wine without much character and Valpolicella, too, lacks a 'serious' image and is viewed as so much alcoholic grape juice to be gulped with enthusiasm.

Of course both of these wines are delightful to drink informally, to gulp if you must. But they also have the right to be seen as serious contenders in the fine wine stakes and certain producers stand out as the individuals most likely to succeed. Their wines may not be the cheapest but they are undoubtedly more subtle and interesting to drink than the mass of exports made under these names.

Soave comes mostly from the communes of Soave; if it originates in Monteforte d'Alpone it may describe itself as Classico. One such wine is that made by Leonildo Pieropan, a consistent leader in tastings and competitions which somehow packs in twice as much flavour as most Soave without sacrificing any of the delicacy of style.

Family pride at Pieropan Soave

AZIENDA AGRICOLA
PIEROPAN,
Soave,
37038 Verona.

Allegrini – a family concern with
the seal of quality

The American authority on Italian wine, Burton Anderson, says that Pieropan's wine stands out from the others 'like a Ferrari in a parade of Fiats', and there is no doubt that sipped on a sunny day in the flowery courtyard of their family cellars it seems the match of any white Burgundy or Bordeaux. Pieropan wine was a prizewinner as early as 1906, when Leonildo's grandfather took the top award in Milan.

Today it is made in a traditional manner with plenty of wood barrels in evidence in the crowded cellars. There are also special racks for drying selected bunches of ripe grapes which will go into a rare and toothsome variant on basic Soave – the Recioto di Soave, rich and pungent. The grapes are grown on the twenty acres belonging to the family and a further seventeen which are rented. This yields only ten thousand cases per year, obviously very much less than the output of a firm like Bolla.

Like Soave, Valpolicella has a popular image and is in fact the best-selling red wine from Italy in the UK. It is a 'Beaujolais' in style, meant to be drunk young and savoured in all its fullness of fruit and aroma of bitter almonds. Seven different varieties of grapes are blended to make the wine, including the Corvina, the Rondinella and the Molinara. As for Soave, a *superiore* is a wine slightly higher in alcohol than the basic 11°, and a Classico comes from a small area just north of Verona in the foothills of the Alps.

The Allegrini family make a delicious Valpolicella Classico Superiore which is delicate on the palate and has been aged in oak casks. This means that not only does this wine taste terrific when young but it also has potential for keeping beyond its first youth and maturing into a subtler and more pungent version of the original.

Pungency is also a feature of the Allegrinis' Amarone. This is made from part-dried grapes as for Recioto (also an Allegrini wine) but instead of yielding a sweet wine with about 14° of alcohol it is allowed to continue fermentation until dry and very strong indeed, a strength which is compounded by ageing in wood. Amarone is a very long-lived wine, too powerful for some tastes but a must if you visit the region. It is a rarity which is offered with pride.

The Allegrini estate covers some seventy-five acres; Giovanni is the winemaker and his sister Maria organises promotion and sales. Like the Pieropans they have been producing wine for three generations, and the experience shows in their results.

If you want to visit Pieropan or the Allegrinis, write in advance to make an appointment. And while you are in the area, be sure to spend some time in Verona itself: the restaurants are excellent and of course the architecture and Shakespearean connections repay exploration at length.

ALLEGRINI,
Fumane di Valpolicella,
37022 Verona.

MAY

Frost in May holds even more of a threat for the grower than earlier in the year because this is the time when the new buds which will sprout next year are forming. So a very harsh frost or, worse yet, a hailstorm will destroy prospects not just for one vintage but possibly two.

Vines are usually self-pollinating and the flowers appear in June, so it is important that they receive plenty of light and some warmth in May. Just before the blossoming period the vines are sprayed against a blight called downy mildew (peronospora); if this attacks a vine the young grapes will not ripen.

'All in the merry month of May
When green buds they were swellin''
The Ballad of Barbara Allen
(trad.)

Barossa Valley dignitaries tasting their wines in South Australia

In Europe, it is time to bottle and despatch the young wines from the previous vintage to market; the dry white wines are usually first to be released with the younger red wines later. Naturally weather conditions affect both the bottling and shipping. Extremes of heat on the quayside can be as damaging as icy winter conditions. Meanwhile in the southern hemisphere winegrowers have already gathered in their harvest and there are celebrations to mark the occasion as early as April (try the Barossa Valley Vintage Festival one year; this South Australian festival takes place in alternate years, with a major arts festival in Adelaide in the years between).

FESTIVALS

In France, several regions have wine festivities this month. The villages of Molsheim and Guebwiller in Alsace are 'en fête' during May, and in the Bordeaux area 18 May is the date to celebrate at Montagne-St-Emilion, one of the satellites of St Emilion itself. At the end of May Pomerol wheels out its wine dignitaries for a 'Grand Chapitre', a robed procession.

For the grower there is a very important wine fair held in Mâcon during May when competitions for all the new wines are held. The much-coveted medals are subsequently displayed with pride on the various award-winning bottles. This is one of the more influential of the open competitions and is by no means for Burgundian wines only – the whole of France is there.

In the Loire Valley, at the Fête du Crottin in Sancerre, you may sample the delights of goat cheese – those tiny cheeses now often served warm over salad – which go well with the acidic wines of the region. There are other French cheeses available as well as the pungent goat.

Mid-May is the time for a wine festival in Tours, with a chance to try red, white and rosé Loire wines. In the Rhône Valley the village of Vacqueyras is host to a festival of all the Côtes du Rhône-Villages wines in May. These are the red wines which are entitled to bear a village name on the label as well as the simple title 'Côtes du Rhône' and a fine collection they are. Try Sablet and Rasteau as well as Vacqueyras itself.

The practical Italians combine other merchandise with their wine when they organise festivals: in the Chianti region, for instance, there is a marvellous Iris Festival which features flowers, honey, olive oil and a variety of other foods as well as the local wines. This is a true entertainment with dancing in the evenings and is held on the first two Sundays in May at S. Polo in Chianti, Tuscany. Later in the month or in early June Florence displays its fine crystal and china as well as wines and foods at the Fortezza da Basso. And the end of May is the time for the Festival of Pinenuts (*Sagra del Pinolo*) – those tiny sweet nuts which combine so well with spinach or ricotta cheese to make delicate appetisers – at Chieseanuova in Tuscany. In the Veneto there is a Soave festival on the first Sunday in May held in the village of that name.

Towards the end of May you might also consider visiting the wine fair at Krems in Austria, the Österreichische Weinmesse, which displays wines from the entire country and is intended for both trade and public. For more information about visiting Austrian vineyards in general, write to the Austrian Trade Commission. If you are interested in courses or tastings, not to mention boat trips on the Danube, then contact the Fremdenverkehrsband Wachau.

Krems – scene of a wine fair this month and an Austrian wine centre

Should your travels lead you towards the Rioja region of Spain at this time, then make for the historic pilgrim town of Santo Domingo de la Calzada, not far from Haro, where there is a fiesta from 10–15 May each year. And at Jerez de la Frontera in mid-May there is a celebration of the horse – the *Fiesta del Caballo* – which, naturally, is an excuse for the quaffing of much delicious unfortified local sherry. The local vineyard owners appreciate horses, flamenco and bullfights just as much as they do fine vintages!

ENTERTAINING

THE TASTE TEST: Comparing wines at home

The wine and cheese party may have passed into the realms of tired cliché along with fondue and folk music but the idea of enticing friends to share their cellars is not a bad one. 'Bring a Bottle' may have the wrong connotations but if tied to a theme the simple gesture of donating one bottle can be the basis for a real wine-tasting at home, not to mention a party afterwards.

With such an inordinate variety of wines now on offer, the theme of your tasting could be quite adventurous. Instead of, say, light red wines of France, why not attempt a tasting of Cabernet from around the world, or compare the sweet white wines of Europe with those of Australia and California? Remember that each bottle may be fairly expensive (perhaps £6–£8) but you need only contribute one per person or couple.

There are no hard and fast rules about a home tasting. If you prefer to sit about on comfortable chairs, pour a little of each wine and discuss as you go, then this is fine. But if you want to keep some sort of written record of the wines, then you will need to provide everyone with paper and pencil and line up the wines on a table.

If the wines are quite similar in style then a single glass will do per person. Simply empty any excess into a bucket discreetly located near the table – or use an empty magnum bottle with a plastic funnel on the table itself. The maximum number of wines should probably not exceed twelve as it is hard to distinguish the flavours beyond that figure. If you sip about 2 fluid ounces of each wine then you will altogether imbibe the equivalent of four typical glasses. On an empty stomach this can have quite an effect, so do provide spittoons in the form of wooden boxes filled with sawdust or simple plastic buckets and have the courage to set the example . . . Professional wine tasters always spit out their wine samples for two very good reasons; they want to keep their palates as 'awake' as possible, and they would obviously prefer not to stagger away from the tasting table part-inebriated.

An empty stomach is unfortunately essential for the best results: even the merest sliver of cheese can make a raw young red taste quite smooth and charming, hence the wine merchants' saying, 'Buy on apples, sell on cheese . . .' If a wine can withstand the sharpness of a tart apple it will taste marvellous alone, but as apples are rather too extreme for the average tasting provide plain crackers such as Bath Olivers and plenty of water to rest fatigued palates.

If all of this sounds fearfully professional and solemn, the only answer is to try it just once. You will almost certainly be amazed at your ability to identify the special aromas of certain wines if you merely gargle them around your mouth and then spit out. What remains is important. It should confirm the first impression gained by sniffing at the wine; nose and palate work together.

Order of Play

1. Cover your table with a white cloth; this helps to define the colour of the wine and its clarity, collectively described as 'appearance'.

2. Arrange the bottles from left to right according to age and sweetness.

The youngest is normally tasted first and the oldest and therefore the most subtle last – all the more reason to spit out the samples inbetween! Any sweet wines should be saved for the end of the tasting as it is very difficult to assess a dry wine after a mouthful of sugar.

3. If you want to add an extra dimension you could wrap all the bottles in brown bags or tissue paper to hide their identity and then vote a winner from this 'blind' tasting. Seeing the label can prejudice people one way or another: some wine lovers, for instance, feel Australian wine could never compete for quality with French so would mark it down automatically – and vice versa, maybe, if one of your friends is an Australian . . .

4. Number the wines from left to right by writing on the cloth if paper or on the bottles themselves. Each guest then takes a glass and begins with number one, noting reactions to the wine on a piece of paper. People are very chary of expressing themselves about wine so these notes might be for private purposes only, possibly using a marking system out of 10 or 20 (some tasters even mark out of 100), with a general vote for the three best wines at the end.

5. When tasting, first hold the glass up to the light and check the wine is clear, then try to describe its colour – think of jewels like garnet or ruby to help here, or shades of gold for white wines. Next take a tentative sniff at the glass, then a deep breath, and try to write down all the smells the wine brings to mind, good or bad. Everything from apple blossom to wet dog is permissible as this is for your eyes alone and an *aide-mémoire* for when you next encounter this wine. Finally, draw in a little wine and suck it along the sides of your tongue – swish it around the mouth then spit out. Again, quickly write down all the flavours and sensations it hints at – salt, velvet, steel, berries, oiliness, wood scents. From these notes try to decide if the wine seems balanced to you: a good wine has plenty of definite, healthy flavour (nothing chemical) both on the nose and the palate. Tasters describe the lingering sensations that remain after spitting out your sample as the 'finish'. A 'long finish' tends to be the sign of a well-made wine, possibly a good vintage. Younger wines finish shorter and as a rule white wines are much lighter and the fruit flavour much more important than for red wines. Any wine which looks brownish (unless it is fortified) is suspect and is probably oxidised.

Hans Crusius of the Nahe (see *June*) tastes his Riesling with obvious relish

What to Taste
A few ideas for wine combinations:

– Cabernet Sauvignon from around the world (Bordeaux red versus the rest)

– Chardonnay from around the world (white Burgundy and Chablis as opposed to Bulgarian or Australian examples)
– the mid-priced red wines of France (Vin de Pays and similar)
– lesser-known white wines of Europe (eg, Jurançon, white Rhône wines, Bulgarian white wines, a few Italian and Spanish examples)
– rare sweet wines of the world (for the affluent or extravagant)
– inexpensive sweet wines of the world (for the adventurous with a sweet tooth)
– Champagne versus sparkling wines of France (and elsewhere)
– a 'vertical' tasting; several vintages of the same wine
– a 'horizontal' tasting; several similar wines of the same vintage
– quite simply, a selection of favourite red or white wines within a certain price range arrayed together
– a comparison of all the different styles of port, Madeira or sherry you can find (spittoons certainly desirable at this one!)

MERRIE ENGLAND: THE RETURN OF THE VINE TO BRITAIN

'Go down to Kew in lilac-time, in lilac-time, in lilac-time; Go down to Kew in lilac-time (it isn't far from London!)'
ALFRED NOYES, *Barrel Organ*

During Alfred Noyes's lifetime (he died in 1958) you might have had to travel to Kew, to Hampton Court or to a private house to see vines growing in England. For the most part, they were cultivated for table grapes and usually protected in greenhouses or conservatories. It seemed that the ancient art of English winemaking was virtually extinct.

Yet there were stirrings in the south. In 1951 Maj. Gen. Sir Guy Salisbury-Jones planted a vineyard at Hambledon in Hampshire (also renowned as a home of cricket) and his lead has been followed with growing enthusiasm and increasing expertise over the twenty-five years since. The idea of vines growing on a grand scale on our tiny island may seem new, but in fact it has been tried before. The Romans decreed that wine grapes should be planted to slake the thirst of their legions here as elsewhere in Europe and in the so-called Dark Ages a winemaker was a person of some note. King Alfred imposed stiff penalties on anyone caught damaging a neighbour's vineyard.

The French were our undoing, in more senses than one. When, in 1154, Britain acquired Aquitaine through the marriage of Henry II to Eleanor, the French began to ship their 'claret' and soon undermined the native production. Even war did not stop the influx of wine from Europe, as Spanish 'sack' (sherry) and Madeira grew in popularity.

Over the next three centuries, the monasteries were leading grape growers and winemakers, but many of the establishments were closed by Henry VIII in the sixteenth century and even more were decimated by the plague of 1665. By the eighteenth century the romance of winemaking was as firmly associated with France in the British mind as it is today:

Thus the new generation of English winemakers has been reversing a trend established over very many years. The English Vineyards Association has declared our day 'the Golden Age of English wine' and since none of us is old enough to have tried any earlier examples we are not in a position to contradict. When talking of 'English' wine, however, it is important to remember that this is something quite different from 'British' wine which has been made and sold for many a year.

British wine and sherry are made from concentrated grape must which is imported from elsewhere in the grapegrowing world to be converted into various styles. In the parlance of the wine trade it is known as 'made wine', a marvellously medieval phrase which very neatly sets it apart from English wine. But sadly, because of labour costs and taxation, it is unlikely that true English wine will ever be as inexpensive as that termed British.

There are now more than a thousand acres of vines spread over the British Isles, some cultivated for winemaking by the producer, others destined for a co-operative crush as elsewhere in Europe. To date, few vines have thrived above a rough geographical divide from the Wash in the east to Bristol in the west; Hampshire, Wiltshire and the Isle of Wight boast some of England's finest vineyards, but there are also concentrations on the Suffolk-Essex borders, and in Kent, Sussex and even the Thames Valley, all producing some excellent wine.

Planning A Vineyard Visit

If you have a fine day in May, or perhaps a sunny weekend to spare, write to the English Vineyards Association for a copy of their current list of vineyards open to the public. You should also make contact with the English Wine Centre in Alfriston: this is where the annual English Wine Festival is held each July and awards are made for the best wine and best packaging, an important aspect of production for these still little-known wines.

Which vineyards should you select from the list? Closest to London, little further than Kew Gardens, are the Thames Valley vines. Westbury (not far from Reading) makes an interesting stop as they make some drinkable wine from the Pinot Noir grape as well as using the more popular white varieties. There are sixteen acres of vines and these are well-organised for the visitor. Some miles further on, you might go and see an example of a wine co-operative in the making at Chiltern Valley in the *other* Hambleden, near Henley-on-Thames, Oxfordshire.

As a rule, the wines produced do not support the cost of the vineyard and tourism is very welcome as a supplementary income. A series of

'England, with all thy faults, I love thee still –
My country!
I would not yet exchange thy sullen skies,
And fields without a flow'r, for warmer France
With all her vines.'

WILLIAM COWPER,
The Timepiece

Bernard Theobald, the Sage of Westbury Vineyard near Reading

good vintages helps to lessen the burden, but this is rare in England. New plantings are still frequent and this involves a four-year wait for fruition and the first wines.

South of London, one obvious stop is the Beaulieu vineyard in an area of great natural beauty. From there you might hire a boat and make your way to the Isle of Wight where both Adgestone (see profile below) and Barton Manor next to Queen Victoria's Osborne House both merit a visit. Back on the mainland and moving east into Sussex you will find the Carr-Taylors' vineyard at Westfield near Hastings. This family pioneered the export of English wines and even took a stand at the giant Salon des Vins in Bordeaux one year. Also in Sussex is Chilsdown in Singleton, near Chichester. Ian Paget has done a good deal of work to promote English wines and his vineyard is well worth a visit.

In Kent, near Maidstone, you may enjoy seeing the vines at Leeds Castle, one of the prettiest small castles in England. Another must for those keen to learn more about grapegrowing in this country is Lamberhurst near Tunbridge Wells. Kenneth McAlpine often wins awards for his wines which are made by a German — appropriately enough as so many English wines are not only made with German grape varieties but in weather conditions as harsh as any Germany has to offer.

Vines grow in the perfect setting of Leeds Castle, Kent

WIGHT WINE: THE VINEYARDS OF ADGESTONE

Brading is quite close to all the popular resorts in the Isle of Wight – Ryde, Sandown and Shanklin – yet it can be difficult to track down Adgestone Vineyard nonetheless as the site is tucked away from the holiday crowds, not for privacy but for the sake of the wines. It has all the requisite features for a fine vineyard: a good southern aspect, meaning that the vines catch every ray of sun from dark to dusk; good drainage; shelter from the worst winds provided by the trees on the hill tops around; and good soil, a chalky loam akin to those where many of the world's finest white grape varieties are cultivated. In addition, the Isle of Wight offers a generally benevolent climate – cool but not excessively harsh winters and a fairly long period of sunshine over each summer.

There is a well-preserved Roman villa near Brading and the owners of Adgestone like to imagine that vines were grown in the area as early as the fourth or fifth century (the last time the villa was inhabited) for the pleasure of the local Roman gentry. Today the wine is made by Ken Barlow, once a tobacco planter in Africa and India, now back home in the gentle surrounds of the Isle of Wight: he returned in 1968 with plenty of agricultural knowledge which he has put to excellent use.

By 1970 commercial quantities of wine were already in production, still quite an early date in the English 'wine renaissance'. 1976 was the record-breaking hot summer which finally put English wine on the map and Ken Barlow was awarded a Gold Medal by the English Vineyards Association for the Best Dry Wine – quite a feat in a year when many wines were of fine quality. In 1978 he won the Gore-Brown Trophy for the Best English Wine at the annual festival.

This award is highly respected in English wine circles: it was established by a pioneering wine family and is now contested by about two hundred wines. Since 1978 Ken Barlow has received either an EVA (English Vineyards Association) Seal or Medal for each of his vintages. The Seal is an attempt by English winemakers to establish quality controls like those in France and Germany. It is worth looking out for as it certainly guarantees a good standard of wine.

Ken Barlow at ease at Adgestone

There is only one wine made at Adgestone. Although various grape types are grown they are blended each year according to yield to make a single wine; thus each wine will be very different, depending on how the grape types fared in any particular year. Apart from white grapes including Müller-Thurgau, Seyval Blanc and Reichensteiner, Ken Barlow also devotes a couple of his twenty-four acres to Pinot Noir, but these are not grown for commercial purposes at the moment. His white varieties are all high-yielding and sturdy, well-proven in English vineyards, with a full fruity flavour.

The grapes are picked at the end of October or even in November to ensure maximum ripeness; the juice is then allowed to stay in contact with the skins (as for red wine) for a short time to give added richness of flavour. As the weather is cool by now the fermentation continues over a long period, into the New Year. The various grape varieties are made into separate wines which are then blended when ready, with the addition of a little *Süssreserve* (unfermented grape juice). The finished wine is bottled during the summer.

JUNE

In most of the world's wine regions this is a crucial month. The vines blossom and set the embryonic grapes and the whole harvest can be destroyed at a stroke if this process is interrupted for any reason. *La vigne en fleur* has a romantic ring and indeed the rather unromantic greenish grape flowers do have a glorious if subtle fragrance, but for the growers it is another period of very hard work.

Temperatures need to be around 18–20°C during the flowering and if the warmth is accompanied by calm conditions, so much the better. Rough winds may shake the 'darling buds of May' but damage to the flowers of June is far more serious. When the flowers are over the vines are normally sprayed against mildew and some of the developing shoots are tied to the wire, selected for this year's growth. If nitrogen-producing plants such as mustard have been planted between the rows of vines then these may be ploughed in at this stage, otherwise an assessment is made of the soil to see if further nitrogenous compounds need to be applied. This addition of nitrogen must be done after flowering as too much during blossomtime can jeopardise pollination, a condition known as *coulure*.

In the cellars this can be a very busy time as wines not already shipped must be despatched before the very warm summer weather. So wines for sale this year are bottled and labelled, while those which are to remain in the cellar for further ageing are racked, ie, transferred from one barrel or vat to another. This process is normally carried out several times in the life of a wine and has the effect of removing impurities and producing a clearer, cleaner wine. For the final filter the winegrower uses a very fine mesh and a variety of compounds to extract the more obvious particles and yield a wine with the brilliant clarity now expected by the consumer. (See *October* for more about these cellar activities.)

WINE GOES TO MARKET: THE STRUCTURE OF THE WINE TRADE

This ancient joke illustrates one age-old image of the wine merchant, an image that still persists however in the minds of many wine drinkers, especially younger ones. For them, a wine merchant is an anachronism in a pin-stripe suit adorned with old school tie or regimental badge, supping his wares noon and night. His taste runs to old-fashioned 'grocers' claret', heavy and overpriced red Burgundy and rather sickly lesser Sauternes.

With this monster in mind, the fledgling wine drinker flees to the local supermarket only to discover that it is almost impossible to select satisfactory wines without any form of guidance as to the relative styles and qualities of the wine, let alone an opportunity to try before buying. So merchants who can offer a halfway house between these two extremes naturally do very well out of all the wine buyers who are seeking neither snob labels nor the very cheapest in plonk.

But where do these forward-looking merchants obtain their wine? The more traditional wine list tends to have a selection of 'agency' lines, familiar wines such as, say, Blue Nun and Mouton Cadet, together with other wines selected on their behalf by middlemen operating in the various regions of Europe. Naturally these middlemen take a commission for their services and this is passed on to the customer. The range of wines tends to be predictable and fairly safe – the kind of wine you see on hotel restaurant lists.

The more enterprising wine shipper will seek out personal contacts with growers and winemakers to ensure quality and character in the wines he lists. In these cases, the suppliers will no longer be able to sit back, safe in the knowledge that his wines are sold often before they are made, regardless of vintage quality. He (or she) will have to maintain standards in order to keep the British merchant happy. This type of amicable friction can only do good to the consumer.

In more traditional areas such as Burgundy it can be tricky to find a grower who will sell good wine direct; the *négociant* has had a stranglehold for many years, not only marketing the wines but also blending, bottling and storing them prior to shipment. But of course the honest broker (the *courtier*) still has a part to play in all this, preparing the ground for a visit by the English buyer and saving time and money during what can be the costly business of choosing new wines at source.

The old-fashioned merchant used to buy a wide range of wines forward – immature wines which needed to age before going on sale. In the past these were shipped to the UK in barrel or bottle and then stored in the merchant's cellars for some time before being labelled and

LADY: *'You mean to say that you never let water pass your lips? What do you use to brush your teeth?'*
WINE MERCHANT: *'A light Sauternes, madam.'*

sold. In the days before EEC regulations this system gave rise to all kinds of abuses, with wines arriving from one region and later appearing in the guise of something much smarter, or even being blended for 'improvement'.

Today, the high costs of storage mean that the early buying of wines can be very expensive for the shipper and he may not be able to afford to have his capital tied up for two or more years. Anyway, fewer modern wines are made in the heavy woody mode which demanded years of smoothing in the cellar. The public demands younger and fruitier wines for rapid drinking. However, the entrepreneurial merchant can still do well for his customers by buying 'futures' in Bordeaux or Oporto, ideally using his knowledge of less famous names to rival the legendary Latour or Taylor. These wines may be sold on to individuals or companies by the case and they then pay the incidental costs of shipment and tax on arrival. But they must have sufficient patience to wait before sampling what they have bought!

In all, both consumer and merchant have come of age. Companies like The Wine Club and Bordeaux Direct have led the way in putting the drinker in touch with the grower, offering a wealth of information about each wine they sell, instead of surrounding famous names with mystique enough to deter any but the very confident and well-connected.

FESTIVALS

If France is your destination in June then there are plenty of local festivals to choose from and in alternate years the major international wine fair is held in Bordeaux (otherwise in Germany). The vast array of wines on display is mainly for the benefit of members of the trade but it is an intriguing event for the amateur also, and the fair also includes food. For more details write to Food and Wine from France Ltd, who are based in London, or wait until you are in Bordeaux itself and contact the Conseil Interprofessionel du Vin de Bordeaux.

CIVB,
1 cours du xxx juillet,
33075 Bordeaux.

On the opposite side of France there is a celebration of the Kugelhopf on 11 June at Ribeauvillé. This rather dry yet delicious cake contains sultanas soaked in kirsch and almonds and is named for its distinctive shape, a fluted dome. Locals serve it with dry Alsace Muscat or with one of the memorable white *eaux de vie* of the region, fiery spirits made with fruits and berries, each pungently scented and served ice cold.

June is also a month for flower festivals in some of the lovelier towns and villages of Bordeaux. There is a Fête de la Fleur in scenic St Emilion on 14 June and during the third week of the month visit

Loupiac, home to sweet wines and an abundance of flowers. The Médoc and Graves regions hold their festivals on 19 June in dozens of small communities – and what could be a more delightful way of heralding summer than by sipping a new Bordeaux white surrounded by June blossoms?

Beaune in the Burgundy region is a veritable tourist Mecca with its marvellous wines and extraordinary medieval buildings including the Hôtel Dieu, scene of the annual autumn auction of rare wines. There is also an exceptional wine museum (see *November* for more about visiting Burgundy). During the first week of June a wine fair is held here, so if you are able to find a room (not easy in the high season) this has to be a stop on your French travels.

The major wine towns of the Champagne region are also 'en fête' in June with the festival of St Jean held on the Sunday closest to 24 June in Reims, Epernay, Hautvillers and other smaller communities. The cathedral at Reims is worth a visit at any time but it is a particularly lovely area at this time of year (see *July* for more about the Champagne region).

Down-to-earth celebration of the vine at Johannisberg, Rheingau, Germany

In Germany the season for wine festivals might be said to open in June, with wine days, wine markets and tastings of all kinds held throughout the summer in all the regions. There is an excellent list of festivals called 'Deutsche Winzerfeste' available from Wines from Germany Information Service. Just as a sample, there is a Mosel Wine Week in Cochem at the beginning of June, wine festivals at Lorch and Hochheim in the Rheingau during the month, and a Freiburger Weintag held amid the picturesque scenery of the Black Forest at the end of June.

Spain and Portugal have many religious festivals throughout the year, but in June northern Portugal, home of port and Vinho Verde, is worth a visit for the Grand Pilgrimage of São Gonçalo at Amarante early in the month and, at the end of the month, for the Festival of São Pedro at Póvoa de Varzim, a resort with wonderful sandy beaches not far from Oporto.

ENTERTAINING

THE GREAT BRITISH PICNIC

Eating outdoors whatever the weather is a favourite British sport. Indeed, it is often combined with a passing interest in some other sporting event such as the Epsom Derby, Wimbledon or the Henley Regatta. These and many other summer occasions drive spectators into a frenzy of rug-spreading, hamper-unpacking and of course cork-popping, with fiendish ingenuity employed to keep the wine at the correct temperature. And for the less hearty, there are musical and cultural events such as Glyndebourne which offer just as great an opportunity for watching one's neighbours at play eating a sumptuous meal outdoors.

Choosing the menu and wines for such festivities can be quite simple if you take the best from your cellar and combine it with a hamper from Fortnum's, but this very pricey option lacks an element of fun. Preparing the food and risking the weather is all part of the entertainment. How often have you seen elegantly attired racegoers huddled under vast umbrellas, gamely consuming their quail and caviare? – only in Britain.

So June has to be the month for an unashamedly British approach to the menu, though this need not mean the exclusion of all foreign wine. English wines, while agreeable, are rather limited in their applications and as yet the red and sparkling versions hardly rival Bordeaux or Champagne. So let the food be British and the wines classic. Extending the notion of those light dry white English wines, think of something a little richer and more flavourful and you have the ideal summer drink – German Mosel or Hock: not an elaborate label with a lengthy title but a simple QbA wine or at most a Kabinett, neither of which should be overpriced. The fragrance of the Riesling grape is just right for the traditional British picnic.

Alternatively follow a 'colour scheme' and serve pink wines with rose-tinted food. This may sound like so much nonsense but just wait until you have tried, say, a rosé from the south of France with cold salmon and mayonnaise followed by strawberry shortcake. The earthiness of the rosé with its crisp clean flavour balances the taste of the food to perfection. If your choice must be red, then let it be light. Think of Valpolicella rather than Vacqueyras, Chianti rather than Chambertin. And the red wines of the Loire Valley (such as Chinon or Gamay de la Loire) are also entirely appropriate for picnics as they too may be served cool; or consider a young Beaujolais or Côtes du Rhône treated the same way.

If your budget is not too limited then Champagne may be an option, but remember this really can be almost unpleasant when served warmish. So take along an unglamorous ice chest in the American style to preserve the temperature of your expensive bottles. If the river is all you have as a fridge, then perhaps it might be wiser to stick to sparkling wine which has a certain fruity flavour and charm even when not absolutely chill. Consider German Sekt, California 'Champagne' or a Blanquette de Limoux.

Some of the following ideas for interesting picnic fare are thoroughly British, some unabashedly a blend of cultural influences. All are easy to eat without an elaborate portable table/chairs/butler, and all may be prepared and stored in the fridge prior to the Event whatever it may be:–

Glyndebourne – quintessence of the Great British Picnic

Elegant Nibbles

This is the type of picnic which might do duty for some hours, perhaps stored in a car boot for later distribution to sundry hungry spectators. The food needs to be easy to eat while on the move and unlikely to spoil if left to linger for a time in the sun/wet. The wine should fare better as the ubiquitous ice chest fits readily into what Americans call the tailgate of a car.

MENU

Hard-boiled quails' eggs served with shell on – the hardy crunch shell and all.

*

Tiny pancakes made with a mixture of wholewheat and plain flour to the consistency of drop scones, similar to Russian blinis. Spread them luxuriously with lumpfish roe from jars or some cream cheese or sour cream – even chopped onion if liked.

*

Rolls of smoked salmon filled with cream cheese and sprinkled with lemon juice for moisture.

*

Cucumber segments part-peeled (keep some skin on to retain shape and moisture), their centres filled with tiny shrimp sprinkled with cayenne pepper.

*

Greek humous bought or made to spread on pita bread.

*

Black olives and green olives rolled in herbs and fine oil.

*

Brie (not too ripe) in a large piece; French 'biscottes'.

*

Grapes or fresh figs to conclude, with some rich cookies or cake for those sweet of tooth.

*

Wines: The unusual will fit well here, so experiment with Bulgarian Chardonnay, Vinho Verde, or a lighter German wine such as a Halbtrocken. Those with a taste for such things might even serve real Greek retsina – if they can obtain it. And try a sweeter German wine with the fresh fruit; a Mosel Auslese from a good year.

The Food's the Thing

This smarter picnic presupposes that your guests have an hour or so to spare from the exhausting business of wandering around in search of sport. A rug with tablecloth will suffice although of course a real table and chairs might make it more of an occasion. Use proper china and glasses; the food and wine warrant it:

MENU

Canapés Basques and Miniature Mushroom Quiches.
For the canapés, toast stale white bread lightly and brush with melted butter in advance. Mash up a can of good-quality sardines with plenty of unsalted butter, a dash of white wine vinegar, a tablespoon of Dijon mustard and chopped fresh parsley and tarragon to taste. Add ground black pepper to taste and blend well. Spread on the toast just before serving to preserve crispness.

*

For the small quiches, bake shortcrust pastry with 8 oz flour and 4 oz butter to make 24 small tartlets and allow to cool. Chop 2 lb button mushrooms and add a bunch of spring onions (also chopped) and lemon juice to taste. Sauté in butter for 2 minutes, then add a small carton of single cream or the same amount of milk and cook slowly for about 15 minutes. Mix with 2 beaten eggs and a small carton of double cream, top with grated cheese and nutmeg, then bake in the shells in a fairly hot oven (190°C/375°F/Gas Mark 5). Serve cold or warm.

*

A good-quality game pie which may be bought from top butchers or stores *or* a terrine made at home with chunks of ham, pork, tongue and plenty of parsley, like *jambon persillé* popular in Burgundy.

*

Green salad using various types of leaf eg, lettuce, radicchio, watercress, endive, and lightly dressed with walnut oil.

*

Tomato salad dressed with Dijon mustard and sunflower oil. Gradually beat the oil into the mustard to make a creamy mixture. Add chopped chervil if available.

*

Wines: White Burgundy such as Meursault if the budget is sufficient, or try a Mâcon Blanc or St-Véran as a good substitute. Red Burgundy for the game pie, or a fruity St-Emilion from a good year like 1983.

THE WINE WANDERER: German wines and VINEYARDS

*'Kennst du das Land, wo die
Zitronen blühn? . . .
Kennst du es wohl?*
Dahin! Dahin!
*Möcht ich mit dir, o mein
Geliebter, ziehn!'*

('Know you the land where the
lemon-trees bloom? . . .
There, there I would go,
O my beloved, with thee!')
GOETHE, *Wilhelm Meisters
Lehrjahre* (translated by Carlyle)

The German soul is full of romance. The climate may well be too cool for lemon trees but some of the scenery in south and west Germany is true story-book, and the vineyards are to be found in the most attractive settings.

To preserve the romance you may prefer to abandon modern transport and choose instead a Rhine or Mosel steamer. Your journey could take as little as a single afternoon or as much as ten days but however long you spend on the river, this is an ideal way to see the vineyards and to relax and enjoy yourself as well. As a rule, the boats are very modern and comfortable, and the catering is of a high standard. Contact the K-D German Rhine Line in Cologne for more information.

Trains may be more prosaic but they are undoubtedly efficient and have charm for those bored with car travel. It is possible to explore all the major German wine regions by rail: start in Cologne or Frankfurt and there are connections for the Rheingau, Mosel, Nahe, Rheinpfalz, Rheinhessen and Baden in the south. The German National Tourist Office in London will help you to plan your trip.

Regarding the wines themselves, arm yourself with some brochures from the Wines from Germany Information Service for basic information and be prepared to learn a great deal as you go about wine law and lore. If your impression of German wine is of a pleasant but rather 'soft' drink then it is likely you will change your attitude by the time you return. One point to remember is that fine German wines are consistently undervalued in Britain and are good buys for your home cellar.

The scale of wine production in Germany rarely rivals that of central Spain, southern Italy or the Midi area of France. Yet there is a very high concentration of quality wine, as well as excellent table wine: this is not normally exported so may come as a pleasant surprise if you know only those rather dull 'Euroblends' (actually part Italian in origin) sold as *'Tafelwein'* in Britain.

NB for more details about German labelling and wine law, see appendix 179.

The eleven German wine regions are relatively close together and the contrast between them is not so dramatic as, say, the difference between the Champagne region and the south of France. Wherever you go during the summer seaon and into the autumn you are likely to encounter local village wine festivals, with stands set up in the cobbled streets beneath half-timbered houses. Singing and dancing in the streets are commonplace, with a local brass band often taking part in the festivities. Sausage, cheese, cold chicken, pork steaks roasted over an open fire and pickled pork are typically sold to complement the wines.

If your visit does not coincide with a festival there will still be plenty of tasting opportunities without any formality. As in numerous wine regions all over the world, a great many wines are made by families who, in the tourist season, set up tables by their front door with a sign declaring 'Weinproben' – tasting. Wines may be sampled by the glass for a small charge and you will have the opportunity to try the whole range of styles from Kabinett, through Spätlese, to Auslese and even Beerenauslese and Trockenbeerenauslese. Food may also be on offer and sometimes there are rooms to rent so that you can take a closer look at the vineyards and the winemaking equipment.

Germany is a place where you can easily take the family with you on a wine holiday. The atmosphere is casual and there are many simple guest houses, or good camp sites if you prefer, all close to the vineyards. The active can combine tasting with vigorous hiking by following the *Weinwanderweg* footpaths which are well marked and lead to the cellars of local producers. To recover from the exercise you might visit a spa town such as Bad Dürkheim in the Rheinpfalz, Bad Kreuznach in the Nahe or the elegant Baden-Baden for some rest and recuperation with glass in hand.

'Uber allen Gipfeln
Ist Ruh'.'
('Over all the mountain tops is peace.')
   GOETHE, *Wanderers Nachtlied*

Take the *Moselweinstrasse* for a very picturesque journey along this winding river, tasting the light, fresh local wines as you go. Trier is an

Precipitous terraces along the Mosel Valley

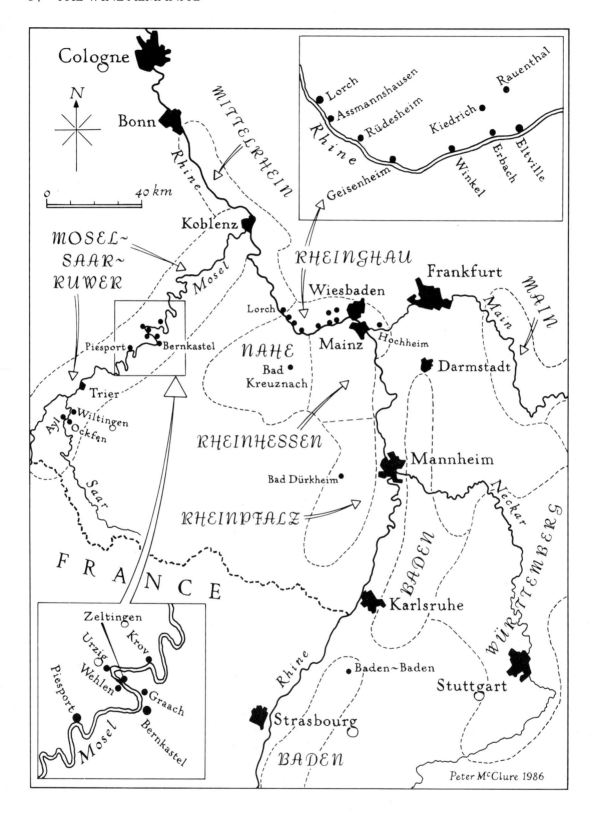

Cologne

N

Bonn

40 km

Rhine

MITTELRHEIN

Koblenz

MOSEL~
SAAR~
RUWER

Mosel

Piesport   Bernkastel

Trier

Wiltingen
Ayl
Ockfen

Saar

F R A N C E

Zeltingen
Urzig   Krov
Piesport   Wehlen   Graach
Bernkastel
Mosel

Lorch
Assmannshausen
Rüdesheim
Geisenheim
Winkel
Rauenthal
Kiedrich
Erbach
Eltville

Rhine

RHEINGHAU

Wiesbaden
Lorch
Mainz   Hochheim

NAHE
Bad
Kreuznach

RHEINHESSEN

Bad Dürkheim

RHEINPFALZ

Frankfurt

Main

MAIN

Darmstadt

Mannheim

Neckar

BADEN

Karlsruhe

WÜRTTEMBERG

Rhine

Baden~Baden

Stuttgart

Strasbourg

BADEN

Peter McClure 1986

interesting city to visit, with Roman origins and two thousand years of winemaking history; it is still a centre for wine producers and shippers. Drive on from here or walk along one of the *Weinlehrpfade* (wine footpaths) leading away from the city to sample wines from local cellars: these will take you through the vineyards and as you go you will see exhibits giving details of grape varieties and viticulture in general. And using Trier as a base it is easy to visit the vineyards of the Saar, situated on steep slopes covered in slate. The best known villages in this area are Ayl, Wiltingen and Ockfen.

In the opposite direction there are some more famous names such as Piesport (a dream for photographers); Bernkastel in the Mittelmosel, home of the Doktor wines; then Wehlen with the noted Sonnenuhr (sundial) vineyard. Zeltingen also has a Sonnenuhr vineyard, then there are Graach, Ürzig and Krov, the latter renowned for its cheeky label 'Nacktarsch' showing a bare-bottomed urchin.

The famed Rheingau region is only some 30 km in length, yet it is home to many of Germany's greatest wines. Set out from Frankfurt at one end, or from Koblenz at the other and follow the river Main through its amazing gorge past the many fairy-tale castles. Look for the signs marked Rheingauer Riesling Route, which begin at Lorch if you set out from Koblenz. If your budget is generous stay near Assmanshausen at the Hotel Krone, renowned for good food and wine, especially the unusual red which is made in vineyards belonging to the hotel.

Continue on to Rudesheim which can be a 'tourist trap' in season but is worth a visit for its classic German Hock full of fragrance. Next is Geisenheim, where experimental grape varieties are developed, of interest to grapegrowers not only in Germany but also in New Zealand and California.

Be sure to stop at Schloss Johannisberg, a sight impossible to miss as it is perched high above the river, said to be the home of the *Edelfäule*, grapes made with noble rot. Another aristocratic estate is Schloss Vollrads near Winkel, occupied by the same family for some eight hundred years. Kloster Eberbach is another interesting stop as this beautiful monastery dating from the twelfth century is home to many wine seminars and courses as well as a museum of wine equipment. It also houses the German Wine Academy. Tastings are on offer to the passing visitor for a small charge. Write to the German Wine Academy in Mainz if you would like to learn more about their courses.

So onward to Kiedrich, Erbach and Eltville, and the road turns upwards into the hills of Rauenthal where the wiens are heavier and more pungent than those made below. Finally you will reach Hochheim, the origin of the name 'hock' and once the major port for shipment of the local wines. One of the vineyards, the Königin Viktoria Berg, is named after Queen Victoria, recalling her visit in 1850. To this day it produces a very superior wine.

NAHE QUALITY: The wines of Hans Crusius

The Nahe Valley is not on the obvious tourist route. It lies between the Rheingau and the Mosel and you will often read that the wines also fall somewhere inbetween in terms of style. This is not really doing them justice as they show a distinct character of their own, with a clean taste compared by Hugh Johnson to the wines of Sancerre, 'a delicate hint of the blackcurrant leaf with a delicious mineral undertone'. Certainly the drier wines made in the area show this mineral quality at its best – this has to be the drinking man's (or woman's) ideal mineral water.

The styles known as *trocken* and *halbtrocken* are a relatively new concept in German Wine Law and reflect two trends: the desire of the Germans to drink lighter wines with their meals, and the desire of the producers to compete with Soave and Muscadet in the export market. The first of these aims is a healthy one – it has to be a good thing that an increasing number of German wines are dry enough to drink with any dish. The second is more debatable, however, as Mosel is not Muscadet and fails when it tries to imitate too closely.

Hans Crusius makes a good deal of dry wine, but although his wines certainly sell well, he is not making them with solely commercial aims in mind. Despite the fact that his family have been making wine in the same place since 1570 he is a man remarkably open to new ideas. Having begun to produce drier wines he has now firmly decided in their favour, so much so that he declares in his colourful English that 'I'd give £100 to the church if all my customers wanted dry wine.' At present only half of his output is dry, the rest sweet. They are clean, classy wines and have a long finish, and even in the richer varieties there is not too much sweetness.

Over the past ten years the wines of Hans Crusius have become noticeably dryer but this does not mean he has abandoned ttradition; he still makes all the other class *QmP* styles, including the rarer sweet Beerenauslese if conditions permit. In Crusius's opinion, dry wines are more honest than sweet. A good dry wine cannot lie, cannot hide mistakes under a layer of sugar. He enjoys rising to the challenge of such a wine, yet there is a paradox. To make a good dry wine he feels the grapes need to be very ripe, ripe enough to make a Spätlese or Auslese if fermented in the traditional way. Grapes of Kabinett quality are too light, have too much acid, he feels, to make a superior dry wine of the type he appreciates. Unfortunately the drier styles do not keep for as long as the sweeter.

Hans Crusius and his son, Dr Peter Crusius

Hans Crusius's winemaking involves a mixture of ancient and modern processes, with wooden casks used for fermentation and for ageing the wines afterwards, and the very latest in cold sterile filters to render the wine perfectly brilliant before bottling.

The vineyards themselves are in very fine locations, notably that on the Bastei, a rocky outcrop perfect for Riesling and the pride of the company. The nearest town is Traisen, hence the name Traiser Bastei for this wine. A larger part of the crop comes from a steep cliff of porphyry rock called the Rotenfels (it really *is* red), again ideal for Riesling but also suitable for Müller-Thurgau, Weissburgunder and Kerner, a fairly new part-Riesling crossbreed with a slight Muscat aroma.

Overall some seventy per cent of the production is in Riesling, the noblest and trickiest of German varieties. All the wine is estate-bottled and labelled with the old-fashioned traditional style of Hans Crusius's grandfather. Hans's son Peter works with him (he has a doctorate in oenology, wine science) so the unbroken line will continue for the foreseeable future. Their latest product is a sparkling version of their wine, properly fermented in the bottle, as befits a wine of such aristocratic allure.

JULY

Whether you take the romantic or practical view of travel, July is certainly an ideal month for summer holidays. And whether your aim is total relaxation or cultural enrichment, combine your trip with a look at some local wines or vineyards. If you choose any of the regions mentioned in this book the wines will be impossible to avoid and the simplest enquiry at a hotel desk will almost certainly yield plenty of information about where to find out more about their origins.

In the vineyards, the true warmth of summer means furious growth and consequent trimming back of the vines so that this energy is not wasted. If good berries are to be obtained then the long suckers thrown up by the vine must be removed together with any leaves which may overshadow the young grapes and slow their ripening. In scorching southern climes, however, the leaves remain and are encouraged to hang down over the bunches (particularly of white grapes) protecting them from the effects of excessive sun. Remember that raisins are simply dried grapes, but wine made with raisins – apart from a few very rare exceptions for wines made with grapes deliberately dried (see *April*) – tastes very odd indeed.

Weeds spring up between the rows, stealing valuable nutrients from the soil, and these must be hoed or sprayed. And the vines themselves need to be sprayed against the various forms of rot and insect infestation which threatens them in these warm months. Mention 'red spider mite' to a winegrower this month and he will visibly pale.

Indoors the wines are not usually bottled at this time of year unless there is a cool modern bottling plant – in the hot weather it is hard to keep them stable. But the casks that have been emptied must be thoroughly washed and dusted with 'flowers' of sulphur to keep them in good condition for the coming vintage. Some are filled with water and a touch of dissolved sulphur to kill 'bugs' so that they will not shrink in the heat.

FESTIVALS

Alsace is a stunningly pretty part of France with its fairytale decorated houses and flower-bedecked squares, and in July it is the centre for many small festivals including one at Barr in mid-month; an 'open house' for the cellars of Dambach-La-Ville on the second Sunday; a festival at Ribeauvillé towards the end of the month; and a celebration of the Riesling grape at Riquewihr during that same week. Riesling made in this area is quite unlike its equivalent from the far banks of the Rhine: it is quite dry and contains the very essence of the fruit without too much fragrance – a perfect summer drink.

Picture postcard vineyards at Katzenthal, Alsace

The Alsace wine town of Eguisheim bedecked with flowers

Touring the southern Rhône Valley is another way to spend part of a holiday, viewing both the Roman remains such as the amphitheatre at Orange and a wine exhibition in the grotto there. Away from the coast the heat may be intense, so the shade of a grotto might offer just the right temperature in mid-July.

If you are travelling in Germany it is highly likely that you will come across wine festivals in villages on your route. Consult the invaluable guide already mentioned (page 77). In Geisenheim on the Rhine, there is the charmingly-named Lindenfest (lime tree festival) in mid-month.

If Rome itself seems a little too steamy at this time of year, then take to the wine hills which surround the city. The famous name here is Frascati, another ideal summer thirst-quencher. Make for Lake Nemi to

The gardens of Castel Gandolfo
– summer residence of the Pope

the south of the town of Frascati, a dark-tinted expanse of water evocative of the pagan rites which were once celebrated here in honour of Diana. In June there is a special festival in the nearby village to mark the ripening of the wild strawberries – the Sagra delle Fragole. To the north is Lake Albano, a water-filled volcanic crater. Castel Gandolfo, by the shores of the lake, is the Pope's summer residence and scene of another wine festival in July. For more about these and other festivals in the Rome area contact the Italian Institute for Foreign Trade.

One of the major wine towns of the Spanish Rioja region is Haro, not a tourist attraction in itself but definitely an important stop for those who enjoy these wines, as many of the major producers are based here, including CVNE, Muga, Paternina and Martínez Lacuesta. Haro is a centre for good eating and drinking with an interesting old quarter. Try to visit towards the end of the month as 29 July is the date of the Romeria, a folk festival which involves much wine drinking and even a Batalla del Vino (battle of wine), much promoted by the authorities as an event of major touristic interest.

BUYING TO BRING IT BACK HOME: HINTS FOR THE WINE TOURIST

If you are travelling by car, then it can be very tempting to fill the boot (and any other spare space) with bottles and even cases of wines which have attracted you en route. Producers, too, can be very persuasive when you taste their wares and you may well find yourself burdened with far too much sparkling rosé and not enough of anything you would normally drink at home.

Of course holidays are a time to experiment and to find new wines or at least to compare those you love with their neighbours and rivals. And prices can look very reasonable until you stop to consider that if you bring in wine in excess of your customs limit then there will be quite a bit of duty to pay per bottle (see below for a breakdown of your allowances).

As a general rule, it is not really worth bringing back very cheap wines from a supermarket or co-operative. The prices may be low but after their journey these wines may seem dull and lifeless or even unpleasant. Far better to choose a small range of bottles which are really delicious, rare and intriguing for future dinner parties. If you are the kind of host who delights in puzzling guests with 'mystery' wines, this is your moment. Finer wines and those fairly high in alcohol will also survive the journey back home far more successfully than simple table wines, and bottles with corks are normally better than boxes or plastic containers. But let the wine rest for a few weeks on its return to recover from a (quite genuine) condition the wine merchants call 'bottle sickness'.

If you plan to buy more than, say, a case of wine per person in the car, then you may find the customs authorities are curious and want to see documents, so be prepared. At this stage you may well decide in favour of leaving the whole process to your wine suppliers at home in the future. You may also have to pay local taxes such as VAT (TVA in France) at the point of purchase, even though the goods are for export, because the paperwork to 'exempt' the wines is too complex for a small quantity. This can bump up the price of an apparent bargain.

Whatever you decide about quantity, here is an outline of the current allowances for wines and spirits you may bring into the UK:

Drinks bought in an ordinary shop or supermarket in the EEC (per adult):
If you decide to buy *wine only*, you are allowed 8 litres. A bottle will contain either 70 or 75 cl. if it is of a standard size, so you can calculate accordingly – approximately 10 or 11 bottles (a full case contains 12). If you want to bring in spirits as well, you may buy only 5 litres of still table wine and 1.5 litres of spirits over 22% vol. ie, most spirits and liqueurs – 2 standard bottles. If you want to bring home Champagne, sparkling wine or fortified wines, or lower-strength spirits such as Pastis or some Crème de Cassis, then this allowance is only 5 litres if you have any other categories of drink.

Drinks bought in a duty-free shop
This arrangement is less advantageous but could producing savings for the spirit drinker if you have a preferred brand. You are only allowed a total of 4 litres of table wine if that is all you plan to bring in ie, about 5 bottles. Only 1 litre of spirits comes in without payment – probably 1 bottle as many are sold by the litre in these shops – but you may bring 2 litres of table wine as well. For the mid-range wines including sparkling and fortified examples, you may have 2 litres but this means you sacrifice 2 litres of your allowance on table wine and may only have 2 litres total.
NB If you mix supermarket with duty-free this is usually accepted within reasonable limits, so you could buy your wine from a shop and your Scotch on board.
Extra Duty on wine is currently £1.94 per *litre* for table wine and £1.86 per litre for sparkling or fortified, both *plus* VAT @ 15%.

ENTERTAINING

OCCASIONAL SPLENDOUR: Entertaining in THE GRAND STYLE

In spite of our precarious English summer, July is a month for brides, buffets and extravagance. Roses bloom and even the rainfall seems mild compared with the icy sleet of winter or the torrential showers of spring. The secret hedonist in us all is revealed, probably in a marquee, sipping *real* Champagne with a sensation of sinful excess. The food, too, is likely to be rich and heavy with a preponderance of mayonnaise and rich dressings on cold meats and salads which may not be at the peak of freshness due to the warmth.

So if you do decide to lash out and entertain with conscious opulence, for whatever reason, how best to do it in high summer? Lessons in the art come from two contrasting sources: the French, as always, have a way of combining Champagne with just the right food, and the Americans know how to dazzle the eye and palate with a warm weather collation served indoors or out.

The French Grand Style
Here is a special lunch or dinner you might imagine served by a butler in white gloves, with a wine waiter similarly attired hovering solicitously in the background with perfectly-chilled Champagne. It is the kind of occasion you might actually be invited to in France as French families occasionally hire staff like this for a momentous family event. Food is

Entrance to the offices of Möet et Chandon Champagne

served in small portions but second helpings are normally offered and you are expected to toy with a second sample of each fine dish. It would not be at all unusual to drink Champagne throughout such a meal, with Cognac to conclude. The classic exponents of this type of luxury are the Champagne houses themselves, notably Moët et Chandon with their own château not far from Epernay where a lucky few are regularly invited to dine or even stay for a sybaritic weekend.

MENU

Saumon en brioche or mousse de saumon

*

Roast leg of lamb (gigot) or rolled roast of veal

*

Salad

*

Cheeses

*

Bavarois aux poires or Muscat jelly with grenadine

*

Wines: The salmon should be accompanied by a dry Champagne (brut), a good sparkling wine or some white Burgundy. With the lamb or veal, either continue with the same or offer a light claret such as a five-year-old Médoc or a light Burgundy (Santenay or Volnay perhaps). No wine with the salad, red or white with the cheese, and with the bavarois, either more dry or semi-sweet Champagne, or a good sweet white wine (Sauternes or Barsac).

For the saumon en brioche make 2 lb brioche dough using yeast (any good French cook book has a recipe) then prepare the stuffing for the fish. (For 8 people you will need a salmon weighing about 4 lb.) Mix 3 oz breadcrumbs with about ¼ pint fish stock or chicken bouillon, 2 large onions and 1 lb well-chopped mushrooms lightly sautéd in butter and parsley, salt and pepper to taste. Bind with an egg yolk then fill the fish cavity and sew up with thread. Place the fish on a flat rectangular piece of brioche dough and pull up the edges, then place another piece of dough on top and shape the two around the fish. Brush with egg, then decorate with 'scales' and the outline of the head if you have an artistic bent. Bake in a moderate oven (190°C/375°F/ Gas Mark 5) for 45 minutes until golden brown. Serve tepid rather than very hot with a simple Hollandaise sauce.

The cheeses should be in perfect condition (freeze some very ripe French cheese in foil – Brie, Camembert, Chanmes and St André all freeze well – when next you return from a holiday there).

For the bavarois, poach 1 lb William pears (peeled) in a syrup made by boiling half a bottle of Sauternes (or another good sweet white wine) and sugar until the pears are soft. Purée the fruit and add 2 sachets of gelatine – keep warm. Put 10 egg yolks into a double boiler and beat for one minute then add the hot pear syrup and continue to beat for 5 minutes. Remove from the heat and beat until creamy in appearance. Whip a small carton of double cream with a dash of vanilla essence; when thick add 2 tablespoons of icing sugar and whip again. Put the pear mixture over a bowl of ice cubes and beat until cool, but fold in the cream before it sets. Dampen a 4-pint mould and line the base with baking parchment. Fill with the mixture and cover with baking parchment. Put in the fridge to set for at least three hours.

For the Muscat jelly see *April* – also for more suggestions about sweet wines.

A French Regional Repast

MENU

Filets de Sole au Champagne

*

Canard au Bouzy (duck in local red wine sauce)

*

Cheeses

*

Sorbet au Champagne

*

Wines: Dry Champagne throughout or serve rosé Champagne with the duck and cheese *or* a very light red wine such as Bouzy (hard to obtain) or a red wine from the Loire. Demi-sec Champagne goes well with the sorbet.

If Champagne were not so light and digestible (often recommended to wealthy invalids and expectant heiresses) this menu might look like overkill, but it is not too heavy and very delicious.

Take two fillets of sole per person and poach in ⅓ bottle Champagne with salt, pepper, a chopped onion and a knob of butter for 5 minutes; the fish should be barely cooked, and certainly not soft. Lift the fillets on a slotted spoon on to a warmed serving dish. Reserve the cooking liquid. Melt 2 oz butter in a pan and add 2 egg yolks and a small carton of double cream. Beat over a very gentle heat (or in a double boiler) until you have a creamy sauce; add some of the cooking liquid to reach the right consistency. Taste and add more seasoning if necessary. Pour over fillets and decorate with fresh parsley or chervil.

A typically French duck should be pink on the inside with a crispy skin, so roast at a high heat (220°C/425°F/Gas Mark 7) for 15 minutes then reduce to 180°C/350°F/Gas Mark 4 for remainder of cooking time ie, a 6 lb duck will serve 4 people and takes 2 hours plus the initial 15 minutes. Remove the cooked duck from the oven and let it 'rest' for 20 minutes, then transfer to a platter. Skim the fat from the juices then add about ⅕ bottle red wine (Bouzy for authenticity) to the pan and bring to the boil. Let this reduce by about half and then add 4 oz mushrooms (chopped finely) and 2 chopped shallots or a small onion. Simmer for 5 minutes. Meanwhile carve the duck breast into thin slices and arrange on a warm serving dish with legs, wings and thighs; offer the sauce separately. Vegetables need only be of the simplest; some tiny steamed young turnips and carrots are ideal, with some green beans or spinach for colour.

The sorbet is made with an entire bottle of brut Champagne or sparkling wine (to serve 4–6). Make a sugar syrup by boiling 1lb caster sugar in one pint of water until the sugar dissolves. Mix this with the Champagne and the juice of 2 lemons, then freeze for 45 minutes. Remove from the freezer, beat and freeze again for about 3 hours. Serve in Champagne glasses (flutes) and decorate with a tiny strip of lemon zest.

THE CHAMPAGNE REGION

Somehow the Champagne region does not seem to fit the wine it produces: the austerity of northern France with its vast flat fields and gloomy vistas of military cemeteries is at odds with the glamour and vivacity of a wine with its own sparkle. Even the two major centres for production – Reims and Epernay – seem a little lacking in excitement.

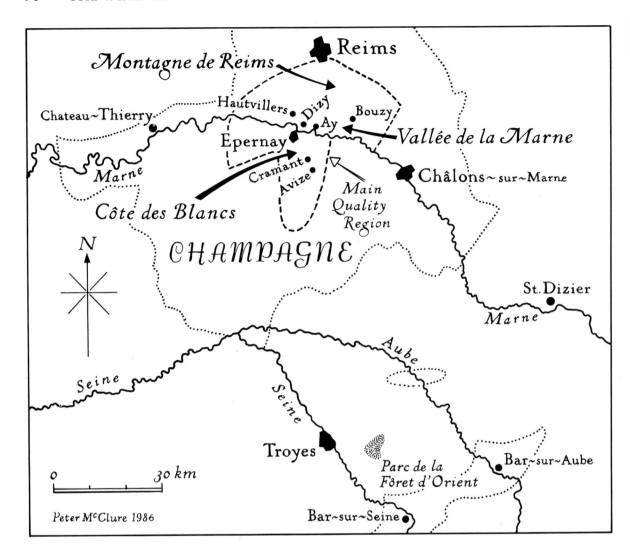

Montagne de Reims

Reims

Chateau~Thierry

Hautvillers · Dizy
Ay   Bouzy

Epernay   Vallée de la Marne

Marne   Cramant · Avize

Côtes des Blancs   Châlons~sur~Marne

N   Main Quality Region

CHAMPAGNE

St.Dizier

Marne

Seine

Seine

Aube

Troyes   Bar~sur~Aube

0   30 km   Parc de la Fôret d'Orient

Peter McClure 1986   Bar~sur~Seine

The Champagne blender creates
his 'assemblage'

The towering façade of Reims Cathedral is impressive yet stark. Similarly, the mansions which are the 'fronts' for the major Champagne houses are substantial rather than exquisite.

This is the simplest destination of all for the British wine lover. Across the Channel to Calais or Boulogne, then a clear stretch of motorway will bring you to the heart of Champagne. The vineyards themselves are hard to see at first and you are more likely to notice the remains of vast imperial forest where wild boar is still hunted, or the open wheat fields. Like most of the people you may encounter here, the vines are unassuming, but once you turn from major roads to the 'wine roads' recommended to visitors, then it is time to admire the symmetry of the vines which must be among the best-kept in all of France. And there is good reason for the careful attention paid to the vines: the grapes they yield are carefully graded according to situation and are very valuable to the growers.

There are two major areas of Champagne production – the Montagne de Reims for red grapes and the Côte des Blancs for white grapes. Between these poles is the Vallée de la Marne with its centre the village of Ay, famous as the home of Bollinger Champagne. Not far away is the village of Dizy, and to the north the Abbey of Hautvillers, where Dom Perignon is said to have perfected the art of Champagne-making. It was he who found a way of keeping the bubbles in the bottle by making secure stoppers and encouraging the use of sturdy bottles to avoid explosions. In addition he and his colleague Dom Ruinart are credited with developing the method of blending so vital to the style of Champagne as we know it today.

To the east lies the village of Bouzy, the source of good red wine used to tint Champagne its very special shade of pink and also good to drink by itself. Unfortunately none of the grapes in this area are cheap and hence no wine is inexpensive in the shops. A still Coteaux Champenois made with the local Chardonnay grapes may well cost you almost as much as its sparkling cousin.

Reims is the northern point for Champagne production and Epernay is at the heart of the region. To the south of Epernay is the Côte des Blancs where the Chardonnay grape thrives. Many growers in this area make their own Champagnes rather than selling to the famous name houses and their Blanc de Blancs can be very delicate and fine. In fact the success story of the small growers, known as *récoltants-manipulants*, is a fairly recent phenomenon and today they sell their wares in other parts of France as well as locally. (See the section about Bruno Paillard for more about how these wines are distributed.)

The major towns in the Côte des Blancs include Avize (home of a large co-operative) and Cramant which gives its name to a very subtle and lightly-sparkling style of Champagne called the Crémant de Cramant. If you visit the region you will be able to try all these styles for yourself, from the 'meaty' blends of the Montagne de Reims with a high proportion of red grapes, to the lightest of Cramants, with perhaps just one vintage wine to make a memorable experience.

South again is the ancient city of Troyes, once the capital of the region and the seat of the powerful Counts of Champagne. Its medieval streets with their half-timbered houses are most attractive and there are impressive parks and forests nearby, notably the Parc de la Fôret d'Orient. Champagne is also made around the towns of Bar-sur-Seine and Bar-sur-Aube, and these outlying vineyards are known collectively as the Aube vineyards.

Once as far south as Troyes it is not all that far to Dijon and the beginning of the Burgundian vineyards, so you may like to combine

Typical chalk cellars adapted from the caves beneath Reims and Epernay for storing Champagne

visits if you have at least a week to spare. The food in both regions tends towards the filling as well as the mouthwatering, and after ten days of pastry filled with snails and mushrooms, duck in wine sauce, boudin (black pudding), andouiltette (spicy tripe sausage), blanquette de veau (veal stew) and a range of marvellous full-cream cheeses such as Chaource and Chambertin, you may need to spend the rest of your holiday concentrating on scenery and exercise rather than further gastronomic and alcoholic delights . . .

The Champagne Method

If you visit any of the old and famous Champagne houses during your stay in the region, you will be able to wander in the endless miles of ancient chalk caves under the towns of Reims and Epernay and see the Champagne method for yourself. Put simply, it is a way of retaining the bubbles produced in a bottle of wine by bringing about a second, artificially-induced fermentation.

Not that 'artificial' means the introduction of mysterious additives. A selection of still wines are skilfully blended by an expert *chef du cave* to suit the style of the house, then a small amount of liqueur made from pure cane sugar and old wines is added to each bottle of this blend, together with yeasts. The bottle is capped (not usually corked at this stage) and the second fermentation begins. Once it is finished there is carbon dioxide in the wine in the form of fizz, and there is also a sediment of yeast particles and other by-products of fermentation. The young Champagne rests on this sediment and establishes its special 'toasty' flavour. If the original wine is very fine this may be selected as a vintage bottle and allowed to rest on its lees (sediments) for a longer time to obtain a richer flavour.

Once this part of the process is concluded, the sediment must be separated from the wine. Through a method called *remuage*, said to have been invented by the Veuve Clicquot on her kitchen table, the bottles are inserted into special racks called *pupitres* and very gradually tipped and twisted over a period of at least seven weeks, progressing from a near-horizontal to a near-vertical position. During this time the fine deposit in the bottle makes its way to the neck. The *remueurs* who carry out this technique are highly skilled but sadly today there are machines which are threatening to replace them – catch one while you can.

The block of sediment in the neck of the bottle is now frozen by dipping the bottle into dry ice, then the crown cap is swiftly removed, the plug of sediment flies away and the bottle is corked with the typical thick Champagne cork we all recognise once it has taken on its mushroom shape inside the bottle. Just before corking, a dash of cane sugar and old Champagne is added to replace any liquid lost. The amount of sugar determines the style of the Champagne: brut is the dryest commonly available; extra sec is also dry; demi-sec is medium sweet; doux is very sweet indeed.

Note: If you see Premier Cru or Grand Cru on a Champagne bottle this refers to the quality of grapes used in the blend. The price is fixed at the beginning of each season. Grand Cru vineyards charge 100% of the market rate for their grapes; Premier Cru 90–99%; all the rest proportionately less down to 77%. It may seem ideal to use all Grand Cru or all Premier Cru grapes but in fact the grapes from the 'lesser' vineyards are also treasured as integral parts of the blend, giving character and what tasters call 'backbone'. (See the section on Cognac in *November* for a similar story of blends.)

Visiting the Champagne Houses
Most major producers have organised tours, and most have English-speaking guides. In the summer season you may find yourself escorted by an elegant public schoolboy who is filling in time before college. It is cold in the caves so wear a sweater or coat, and flat shoes for the walk, except in Mercier (Epernay) and Piper Heidsieck (Reims) where you take the trip in a special electric train. Some producers charge for the tasting afterwards (Piper-Heidsieck, Ruinart and the Mailly Co-operative among others) and this is hardly surprising when you consider the value of their product and the number of visitors. Some, like Bollinger, Perrier-Jouët and Pol Roger will show you round only if you have an appointment, so write in advance. For a full list of the producers write to The Champagne Bureau which represents the producers in this country.

HOUSES GREAT AND SMALL: THE HOUSE OF MUMM AND BRUNO PAILLARD, BROKER AND CHAMPAGNE MAKER

There is a definite social structure in the Champagne world: there is a division between the acknowledged great houses and more inferior producers just as there is between those who can afford the 'real thing' and those who cannot. But there is a difference. There is really no substitute for true Champagne once you have a taste for it, but there is for the *marques*, the famous names like Moët et Chandon, Taittinger and Mumm which appear to dominate the market.

It is impossible to deny that all the famous houses make excellent Champagne, some blander in style than others. Some, like Krug and

Entrance to the Mumm cellars;
the real glories are underground

G. H. Mumm & Co
34 rue du Champ-de-Mars
51100 Reims

Bollinger, have a power and distinction it would be hard to beat under any circumstances but they have the resources to get it right. As Hugh Johnson has remarked, 'The great houses push to the limit the polishing and perfecting of an agricultural product.'

The House of Mumm at first sight looks too commercial to be attractive. After all, it is a public company and the majority shareholder is Seagram, the world's largest liquor company originating in Canada and now dominant in the entire drinking world. Perrier-Jouët (famed for its exquisite 'Belle Epoque' bottles) and Heidsieck Monopole are under the same ownership.

The standard non-vintage wine produced by the company is not the most exciting to taste. It is very well made and has no obvious faults but no highly distinctive style either. Yet this is as it should be. The aim of a 'house' Champagne is to be subtle, reliable and consistent from year to year.

When it comes to the vintage wines, however, there is excitement and character to be had. The major brand is Cordon Rouge, which is also sold as a vintage wine in suitable years. Then there is a notable Cordon Rosé which has all the tinge of earthiness from the Bouzy rouge wine and the toastiness of a good vintage Champagne combined. Beyond this is the exclusive René Lalou, their deluxe offering in the Dom Pérignon category. This is extravagantly packaged in what looks like a giant scent bottle but ignore the marketing, try the taste, and you will find it full of complex flavour and richness albeit quite dry. Most interesting of all, perhaps, is the Crémant de Cramant made from the Chardonnay grapes grown in the village of Cramant, less sparkling than the standard Champagne and an exquisite apéritif for those who appreciate its delicacy.

At any one time Mumm has stock of some twenty-five million bottles of which around eight million are sold annually. The visit to their caves and bottling cellars is one of the better-organised tours and worth your while if you are in the region. Tours run Monday to Friday except on public holidays, but note that the company closes for lunch between 11.15am and 2pm! No appointment is necessary.

BRUNO PAILLARD: THE NEW FACE OF CHAMPAGNE

The broker is a very rare animal in the Champagne region. Whereas in Burgundy you seem to hear of nothing but *négociants* and in Bordeaux of *courtiers*, all anxious to negotiate wine sales on behalf of others, where Champagne is concerned the procedures are all very seemly. The big houses have their highly professional marketing operations and the small growers have their contacts and the prestige that comes from being written up favourably by Gault-Millau; they are avidly sought out by connoisseurs who drive from Paris to stock their large cars with supplies of good Champagne.

Rémy Paillard has managed to break this mould and do very well at the business of broking. Being impartial in Champagne is no bad thing when so many prickly egos are in evidence and so much money involved in production and overheads. Beyond the famous names and the small growers are a multitude of labels, designed for the needs of a particular customer, and this is where a broker can be invaluable. He can select without prejudice from the many wines available each year, blend them if he so desires, and offer a Champagne geared to suit a certain palate. The label is no problem: for a franc a year he may register any name he chooses – Paillard Champagne perhaps.

Bruno Paillard is the son of Rémy and he has not only embraced the profession of broker with great success all over the wine-drinking world, but also become something of a *marque* himself. The fine Champagnes which he 'assembles' (as the locals would say) in his modern cellar facility are now on their way to rivalling those from the major *marques* and he is ably assisting them with such publicity coups as selling his Brut non-vintage to the English section of the Orient Express, and by commissioning marvellous labels for his vintage wines from notable artists.

The only other French wine famous for this practice of 'designer' labels to date is Château Mouton-Rothschild, the Bordeaux first growth claret. Paillard is moving in elevated circles and he intends to stay there. And if the quality of his vintage remains high and his selection standards as scrupulous there seems little doubt that he can challenge the establishment to great effect. Go and visit him in Reims and sample his wares!

CHAMPAGNE BRUNO
PAILLARD SA,
rue Jacques Maritain,
51100 Reims.

Bruno Paillard demonstrates his skill with an audience

Labels: The Paillard label style both classic and artistic

AUGUST

Throughout the winegrowing world this is still the traditional time to plan a holiday. The only people who must be exceptions to this rule are the winemakers themselves, for although harvest time is not for another month (apart from some early-ripening varieties of grape) the work in vineyard and winery must go on apace in preparation for the near-frenzy of vintage. Despite all the assistance offered by modern technology there is still one simple and crucial fact about the production of a good wine – it must be made with grapes picked at the peak of condition. In this final month before the harvest, therefore, the work of the vinegrower centres on preserving the abundant bunches of grapes for a healthy crop.

Depending on the region, the ripening grapes will need to be exposed to the sun by trimming back the vine leaves, or alternatively shielded from its glare by allowing them to grow densely. In Germany, for instance, the days may be sunny yet not very hot and every ray will help the grapes to ripen naturally. If they cannot produce sufficient sugar to give a minimum level of alcohol, the juice may need the addition of cane or beet sugar before fermentation. This process is known as chaptalisation and it is important to understand that all this added sugar is used up in the transformation of sugar to alcohol so the wine is not actually 'sweetened'. Minimum alcohol levels are an essential feature of all quality wines to ensure that they will have good keeping qualities.

The fierce heat of the August sun is much appreciated by certain makers of pungent red wine. All that warmth helps to ripen, colour and flavour the grapes to give the much-desired 'complexity' – a favourite term used by tasters when describing full red wine. A good example of this affinity with sun is Châteauneuf-du-Pape, made with no less than thirteen different grape varieties including the spicy Syrah and the earthy Grenache. Its minimum alcoholic strength is a head-turning 12.5%, readily achieved by growing the vines low to the ground which is scattered with flat stones. This lunar landscape, home to sagebrush, lavender and thyme as well as the vine, draws in the sun's fire during the day, then during the cooler night slowly releases the heat to continue the ripening of the grapes over twenty-four hours.

A total contrast to this sultry wine is provided by the Vinho Verde of Northern Portugal, which is made with grapes high in acidity, grapes which have a tart, 'green' taste. This sharp quality in the wine is especially delightful in hot weather as it is coupled with a perfectly natural slight sparkle. This particular finesse is achieved by training the vines to grow on high trellises so that the leaves drape themselves over the grapes and prevent premature ripening. In fact the vines are often grown as a surround to a very mundane planting of sweetcorn or tall scrawny cabbages used in the making of the traditional Portuguese soup *caldo verde*.

Rainfall can be scant during the dog days of August and this is ideal for grapes which have already seen their fair share of moisture earlier in the season; indeed, the highest quality yield is obtained from vines which have seen almost no rain after the flowering in June. Without rain to dilute the juice, the grapes swell just enough to retain all the flavour and character which will mean a good wine later.

For those regions which truly suffer from lack of rain, so that the young grapes turn to raisins before they can even be said to ripen, then irrigation is an answer. This is considered almost immoral by the major European areas and no quality wine is produced from irrigated vineyards, but in central California there might be no harvest if the vines did not receive some extra water. Left to themselves, vines will seek water from deep underground but in an arid region this may not suffice to swell the young grapes.

Sudden summer storms are a nightmare for the winegrower. Just one may not have any effect, but repeated downpours can lead to rot on the grapes, either mildew or oidium. Of course, in certain vineyards, *Botrytis cinerea* or *pourriture noble* is actually welcomed but as a rule mould is a plague and sprays are used to control and prevent any outbreak.

With rain comes sudden growth, but as with roses in an English garden, most long trailing new shoots take away from the essential flower and fruit and so must be removed, either by hand or sometimes by machine. Likewise, weeds which flourish between the rows of vines are stealing needed nutrients and must be eradicated.

If the winegrower has all these potential problems under control, August is a profitable month, a time to overhaul equipment for crushing, pressing and fermenting before the harvest. It is certainly a good time to visit the vineyards as the grapes are at their best and are spectacular to view.

HOLIDAY CLASSICS

Assuming that you are not necessarily a dedicated wine bibber and hence not intending to make wine-tasting the first priority on your annual vacation, then what should you try when visiting some typical holiday destinations?

In France, you will find most regions have some local Vin de Pays which bears sampling and is all the better for drinking with local gastronomic specialities; you may also discover that to buy a bottle of Burgundy in Bordeaux is often viewed as an outrage, and an impossibility. So concentrate on the regional production and trust the locals to match food with wine. If the Vin Jaune of the Jura tastes curious with rabbit and morel mushrooms, just put it down to experience.

Greater difficulties come when you venture beyond France, Germany and Italy, all of which have fairly clear-cut regional wine identities, and into the undeniably hedonistic territory of Greece, her islands, and all those other sundrenched parts of the Mediterranean.

Terraced vines in the scorching heat of Samos, Greece

Greece. Even before the Romans compelled the conquered people of Europe to plant vines, the Greeks had been using their wines as a valuable commodity in exchange for all manner of goods. Today most Greek wines are hardly worth their weight in silver but many are agreeable and the influence of EEC membership means better standards of quality year by year. Away from the mainland, the island of Crete is an important producer (the third largest region) and wines here are likely to be red, heavy and alcoholic, as well as slightly sweet. Names to look for include Daphne, Archanes and Peza – this last is made at a co-operative.

The universal alternative to heavy red or white wines is retsina, that curious beverage which tastes of floor polish when you drink it at home yet somehow contrives to be just right when served chilled with some fish fried in olive oil and a pungent tomato salad with feta cheese. The flavour comes from pine resin which is added during fermentation.

Corfu is the best known of the Ionian islands which produce rather everyday wines. Best of these is the Verdea, a full dry white or red. Contrast this with the sweet dessert wines such as the Muscat and Mavrodaphne which are made in many Greek regions. The most famous Muscat is made in Samos, one of the Aegean islands. Another good example is made in Rhodes where the other wines produced, collectively known as 'Rhodos', are of sound quality.

Yugoslavia Perhaps the most popular holiday resorts in Yugoslavia are on the southern Adriatic coast, in Dalmatia, where the wines are meaty reds or rich, oily whites, not as sweet as those of Greece (although beware a rather sticky drink called Prosek) but high in alcohol and often served mixed with mineral water to avoid headaches. Best of the red wines is Dingac; best of the white is Posip.

Spanish Riviera and Balearic Islands The finest regions of Spain are not in the famous resort areas but to the north – around Barcelona for the fine wines of Penedes and for sparkling wines, and north again and inland for the bare countryside of the Rioja. The Alicante area produces rather dull tourist wines, most of which are sweet (including moscatel), and rosé as well as white and red table wines. Fortunately wines from other Spanish regions may be found fairly easily: try those made by Torres or some of the red and white Rioja.

On Majorca and Ibiza most everyday wine is imported in bulk and bottled locally. Everyday red wine is also produced on Majorca, including a large quantity at the Felanitx co-operative. The best local wines are made by José Ferrer at Binisalem near Inca. His red can be excellent and should be sampled on the spot as too little is made to allow for export.

Portugal – The Algarve As in Spain, the north of Portugal seems to have all the glory for table wines, and for port as well. The sunny Algarve on the south coast is not considered a fine wine region although efforts are now being made to raise the quality, notably of the wine called Lagoa which has the typical 'burnt' aroma of wine made in a hot climate. As an alternative try a Vinho Verde or Dão from further north.

FESTIVALS

While some of the grander wine regions such as Bordeaux and the Rioja may disdain August as a month for festivals of wine, others are not so fussy and the roaming holidaymaker may light upon some very festive occasions including the following:

ALSACE During the first fortnight of August there are local festivals in Turckheim, Obernai, Dambach-la-Ville and in Colmar as well as the Fair of the Almond Trees in Mittelwihr. The storybook villages of the area are at their most glorious this month with every house smothered in flowers.

CHAMPAGNE Once every three years there is a notable festival of

Champagne organised by the wine growers of the Aube. This is held on the last Sunday in August and the next festival will be in 1987.

LOIRE The first Sunday in August sees a wine fair at Montsoreau, then in mid-August there is a fair in Vouvray, famed for both its still and sparkling white wines. To sample Loire reds, try Bourgueil at the Amboise, Montlouis and Bourgueil festival on 15 August. Finally, the last weekend of the month is the time to enjoy the dry delights of Sancerre, an excellent wine often overpriced through no fault of its own.

GERMANY The marvellous German *Winzerfeste* continue during August, with some notable festivities in Franken, not far from Frankfurt, at Volkach and Sulzfeld among other towns. The wine festival of Rudesheim in the Rheingau is held in mid-August, then at the end of the month there is a special *Fest rund um die Naheweinstrasse* which encompasses all the little villages of this area. In the Palatinate, the famous village of Nierstein celebrates in early August and Worms, famous as the home of Liebfraumilch and for sparkling Sekt, has a festival later in the month.

AUSTRIA On 13–15 August there is a wine festival at Weissenkirchen in the Wachau region, a picturesque village with a folklore museum. This area is not far from Vienna, on the main Salzburg road.

ENTERTAINING

Whether you spend August at home or abroad, the likelihood is that you will want to spend a good deal of the month outdoors. Even in Britain, renowned for unpredictable summer weather, we attempt to picnic and barbecue just as if we were in Corfu or California. Away from home, Britons are among the first to join in beach barbecues and cookouts – eating outdoors seems the essence of a summer escape. For the citybound, restaurants open their terraces for a breath of balmy air while dreaming of a beach taverna in a warmer clime.

At this time of year, the formality of cork and bottle somehow seems out of place. The plain carafe or jug of equally plain wine fits the style better. Perhaps August is the month for the unpretentious wine, for wines which are no grander than Vin de Pays, or even simply Tafelwein, Vino da Tavola or EEC-blended wine from 'various countries of the EEC', all of which can make delightful drinking at the appropriate moment.

Hot weather makes us yearn for a cool drink, and even if the sun fails

A dream of a Greek meal; fish cooked in olive oil served with Retsina and ripe fruit

to shine in August a cool drink must be served to maintain the spirit of the holiday month. So choose wines which will take some ice or, alternatively, decide you need a really long drink and add soda water or fruit juice and create your own version of those newly-fashionable 'coolers' which are actually quite traditional.

A *spritzer* is American for a fruity white wine such as California Chenin Blanc or perhaps Yugoslav Riesling mixed half-and-half with soda or sparkling mineral water. In Edwardian England followers of Oscar Wilde would have called this a 'hock and seltzer'. German wines lend themselves well to this treatment as the fragrance of Riesling or Sylvaner grapes is not diminished by adding a mixer. Add ice if the weather is really hot, and a slice of lemon for effect.

A *mimosa* is American for the British *Bucks Fizz*, a mix of well-chilled Champagne or sparkling wine with orange juice. Half-and-half works best and again a fruity sparkler fights back more than the very best Champagne. Use still wine as an alternative: a slightly sweet style, such as a Muscat, will be quite delicious. Add ice and serve from a glass jug decorated with mint and orange slices.

A *Kir* is the classic for wine merchants and all 'foodies' – the gourmet's cocktail. It is simply a glass of very dry white wine with a small dash of Crème de Cassis, a blackcurrant liqueur. Originating in Burgundy it is made there with Bourgogne Aligoté and local liqueur; for a variation try a different fruit liqueur such as Crème de Myrtilles (bilberries) or Crème de Framboises (raspberries). A *Kir Royale* is the same drink made with sparkling wine or Champagne.

GOING WEST: The Vineyards of California

For some reason California wines have the reputation of being rather exclusive and expensive but take one trip to the West Coast and you will prove the opposite. Not only are there table wines in abundance at the most ridiculously low prices but even respectable 'varietal' bottlings are rarely out of reach. Of course there are also the rare bottles from the so-called 'boutique' wineries to contend with. Many of these appear to be made for wine masochists prepared to part with at least £20 for a single bottle of their preferred nectar.

   While you are in California, try to see both sides of the picture. Our rates of exchange may fluctuate but whatever the situation you will be forced to admit that it is possible to drink some very agreeable bottles for far less than you might at home – or even in France. When planning your tour sample a few wines with food first, perhaps in one of San Francisco's marvellous seafood restaurants (not all of which are on Fisherman's Wharf, incidentally – try the various piers). Accustom your palate to the fruit and richness of the wines so that your judgement will be rational. California wines have a decided force of personality which they share with those of Australia. Try as they might, the local winemakers cannot make their wines conform to the restrained European model. It seems California Riesling will never be Blue Nun and some might see this as a positive virtue.

Naturally there are exceptions to the rule and certain microclimates (a favoured California phrase) favour the production of lighter and more elegant styles (as described in the profile of Bill Jekel which follows). High Tech has quite a hold on the wine world here, either overtly in the form of the giant stainless steel tanks seen outside the Central Valley winery/refineries, or less obviously inside the *chais* which house the very latest in centrifuges and filtering equipment. Yet try not to seize upon this aspect as proof that all California wine must therefore be 'manufactured'. The opposite is really the case.

With the help of the University of California at Davis, growers have made startling progress since the unfortunate hiatus of Prohibition in the 1920s. Although grapes had been grown in the area since the gold rush days, the Volstead Act meant a temporary lull and the collapse of many vineyards and businesses. Canny producers created underground tunnels for distribution and cellars hidden beneath bedroom closets, but these individuals tended to belong to the Italian fraternity and had a reliable 'family' of contacts for sale. In the main, the industry has built itself since the Second World War so that where once the local wine was quite a joke, now it is *de rigueur* for fashionable parties.

Start your investigations in San Francisco by sampling the wines, visiting wine stores (likely to be very informative) and the Wine Institute, which will provide you with a useful guide to the wineries with maps and visiting times. Then make your choice between Napa and Sonoma to the north or the various regions which lie to the south.

If you have only a very short time to spare, then you should of necessity choose Napa where the wineries are well organised to receive visitors and seem pleased to welcome you, although some are naturally more commercialised than others. Tastings tend towards the liberal, so consider yourself duly warned! Note that although the early August mornings in San Francisco may be cool and overcast, by lunchtime there could be blazing sunshine. One delightful note – rain is virtually unknown in a California August.

In the tasting room remember that California wines (note – they are never Californian) divide into two groups – varietals and generics. Generics are simple table or 'jug' wines often described as Chablis or

Inglenook; one of the original Napa wineries still important today

WINE INSTITUTE,
165 Post Street,
San Francisco.

Burgundy even today. Varietals are made with a named grape type such as Cabernet Sauvignon or Chardonnay which, incidentally, are two of California's success stories. Other notable varieties to sample are Sauvignon Blanc (often described as Fumé Blanc since producer Robert Mondavi introduced this title), with its wonderful 'vegetable' aroma; Chenin Blanc, which may be medium-dry and uninteresting but at its best tastes of fresh melon; Colombard or French Colombard, acidic and light; Grey Riesling, fragrant and extremely easy to drink (this is the Chauché Gris of France); and of course the mysterious red Zinfandel, the 'workhorse' of California grapes, mysterious because of its name and character which seemed to defy experts searching for its origin until they came upon a humble southern Italian variety called the Primitivo. This appears to match the Zinfandel in terms of botany but not in terms of style for the California variety can yield wines from the frankly earthy to the sublimely subtle. Judge which is coming your way by the price and amount of detail on the label . . .

Mr and Mrs Robert Mondavi beside their distinctive winery in the Napa

Many of these varieties were introduced in California as a result of the efforts of one Count Haraszthy, who is remembered as a founding father of the West Coast Wine business. Count Haraszthy was a Hungarian who made his fortune during the Gold Rush and was commissioned by the California wine industry in general to collect vine cuttings and bring them to stock the new American vineyards between 1851 and 1860. His work was in the Sonoma Valley at Buena Vista, still in operation today and well worth a visit. His descendants run the Haraszthy winery, also in Sonoma. Be sure to see the town of Sonoma itself during your tour as it has a marvellous Western feel, with enough palm trees for any spaghetti Western – and excellent Italian food at the local restaurants. And while in the Sonoma region make an appointment to see the unusual architecture of Hanzell, based on the Clos de Vougeot in France. Their wines are superb Pinot Noir and Chardonnay, both rare and unlikely to be available for tasting due to demand. More accessible is Sebastiani, a major 'brand leader' but making good drinkable wine, notably full-bodied Zinfandel and Barbera. The visits here are both friendly and generous.

Moving on to Napa there is an embarrassment of choice. See at least one of the old-style establishments with interesting buildings such as Beringer or Chateau Montelena; at least one of the new showpieces such as Sterling, which looks like a hilltop Greek monastery, or Joseph Phelps, a very upmarket redwood barn where exceptional wine is made; and Domaine Chandon for sparkling wine made in collaboration with Moët et . . .

South of the city are a number of scattered wineries, near San José and then further south around Monterey, collectively known as the Central Coast. Among these try to see Ridge Vineyards or Chalone, both perched high in the hills, or neighbouring Calera. These last two are situated on chalky outcrops and produce some excellent Pinot Noir wines, rarely this successful in California. Ridge is renowned for Cabernet and for Zinfandel at its best. Contrast one of these 'boutiques' with a look at either Paul Masson or Almadén, both large-scale producers of a dizzying assortment of wines and even brandy.

Bill Jekel demonstrates the quality of his rather special wines

JEKEL VINEYARD
4055 Walnut Avenue
Greenfield Ca. 93927

MONTEREY ARTISTRY: THE JEKEL VINEYARD

Bill Jekel's wines are generally reckoned to be among the best in California but he came to vineyards relatively late in his career. Until 1972 he was involved in a film company (his brother works for the Disney studio) and his interest in wine was no stronger than that of the informed amateur able to indulge his taste. But by the end of the 1960s he had already resolved that the wine business was for him and begun to search for the right location.

The Monterey region is one of the coolest in California, with temperatures near the Pacific Ocean similar to those of Northern European vineyards such as Champagne, Burgundy and the Rhine. This is technically known as Region 1 and it is between Regions 1 and 3 that the ideal conditions for the production of fine wine are to be found, calculated according to the heat over a typical growing season. Monterey as a whole has the conditions of all three Regions but Jekel Vineyard is definitely in the cooler zone. This is a beautiful part of California to visit with its rocky coves and interesting wildlife (sea otters, chipmunks and monarch butterflies); it is something like an exotic Cornwall.

Bill Jekel and his winemaker are convinced that the longer cooler growing season is the key to quality, especially for 'fussy' grape types such as Riesling and Chardonnay. As a rule white wines are supreme in the region although some good Cabernet Sauvignon is also made, providing there is enough warmth to ripen the grapes. Jekel Vineyards make twice as much white wine as red, with plantings of Chardonnay, Riesling and Cabernet.

'Cool' is a relative term. In summer the maximum temperature hovers around 25°C but the area acts as something of a wind tunnel and the proximity of the ocean means cool evenings and nights. There is very little rainfall indeed – only about eight inches *per year* – and this lack of rain coupled with the long season of mild weather means grapes may be harvested very late indeed; Cabernet is commonly brought in during the second half of November.

Bill Jekel firmly believes that judicious irrigation is not only successful for vines but is actually an improvement on natural rainfall. With such a paucity of rain he needs to water, and he does this with sprinklers. But although rain is infrequent there is plenty of damp and mist and this causes *Botrytis* on the vines in many years. As a result Late Harvest Riesling is becoming something of a speciality and with time Bill Jekel feels he could produce something really fine in this sweeter category. For the present, however, he is content with the laurels he has earned for his complex yet delicate Cabernet Sauvignon and his Riesling, described by Hugh Johnson as 'ripe but not heavy' – the ideal for the new breed of California winemaker .

Bill Jekel's wines show a very intense yet dry fruity quality like fine Alsace or German wine and he uses the very best in German technology to help achieve this, particularly cold fermentation. He also uses some small oak barrels made not with American oak but wood imported from Europe, to help attain the 'European style'. The effort is worthwhile and gives depth to Chardonnay and Cabernet alike.

Wood-aged wines are not released until they are ready; young yet drinkable, or 'accessible' as Bill would say – four years after the vintage for Cabernet and two for Chardonnay. For the future there will be experiments with Sauvignon Blanc and with Sémillon, the two white Bordeaux varieties which could mean a California 'Graves' to come, or even a 'Barsac' given the special climate.

SEPTEMBER

'Tell me not here, it needs not saying,
What tune the enchantress plays
In the aftermaths of soft September'
   A.E. HOUSMAN, Fancy's Knell

This is a momentous month in the vineyard. In some warm areas the vintage begins in the latter part of the month and everywhere the emphasis is on protecting the grapes from the ravages of weather and pests. Little can be done about excess rain just before the harvest, but it is certainly undesirable as it quite literally dilutes the juice extracted. Weather forecasts take on a vital importance and teams of pickers stand by for the instant of vintage to be announced.

The Ban de Jurade passing ruined *murailles* at St Emilion

In many regions growers announce the earliest possible date for the picking of quality grapes – eg, those for French AC or Italian DOC wines – based on climatic conditions and hence an approximate knowledge of the ripeness of the grapes. Known as the Ban des Vendanges in France, it is announced on 18 September in the Médoc and Graves regions and on the following day in St-Emilion. But it is up to the individual to determine the exact moment by monitoring the vines constantly and regularly taking grape samples for analysis of sugar content. Once the correct level is reached, they must be picked right away – even at night. The advent of machine harvesters means a 24-hour shift is now possible for some vineyards, but many are still old-fashioned or simply too inaccessible to make use of this option and must hope overnight rain will not threaten the success of the harvest.

Each grape variety ripens at a different time and this is a positive convenience for the winemaker. In Bordeaux, for instance, a co-operative knows that it will receive all the Merlot before the Cabernet Sauvignon and can make separate vats without any administrative difficulties. While some varieties are ready by mid-September, others benefit from another month on the vine, and a few such as the Riesling may even linger on until Christmas to become very rare sweet berries for rich and expensive wines such as the Trockenbeerenauslese of Germany and the late-harvest wines of Alsace.

Pinot Noir and Chardonnay grapes are harvested in the Champagne region

The various pests which threaten the grapes now include all manner of greedy birds and sometimes vines must be netted to keep them out. But in many parts of Europe songbirds are quite a delicacy so very few survive to steal the valuable berries. If they are caught *in flagrante* with a bunch of grapes they are likely to be served up next day to the grapepickers who are legendary for their appetite – and their thirst. The famous estates bring in supplies of ordinary table wine rather than use the gallons of their own supplies needed to slake all those parched throats.

Insects, too, have a fancy for sweet grapes. You may occasionally see mysterious pots full of honey and vinegar at the end of a row of vines; these are to attract marauding wasps. Larger creatures such as deer may well attempt a raid on the vines but as a rule fencing is erected to keep them away well before this crucial time of year.

In the winery there is a bout of frantic spring-cleaning as all surfaces must be scrubbed and scoured before the new grapes arrive: bacteria are a great threat to the health of a new wine. The wooden barrels are ready but all the stainless steel requires vigorous hosing and even the floors, grids, presses and filters must be thoroughly washed. Once the tractors start to roll up with their trailers full of grapes there is no time to lose.

All the barrels containing wines from last year's vintage must be moved to a second-year cellar in readiness for the new crop. In many famous cellars dozens of new oak barrels are ordered and assembled each year to give a particular flavour and power to the raw young wine, but this expensive practice is normally reserved for the finest wines as only they can recoup the money invested. Labels of less renown must be sold sooner and do not need the keeping power imparted by new oak.

THE MAKING OF A NEW WINE

As the grapes arrive at the winery they are generally checked for quality. If they are intended for a fairly high-class wine, Champagne for instance, each bunch is picked over and those showing signs of mould or raisining are rejected. If, on the other hand, the wine is to form part of the huge production of a co-operative, then such niceties simply cannot be observed – the volume is too great. Some growers have the capacity to protect their grapes with an inert gas such as carbon dioxide, applied to prevent spoilage before arrival at the winery. For the rest a small amount of sulphur dioxide is often added to protect the fresh juice from fermenting too soon and spoiling.

The grapes are weighed and the producer is paid accordingly, also according to their ripeness. The sugar content is measured on a scale described as degrees Oechsle, Baumé or Brix depending on whether they are grown in Germany, France or California. To make acceptable wine, sugar, acid and pH levels must be in balance according to local conditions (highest sugar levels are normally recorded in California, for instance), and the grapes need to have a potential alcohol level of between 9.5 and 14% by volume. Less than this the wine may be unstable and not survive as long as it should; more and it will be a 'monster', too alcoholic for drinking with food. Of course there are exceptions to these rules and the Germans and Americans have produced marvellous wines at both ends of the scale, but the vast majority of wines still hover around 11 or 12%.

An old-fashioned wine press in action; many are still used

Today the fashion is for wines which have a pronounced fruity flavour yet are relatively dry. Modern technology plays a large part in obtaining this style, especially for white and rosé wines. For white wines the grapes are pressed very rapidly, either in an old-fashioned vertical press (the classic wooden tub with a screw you see everywhere in Italy and Greece) or in a modern horizontal press which may have a series of plates inside, like a newer version of the old style, or else an inflatable inner tube which expands gently to squeeze the fruit. At this stage the partly-crushed grapes are referred to as pomace. The juice which runs out of them is called the 'free run' on its first pressing.

Subsequent pressings yield juice which has a more pungent, rather bitter flavour – this must be used with care.

Fermenting White Wine

As a general rule, white wines are not fermented with their skins; this procedure is reserved for red wines. However, there are still some old-fashioned heavy white wines which are made in this way then aged in oak like red wine, but these (as in Rioja, for example) are now losing popularity and also need a good deal of keeping before drinking. The consumer is impatient – hence the vogue for Beaujolais Nouveau, the youngest wine of all.

Temperature is the key to keeping white wine fresh-tasting. In cooler climates like Germany and northern France temperatures after the harvest tend to be moderate and the winemakers in these areas have the additional benefit of the ancient caves. Further south there are no such natural advantages: the sun warms the white wine as it ferments, hence the famous 'baked' taste of southern white wines which can even verge on sherry.

If the winemakers can afford it, they are able to buy modern stainless steel fermentation vats which will reproduce artificially the cool conditions of the north and make fermentation a much slower process. The vats are cooled by a second skin of metal containing refrigerant or, quite simply, cool water is trickled over their walls. The ideal temperature varies from grape to grape but an average of around 10–18°C is considered cool enough. Most important is constancy of the temperature.

If a very full-flavoured and quite alcoholic wine is required then temperatures may be allowed to rise as high as 25°C. Typical wines made this way include the very richest white Burgundies (eg, Meursault) and California and Australian Chardonnay.

A Note on Yeast

The 'bloom' on a grape is an indication that so-called 'wild yeasts' are present. If the wine has been made traditionally and for dozens of hundreds of years in the same place then the winemaker will trust in these wild yeasts to give the right flavours and levels of alcohol. Indeed, they are said to impart that indefinable 'something' to many of the great wines of Europe. In a less established vineyard, however, notably in America, Australia or South Africa, the risks involved in allowing wild yeasts to run their natural course can be too great. They may not be sufficient to reach the desired alcohol level or they may add unpleasant flavours to the wine. If the alcohol is too low then other bacteria will take over and the wine might spoil permanently. Thus the yeasts are often neutralised by adding SO_2 (sulphur dioxide) to the grape juice (must) or by heating the juice as for pasteurisation and adding artificial yeast. Of course this 'artificial' yeast is still a natural product, specifically cultured for wine production.

During fermentation, as the yeasts transform the sugar in the grapes to alcohol, the wine gives off both heat and carbon dioxide. Once the fermentation is in full swing the heat tends to kill off bacteria and naturally stabilises the new wine. Yeasts can survive temperatures of up to about 35°C then they die off. The greatest natural degree of alcohol they are capable of achieving is around 16%, but as this is generally too strong for a table wine management of temperature is important.

Making Red Wines

Red wines are generally viewed as 'tougher' than whites: witness the success of red wines in some of the world's hottest wine regions such as South America. Even so, to make a fine red wine there are even more factors to consider than for a fine white. For example, the winemaker must decide whether or not to de-stem his grapes, how long to leave the fermenting juice in contact with the skins, and whether to 'pump over' among other technical niceties. And these decisions can make or break a wine. If anything, red wines are more susceptible to vagaries of vintage than white and conditions must be adapted yearly.

On arrival at the winery, red grapes are crushed and the resulting juice mixed with skins, pulp and perhaps stems is transferred to a fermentation vat made of steel, concrete or wood. (Most likely steel or concrete as wood is now old-fashioned and in fact imparts very little flavour to the wine at this stage.) The stems are often separated as they contain a great deal of tannin, that mouthpuckering astringent quality which is familiar from strong tea. They also tend to reduce the amount of 'extract' (colour) obtained from the skins. On the other hand they aerate the must and encourage oxygen to circulate. They are used in the winemaking process when a stronger, longer-living wine is required, in southern France and northern Italy, for example.

Once fermentation is under way, the carbon dioxide causes the solid matter eg, skins, stems etc. to float to the surface. This floating debris, known as the 'cap', is liable to culture bacteria and lead to spoilage of the wine so it must be kept partly submerged and out of contact with the air if possible. At the same time it must remain in contact with the wine as it contains the vital colouring matter, particularly important in a cool climate or for certain varieties such as the Pinot Noir. Today the cap is normally kept submerged by transferring wine from the bottom of the vat to the top by means of hoses – this is 'pumping over'. Alternatively a simple grille may be fitted on the top to prevent the cap rising too high, or the cellar workers have to climb up and push it down with poles. If they fall in survival is not guaranteed – all that warm new wine and carbon dioxide is definitely not good for the health.

Once fermentation is almost complete and the new wine has calmed – 'muté' say the French with poetic flair – then the new 'free run' is drawn off and what remains in the vat is pressed in the same way as the grapes used to make white wine. The remaining skins will give up their pungent flavours and tannins to the press and so 'press wine' is generally strong stuff with plenty of body. The first pressing is often blended, at least in part with the 'free run', to give a balance to macho and delicacy. The second is rarely used directly but despatched into a blend or local Vin de Table. If there is a third pressing this is for industrial distillation and is sometimes collected by the authorities as a form of tax – and what finally remains in the press is spread on the vineyard as fertiliser or processed into cattle feed. There is no wastage in the practical world of wine agriculture; romance is not a feature of the winery, only the resulting bottle.

A Note on Carbonic Maceration
This mouthfilling phrase is now bandied freely around in many wine regions. It is a technique pioneered in France and generally associated with Beaujolais and similar very fruity wines. When this method is used, fermentation takes place not simply in a vat, but *within each individual grape.*

A vat is filled with whole, undamaged bunches of grapes. The weight naturally tends to crush the lower bunches slightly and this sets off the fermentation via the wild yeasts. Carbon dioxide and heat are given off and as the gas surrounds the unfermented bunches so the fermentation continues gradually. It takes about a week for one-third of the vat to become wine, then the rest of the grapes are gently pressed and the resulting must is allowed to ferment out. Finally the two stages are blended together.

The wine made by maceration has an intensely fruity flavour which is balanced by the more conventional second batch. But as light, fruity wines are in ever greater demand this method will no doubt expand in its application and already giant co-operatives have been adapted to make huge volumes of wine in this way.

FESTIVALS

Wurzburg – the heart of the Franken wine region and home of *steinwein* named for its distinctive flask-shaped bottle

Despite preparations for the harvest there is still time this month for quite a few festivals heralding the new vintage. In Bordeaux and its surrounds, you may well be lucky enough to see one of the Confréries, honoured members of the wine trade, dressed in their impressive robes in full procession in the streets; these medieval burghers are in fact quite a recent revival but no less magnificent for that.

In Alsace they celebrate right through the vintage with picking all day and dancing and drinking all night; the first of these revels is the Fête des Ménétriers in Ribeauville on the first Sunday in September. In Burgundy there is a wine fair in Dijon early in the month where you may sample wines from the entire region.

Champagne is celebrated in Bar-sur-Aube on the second Sunday of September; this is one of the outlying regions of production near attractive forested country. Every three years this is preceded by a festival of all the winegrowers of the Aube, held on the last Sunday in August (the next will be in 1987).

If you enjoy the red wines of the Loire, or you have a taste for the earthy writings of Rabelais, then hasten to Chinon for the annual festival on 19 September. Lovers of meatier red wines might, however, prefer to travel to the south of France and sample Châteauneuf-du-Pape in the Avignon region; the vintage festival there is held on 24–25 September.

September also sees an explosion of festive activity in the German vineyards. The wines of the Saar (part of the Mosel-Saar-Ruwer region) are featured at the beginning of the month, as are the wines of the Nahe, a lesser-known area with an excellent wine route. (Each community organises its own 'Fest' so copious sampling is assured.) In Rheinhessen the town of Mainz has its Weinmarkt (wine market) in September and the Rheinpfalz (Palatinate) to the south has a festival at Edenkoben. Further south still there is the Heilbronner Herbst in the Württemberg region early in the month, while to the north the town of Würzburg is host to a wine festival featuring the local Franken wines. You will find more details of all of these in the leaflet available from the Wines from Germany Information Service.

Asti, home of the famed Spumante, is the scene of a fifteen-day festival celebrating the wines of Piedmont, an area known not only for sparkling wine but also some of italy's finest full reds such as Barolo and Barbaresco. In Tuscany fireworks are lit and much delicious food prepared for a festival of gastronomy and Chianti Classico at Greve in Chianti. Contact the Consorzio Chianti Classico in London for more details.

The end of the month sees festivals in both Soave and Bardolino. For more information about fairs in the Veneto region contact the Ente Autonoma Fiere di Verona.

ENTE AUTONOMA FIERE DI
  VERONA,
Casella Postale 525,
371500 Verona.

The harvest festival at Logroño during the second week of September includes bullfights, parades and folk dancing in the street – not to mention the excellent local Rioja wines. Further south in Jerez de la Frontera, the Fiesta de la Vendimia also offers bullfights, fireworks and flamenco dancers. This extravaganza is held on the weekend closest to 8 September each year.

ENTERTAINING

MUSHROOMS AND MORE: Wine with
VEGETARIAN DISHES

September is a month of such a bountiful supply of both fruit and vegetables that meat should become almost irrelevant. Even if you would never normally consider abandoning your steak, this one month of fruitfulness might just convince you to sample vegetarian fare.

The most luxurious and least 'wholesome' of all non-meat dishes must be those prepared with wild mushrooms which taste sinfully rich and succulent: it fast becomes easy to understand why cèpes, chanterelles and, most of all, truffles are sought after and paid for so dearly.

If you are able to gather any of these delicacies yourself, either in Britain or abroad on holiday, the best possible way to serve them is simply sautéed in butter with a touch of crushed garlic and some chopped parsley. Add a little lemon juice if liked then serve on 'croûtes' of bread either fried in butter and drained or baked in the oven, ready-buttered on both sides. And the wine to serve? Something red and redolent of the country where these mushrooms grow: a full-flavoured claret or north italian red wine, or perhaps a less expensive red Bergerac, Madiran or a Cabernet Sauvignon from a lesser-known region such as Bulgaria.

In the Bordeaux region you will find the giant cèpes sold fresh in street markets at this time of year. The price per kilo seems high but for this delicacy it is well worth it – just compare it with fillet steak! To make Cèpes à la Bordelaise slice and sauté them in butter, then season and add a little garlic, some chopped shallots and enough bread-crumbs to absorb about half the butter and juice. Serve as an hors d'oeuvre.

For a more filling version of the same recipe use the mixture as the basis for an omelette, or serve in puff pastry; wrap in fine pancakes or make tiny pasties. These are good even when you cannot find wild mushrooms. Make some pastry using half cream cheese to half butter as the fat content. Roll out and cut into rounds. Fill these either with a mixture of mushrooms, shallots and so on as for the Bordelaise recipe or with a duxelles made with finely-chopped mushrooms and onions cooked together. Shape into pasties, secure firmly and brush with egg before baking in a moderate oven. They make magnificent and filling snacks or a good light supper with salad. Again, the subtle red wines of Bordeaux or Chianti lend themselves as accompaniment.

Eggs form another staple part of the vegetarian diet and are often combined with various vegetables and even fruits. You may read elsewhere that they do not marry well with wine, but that really depends on the recipe. Take, for instance, the superior omelette made with mushrooms already mentioned, or perhaps a similar creation made with young sautéed leeks: both of these are delicious with a light red wine which is not too fruity. The richness of the eggs seems to clash with a very pronounced fruity flavour and certainly a wine such as Beaujolais Nouveau would taste odd with a fried egg. But an egg cooked in butter on a plate suspended over a pan of steaming vegetables or rice – that is best eaten with plenty of fresh-ground pepper and a substantial glass of a substantial red wine. And don't forget the fresh crusty bread with perhaps a few radishes from the garden. The spiciness of a Côtes du Rhône or a Côtes du Roussillon would do well here.

If the weather is warm use your eggs in the Spanish style by serving them stuffed. Mix mayonnaise with salt, pepper, dry mustard and a choice of tomato purée, chopped capers, anchovies or hot pickles. This is one of the *tapas* you might be offered at a café as many of them are made without meat. Marinated mushrooms are another favourite: marinate in a mixture of wine vinegar, olive oil, crushed garlic (about 2 cloves per 2 lb mushrooms), with a sprig of fresh dill if available. Simmer then cool and keep for a day or longer in the fridge. Slice aubergines, sprinkle with salt and drain in a colander for at least half an hour, then fry in very hot olive oil; the vegetables should be sliced 'on the bias' so that not too much oil is absorbed. Make tortilla or Spanish omelette by frying onions and potatoes in a large flat-based pan then pour on beaten eggs. When it starts to set put under the grill to brown the top. Serve cold, cut in wedges for the authentic touch. The wine? Fino Sherry or a light red Rioja.

In the south of France, the pipérade is another combination of eggs with vegetables. Tomatoes, red and green peppers and onions are fried together in olive oil then eggs are lightly scrambled on top. Serve this warm with very fresh bread and a glass of Côtes du Rhône, Rhône rosé or a Blanquette de Limoux for a southern version of the Champagne breakfast.

Ratatouille is a close relative of the former dish, but it can too often be greasy and insipid. The secret is to use very fresh vegetables and a good handful of fresh herbs, basil if possible as this complements the tomatoes perfectly. Cook some onions and crushed garlic in olive oil to start, then add sliced aubergines and courgettes (both salted and drained first as described above to remove bitterness), peppers and fresh peeled tomatoes, preferably those huge Marmande monsters seen in the south-west of France and increasingly in British gardens, where they do well outside in a temperate climate. Finally the basil and seasoning. Simmer down without a lid for half an hour or so. Serve very hot or quite cold – tepid is not all that agreeable. This goes perfectly with a

A typically basque meal from the French south-west including *piperade*

French goat cheese with its
cendré (ash) coating to preserve
the delicate flavour

very dry rosé such as one of those from the south of France, or a dry white which is not too fruity such as a Soave or Vinho Verde.

And after these savoury delights? Perhaps the ideal (and healthiest) conclusion is a platter of cheeses and fresh fruit. Goat cheese and fresh figs make an extraordinarily delicious and unusual combination which tastes marvellous with a southern French red or rosé, or with a glass of good white Graves. Don't choose cheeses that are very ripe or pungent because soft cheeses taste best with the fruits of this season such as pears and melons: a Brie or even a cream cheese perhaps flavoured with herbs is ideal. Pears and Brie are glorious with a demi-sec Champagne or sparkling wine such as California 'Champagne'.

Icecream and sorbets are increasingly popular thanks to the influence of nouvelle cuisine, where a tomato or pear sorbet may well be served between courses. The fashion now is to make them with natural ingredients and there are some excellent machines available which reduce the work involved to a mere peeling of fruit and opening of cream cartons. Combining a sorbet with a wine can be very tricky, however. Some contain a liqueur such as Poire William or Marc de Champagne and so you might match them with a tiny glass of iced spirit to match. When in doubt for a fruit or savoury ice, choose either one of the fruity dry white wines of Alsace (notably Gewürztraminer) or a Mosel from Germany. If icecream is too rich for you, then consider this wonderfully simple combination: very fresh apricots with a glass of good Sauternes. Serve outdoors in the last days of our British warmth and hope that this year will bring an Indian summer . . .

AND SO TO BORDEAUX

Bordeaux is for adult drinkers. This is not to imply that teenagers are not allowed there, nor that there is anything about the city or region which is less than a hundred per cent respectable. Far form it, for this city exudes a thoroughgoing bourgeois satisfaction and completely justified knowledge of self-worth. No, the 'adults only' sign is to indicate that the *wines* of this region need a little experience and time to be appreciated.

Likewise the city and the legendary Médoc region to the north: neither has instant charm, vivacity or welcoming warmth. Rather, they are somewhat severe, closed and elegant – all adjectives applied by the claret-lover to a favourite wine made in one of the famous villages of the area. Without preparation, the towering gates of the châteaux you pass on your journey through the Médoc can intimidate and seem too imposing for a mere amateur wine-taster.

So a little homework will be necessary, both to avoid errors about the wines themselves and to gain access to the sanctions beyond some of those famous portals. The great surprise then will be the warmth and enthusiasm of the welcome you receive, always providing that you reciprocate with due respect for the wines. For there are more fine wines made here than in any other region of France – more Appellation Contrôlée wines, a high proportion of which are exported to markets as varied as Switzerland and Japan, the United States and China.

To throw in a statistic or two, of the 250,000 acres under vine over the region, some 200,000 yield AC wines, and of these wines some 75% are red. Of course, within the confines of the AC there are wines many and various, ranging from reasonable 'grocer's claret' through pleasant 'bourgeois growths' to the very noblest and rarest reds of all. Of the 25% remainder which is white, some is quite dry, such as the excellent wines of the Graves, while some is immensely sweet and rich – Sauternes and Barsac, for example.

Thus Bordeaux has something to offer all-comers from full red wines to sweet whites, with well-made examples of every other style between. Try a Premières Côtes de Bordeaux as an example of a medium-sweet fruity white wine or even an agreeable, inexpensive sparkling wine from the vast cellars of the Café de Paris empire near Bordeaux. It is not always necessary to pay a lot to drink well in the region, but a good deal of sampling is unavoidable to find your bargains – perhaps this may not seem too arduous!

Assuming you start your pilgrimage in Bordeaux itself, there are several important stopping-points to be observed. First, the Maison du Vin where they are well-prepared with information, maps and introductions to answer all your queries. The Maison is in the elegant heart of the city, near the Grand Theatre and between the shopping precinct and the attractive old Quartier St Pierre. To see some representative bottles at this stage, browse in the Vinothèque, a comprehensive wine shop opposite the Maison. In the rue Abbé l'Epée is the Hôtel des Vins which sells a full range of fine wines and accessories and organises tastings and seminars.

MAISON DU VIN,
1, cours du XXX juillet,
33000 Bordeaux.

If you would like a conducted tour to introduce you to the vineyards, then contact either Bordeaux Wine Tours or the Maison du Tourisme. The latter will send you on a guided tour or loan you an explanatory cassette in English to help you as you drive yourself. If you want what the Americans call an 'in-depth' survey of the local wines then you could attend a course run by the Institut International des Vins et Spiritueux (usually a week long). French speakers might attempt the 'Initiation' course run by the university which really does open doors and includes friendly visits to such temples of the grape as Château d'Yquem and Château Margaux – but you do have to work quite hard in the mornings. For information write to the Institut d'Oenologie.

BORDEAUX WINE TOURS,
12, place de la Bourse.

MAISON DU TOURISME,
12, cours du XXX juillet.

INSTITUT INTERNATIONAL
DES VINS ET SPIRITUEUX,
10, place de la Bourse.

The neoclassical château at Margaux seen from the vines

INSTITUT D'OENOLOGIE, 351, cours de la Liberation, 33405 Talence.

Having visited Bordeaux it might be an idea to head south, for in this area you can see the wines of Bordeaux in all their variety. The most famous names in Graves are but a stone's throw from the city gates, with Château Haut-Brion (one of the 1855 first growths) situated literally in the suburbs. Other notable names here are Château La Mission Haut-Brion and Château Pape-Clément, but for more accessible wines try those made by Peter Vinding-Diers at Château Rahoul and Domaine La Grave. Be sure to sample some dry white wines as well as red for an indication of how classy Bordeaux whites can be.

Even classier, perhaps, are the Sauternes and Barsac made to the south where the countryside changes and the rolling hills with their fairytale châteaux recall a medieval illuminated script. Some of the most famous winegrowers are a little reluctant to receive visitors (and probably have no wine to offer them as production is always limited), but try Château de Malle at Preignac for a warm welcome – ignore the entertaining audio-visual presentation and concentrate on the lovely surroundings and the agreeable wine (a second growth).

Continue as far south as Langon if you are attracted by the extravagant idea of a meal at the table of the famed restaurateur Claude Darroze, then double back through the vineyards of St Croix du Mont and

Loupiac – home to less famous sweet white wines – and so along the banks of the Garonne back to the city. You could divert via the Entre-deux-Mers vineyards if time permits but the wines here are not exceptional – mainly light dry whites which go well with seafood and fairly light reds which may only be described as Bordeaux or Bordeaux Supérieur on the label.

A journey along the banks of Bordeaux's other river, the Dordogne, is also highly recommended. Head towards Paris but avoid the motorway – you will find yourself in the neighbourhood of Fronsac, an old-world village with some lovely ancient houses and manors. The red wines made here bear the name of the village itself or of Canon-Fronsac, or simply Côtes de Fronsac. All are typical reliable quite light 'clean' clarets and they are rarely expensive.

Several miles on from Fronsac you reach Libourne, once a major port and still a clearing house for all the region's wines, also a centre for some wine houses. The town was constructed in the thirteenth century as a bastion against the marauding French – not a contradiction in terms as the Bordeaux region was under the rule of the British in those days and in fact the town is named after Roger de Leyburn, the then Governor. From Libourne you may venture towards something rather special yet unimpressive at first sight – the village of Pomerol. Considering that Château Pétrus is a wine fought over by collectors worldwide there seems little excitement or even evidence of wealth here. Yet the wines are all distinctive and quite addictive once you have the taste for their particular richness – sadly not a cheap fancy. Vieux Château Certan is another good name and will welcome visitors with an appointment.

On to St-Emilion – a notable town for wine lovers and a magnetic tourist attraction as it is one of the most photogenic spots in the region with its orange tiles and ancient stone buildings tumbling down the steep slopes of the hill it perches on. Some of the area's most famous wines are made on these slopes (including Château Ausone and Château Canon) while others including the much-praised Château Cheval Blanc are made on flatter ground outside the walls – the Graves St-Emilion, for example. Good everyday wines are also made in the 'satellites' such as Lussac-St-Emilion and Montagne-St-Emilion. Château Ausone may be visited with an appointment and it is definitely worth making the time as the caves where the wine is aged are most atmospheric and draped in decorative moulds; Château Cheval Blanc also welcomes visitors with an appointment and both places have English-speaking members of staff.

This might be a full enough agenda for your second day unless you wanted to press onward and look at Bergerac, source of some excellent red and dry white wines, not to mention a delicious sweet wine with a

The tiled roofs of St Emilion inspire many a photographer – as do the wines

touch of the 'noble rot' – Monbazillac. The Monbazillac Château, although now in municipal hands, is well worth some attention and indeed all the Bergerac wines bear a great similarity to their Bordeaux cousins and are simply unlucky to be outside the charmed circle entitled to the *appellation*.

Finally, the culmination of your visit: a look at the Châteaux of the Médoc. The first stage of your drive from Bordeaux passes through some rather flat, dull countryside but once you reach Cantenac you are on the

The turreted château of Monbazillac now owned by a cooperative venture

Route des Châteaux and famous names proliferate. The first to catch your eye might well be Château Prieuré-Lichine, owned by Alexis Lichine, writer and bon viveur.

As you drive on towards Margaux, you will see the romantic turrets of Château Palmer, a wine most feel can rival the first growths in good years. Then come Château Rausan-Ségla, Château Lascombes and, most dramatic of all, Château Margaux itself, owned and run by the widow of a Greek-born supermarket magnate called Mentzenopoulos. It has the perfect neo-classical façade and an elegant driveway; parts of the installations may be visited with an appointment although the château itself is reserved for invited guests only.

The next major wine town is St-Julien with names like Château Ducru-Beaucaillou, Château Gloria and the three Léovilles – Barton, Las Cases and Poyferré. The Barton name is originally Irish (many of

Château Priéuré-Lichine welcomes visitors without formality

the names in the area are Anglo-Saxon, not French at all) and the current heir to the family fortunes is Anthony Barton, now running the estates for his father and epitomising a particular style of the Bordeaux gentleman – a fascinating blend of French and Irish with the unmistak-able stamp of the British public school.

In Pauillac the stakes are higher with three first-growth wines in one

The emblem of Château Margaux branded on a wooden case of this precious claret

'commune' and corresponding wealth, although there is nothing visibly ostentatious about the area. Château Latour and Château Lafite-Rothschild were first to be classified, then Châteaux Mouton-Rothschild joined them thanks to the efforts of Baron Philippe Rothschild, the grand old man of Pauillac. You may visit the château except in August or over the Christmas period and there is an excellent wine museum there. Latour and Lafite are also accessible but by appointment only.

Most northerly of the notable names is St-Estèphe, supposedly the 'meatiest' and most powerful of the village wines. Château Cos d'Estournel is a rather eccentric château producing some superb wine (open to visit, but make an appointment in the winter months), and north of the village lies Château Calon-Ségur, formerly owned by the Comte de Ségur, who also owned Château Latour and Château Lafite at that time. The wines made here are of the long-lived and hearty variety which is said to appeal to the British palate.

Peter Vinding Diers – an innovative invader on the Bordeaux scene

THE PURSUIT OF PERFECTION: Peter Vinding-Diers and the wines of Graves

It has to be surprising that a Dane who learned his winemaking in South Africa has come to be one of the great innovators in a traditional region like Graves, but Peter Vinding-Diers has undergone a long and hardworking apprenticeship in local vineyards, first with Gilbeys at Château Loudenne – the 'pink' château of the Médoc – then as administrator of an estate in Portets, Graves. This is Château Rahoul, now acknowledged by wine authorities on both sides of the Channel as overdue for promotion to the Crus Classés ranks of the best Graves wines (see Appendix 00 for a listing of the Graves crus).

Château Rahoul has a chequered history dating back to the days of the Revolution when its unfortunate owner was guillotined. Since that time the wine has been made each year but it is only in the past decade that it has gained renown for its quality. In the early 1970s it was owned by an Englishman, David Robson, still a wine merchant back in England today. Despite all his efforts to replant the estate and improve the facilities he had to give up ownership in 1978 and he chose to sell to two interesting and flamboyant personalities: a British financier, Peter Fox, and perhaps the most famous of Australian wine pundits, Len Evans.

Peter Vinding-Diers was engaged as administrator by this partnership and after the financial collapse of the enterprise in 1981 he took over entirely, finding a new partner in Denmark. Since then he has worked

constantly and with great creative flair to improve the quality of both red and white wines. There are thirty-five acres of land at Château Rahoul and of these about six acres are planted with white grapes, the Sémillon only. The red grapes are part Merlot and part Cabernet Sauvignon, the traditional mix for Graves.

Graves wines are the least obviously fruity of Bordeaux styles. Experts claim the reason is the soil, which is of gravel overlying sandstone. Most of the famous crus come from the northern part of the region, close to Bordeaux, and have that quality of 'fine furs' which is beloved of the connoisseur. Further south, where Château Rahoul and Peter Vinding-Diers's other property, Domaine La Grave, are located, the soil changes to clay and limestone, and this favours white wine in particular, although the reds continue very fine, if different from those of the north.

One unusual technique employed by Vinding-Diers is to leave the white grapes on special aerated trays overnight after picking. This allows the enzymes to start working on the grape pulp and begins the

Château Rahoul at Portets in the Graves region

PETER VINDING-DIERS,
Château Rahoul,
33640 Portets.
(Gironde)

fermentation process very slightly. Then the grapes are pressed normally and the result (after various other technicalities such as adding extra enzymes to the must) is a wine of great finesse and not too acidic, as some from the area can be. The wine is aged in new oak casks for a few months before bottling.

The red wines are made with equal care, using the 'tray technique' again; Vinding-Diers also has the bunches sorted by hand so that even in a poor year he is able to make a good wine with the healthy grapes thus selected. A typical example (the 1983) was said by Clive Coates to have 'the Graves' earthy flavour overlaid by a meaty, spicy Merlot character'.

Domaine La Grave is a relatively recent acquisition. It produces only tiny quantities (2500 cases of red and 600 of white at present) but is already gaining a reputation for excellence. Like the white wine produced at the Château Rahoul, it is made with 100% Sémillon and has a very special flavour of apple blossom, peaches and nuts.

If regulations permitted, Peter Vinding-Diers would like to try growing Chardonnay and Riesling, but this is unlikely to happen in an AC area. A pity, as his knack with white wines is obviously something rather special and certainly gives the tired old image of white Graves a completely new face.

OCTOBER

Season of fruitfulness indeed, but also one of treachery, for too often the mild damp weather can change and storms or even early frosts undo all the good done by the summer sunshine. The biblical quotation is of course meant to be a metaphor for human life, but the grapegrower too must tend his grapes with continued loving care right until the moment of picking or risk losing all. And deciding when to pick the grapes is a nail-biting affair.

For a top-quality wine, incalculable good may come from leaving the grapes on the vine for just that week or so longer than your neighbour and rival. If the weather holds, not only more sweetness but also more concentration of flavour may result. But if the aim is to produce a simple everyday wine with a fruity taste then it is probably not worth the extra anxiety involved – modern technology can help to achieve a good flavour from sound and healthy grapes (see *September*).

Keeping the grape-pickers encamped and standing by is a costly business and they may be 'poached' by another vineyard on just the day you decide to pick – or you could find that the communal grape-picking machine is in use elsewhere. Few growers can afford the luxury of their own machine-harvester. A day's delay, a thunderstorm and . . . no quality wine to provide the income to pay all the expenses incurred. In addition to the extra people employed during the harvest, there is the year-round staff to pay, including the secretary or manager who deals with the office work, and the cellar must be maintained and new equipment bought as needed. Finally there is the cost of the fertiliser and those vital sprays to ward off the pests . . .

Thus the 'nuclear vineyard', family-owned and with all the wine produced on the spot, is fast becoming harder to find. Thousands of grapegrowers are opting to concentrate on viticulture and leave the vinification (winemaking) to someone else, probably a co-operative. Those family ventures which do thrive are based on enormously hard work and a devotion to modern methods for maximum quality and sales: behind the quaint old cellars and barns there are likely to be modern computers and winemaking equipment to help keep ahead of the competition. Such is the state of family ventures of a sufficient size

*'Season of mists and mellow fruitfulness
Close bosom-friend of the maturing sun;
Conspiring with him how to load and bless
With fruit the vines that round the thatch-eaves run.'*
KEATS, *To Autumn*

'Let us not be weary of well-doing; for in due season we shall reap, if we faint not'.
THE BIBLE, Galatians IX

Picking grapes trained high to make maximum use of space for a variety of crops

to export, perhaps to a company like the Wine Club in Britain. Of course, there are smaller family concerns still but these tend to aim for self-sufficiency rather than for profit, producing enough wine to meet the family's needs and just enough more to barter for the other goods they need.

AFTER FERMENTATION: KEEPING WINE

White Wines

The majority of white wines produced today are intended to be sold and consumed very young so the most important procedure after fermentation is to stabilise them and make sure they are perfectly clear. The clarity is achieved by racking the wine off its lees – transferring it from the vat where it was made to another, leaving the residue behind. This process is often backed up by the use of a centrifuge which separates any remaining debris from the liquid to make the final wine brilliantly clear.

Occasionally you may have noticed some tiny crystals clinging to the inside of a wine bottle – for the uninitiated they bear an unnerving resemblance to ground glass. These are tartrate crystals which are quite harmless but not very decorative. In the days when wine was kept in a cool place – usually a cellar – for some years before sale, the falling temperatures led to a natural chemical reaction which 'precipitated out' the tartrates on to the wooden casks holding the wine. Now everything happens faster and so artificial chilling is practised to ensure no crystals are formed. But the producers of high-quality wines may well scorn this process and so you should not be perturbed to see a little deposit in, for instance, a good-quality German wine, particularly after a hard winter.

After fermentation, the wine is racked off to another container, either a wooden barrel or a concrete vat depending on the style of wine and its quality. Most red wines then undergo what is called malolactic fermentation – a natural secondary process which is stimulated by the bacteria in the new wine. The sharp malic acid in the wine, which has a taste like green apples, is broken down by the bacteria into the smoother lactic acid (as found in milk). The temperature needs to be fairly high (about 20°C) for this to happen but because it makes the wine smoother in taste and more stable it is seen as desirable by almost all winemakers.

If the wine is to be blended then this will be the next step. Blends may either include wines made with a variety of different grape types or different batches of wine made with the same grape type. They may also include wines of an older vintage if this is permitted under local regulations. Wines made with 100% of a single variety are fairly rare – examples are Muscadet, Alsace wines, Burgundy and some California 'varietals'.

The elusive factor winemakers seek is known as 'balance' and this is most often achieved in a wine which has been blended. For instance, Bordeaux wines usually comprise a mixture of Merlot and Cabernet Sauvignon as well as lesser quantities of several other varieties. Sauternes are a judicious mix of Sémillon with Sauvignon Blanc – both affected by the noble rot. In the south of France the blend is king, with a host of grape types jostling for position in a wine like Châteauneuf-du-Pape and somehow, with time, settling down to an excellent balance.

Of course it takes great skill and practice to blend well and courage to decide when *not* to blend. Great wines made with the Riesling, Pinot Noir and Chardonnay grape are rarely blended (except in the case of Champagne which blends Chardonnay and Pinot Noir). On the other hand, classic wines like port are a triumph of the blender's art. In newer wine regions like Australia and California it is naturally taking time to establish the ground rules for blends and experiments will go on for many years to come.

Ageing Red Wines

When a wine is allowed to rest in a wooden barrel it is gradually altered by a chemical reaction with the air which seeps in very slowly. This is a form of oxidation and the same thing happens over time to the wine in a bottle sealed with a cork. But the wood additionally imparts an assortment of flavours as well as tannins which give a wine potential for keeping.

So red wines are tannic not only because of the skins and stalks they were made with but also because of the wood they age in. The amount of tannin must be determined by the winemaker. In a good vintage the wines are full of the ripe flavour of the fruit and can tolerate a good deal of tannin, but in a poorer year the tannin can overpower the fruit and prevent the wine from reaching a balanced state. It 'dies' before it is really drinkable.

Oxidation is not only a beneficial process which smoothes red wine and gives it 'bouquet' and the much-desired complexity often mentioned by wine lovers, it is also a threat to any wine which is not quite stable. Interaction of air with the wine will eventually bring about browning and a breakdown of the wine's components when it will be 'oxidised' and undrinkable. Occasionally this happens prematurely in bottle and such a wine may with justification be returned to your wine supplier or wine waiter.

White wines tend to benefit less from wood ageing as the pungency of the wood can destroy the delicacy of the fruit flavours. So it is best to age them in bottle – if at all. The modern passion for very fruity wines, both red and white, means that the whole concept of ageing is not even considered by many winemakers who want to *avoid* ageing at all costs. They combat signs of change with extensive filtering to remove any organisms which might bring about chemical reactions. Modern filters are so fine that even tiny microbes may be excluded from the bottle. Alternatively wine may be pasteurised (a controversial process) by heat to kill off remaining bacteria and produce a 'clean' fruity wine which will not age but is probably not too exciting to drink.

Ageing is therefore the process that distinguishes a fine wine from a lesser cousin, with even light wines like Muscadet found to be much improved given some time to age in vat or bottle (see the profile of Metaireau on page 48). A typical claret, for instance, will be kept in barrel for about three years then in bottle for several more. The French themselves drink their red wines younger than other consumers – in Britain it is still about ten years before we sample a red Bordeaux from a good vintage and château.

Of course even a relatively humble wine may improve with some ageing: try it for yourself. Choose a red wine with noticeable tannin (it makes the inside of your lip pucker) and also some fruit and acidity (feel this down the side of your tongue as you swirl the wine in your mouth). Drink a bottle or two and 'lay down' the rest of the case to age for a year or more; the improvement may be startling.

FESTIVALS

If there is time to spare, many wine areas have their own small-scale thanksgivings for the new wine harvest, with church services and tastings of the barely-fermented wine fresh from the vat – a memorable if indigestible experience!

On a more formal level, there are festivals of both wine and food in many parts of Europe in October. The beginning of the month is the time for a wine festival in Würzburg in the heart of the Franken wine region, where they make dry and pungent German wines much prized by connoisseurs and readily recognisable from the *Stein* bottles, also known as *Bocksbeutels*. Other German regions have their own small fêtes, all detailed in the leaflet already mentioned which is invaluable for the traveller in Germany.

A dog gets down to serious work in the hunt for truffles – Piedmont, Italy

Unprepossessing perhaps but a delight for gourmets – the noble truffle

In mid-October, gourmets should hasten to Piedmont, the Asti and Alba areas, for a very rare delight – the Grande Feste del Tartufo, which celebrates this most royal of fungi in great style. There are truffle auctions and special dishes in all the local restaurants, as well as opportunities to sample them with the region's magnificent red wines such as Barolo. Contact the Camera di Commercio di Asti for more information and dates.

CAMERA DI COMMERCIO DI ASTI, Piazza Medici, 8, 14100 Asti.

In Tuscany the humble song thrush has its festival on the last Sunday of the month at Montalcino, home of another of Italy's finest red wines, the Brunello di Montalcino. If your tastes run to small song birds cooked in ingenious ways then this is for you – or just go and watch everyone else struggling with all those tiny bones!

Oysters are another food which arouse passions both for and against, but the true devotee will be drawn like a magnet to Sancerre on the last weekend of this month, there to taste the delicious Marennes oysters washed down with the local wine. Somehow these wines made with Sauvignon Blanc seem the perfect accompaniment for fresh oysters, the claims of brut Champagne and Chablis notwithstanding.

30 October is the date for the Fête Raclet in Romanèche-Thorins, the centre of the Beaujolais region and the base for many well-known shippers. The Fête includes a tasting and exhibition of wines from the Beaujolais and the Mâconnais as most *négociants* here have interests in both areas – and the celebrations are all part of the preparation for the great Beaujolais Race which takes place in November.

Looking back again towards the beginning of the month, there are Fêtes des Vendanges at a dozen of the wine villages in Alsace; check with the Office de Tourisme Colmar for details of places and dates.

In the Veneto, the town of Fumane, home of the excellent Agricola Allegrini (see *April*), makers of exceptional Valpolicella, has its wine festival in October. And for sheer entertainment, try to find a Bal des Vendanges in France or its equivalent elsewhere and join the grape-pickers and villagers as they celebrate a worthy conclusion to all their hard work.

Office de Tourisme,
4, rue Unterlinden,
68003 Colmar.

ENTERTAINING
WINE WITH GAME

'Happy the hare at morning, for she cannot read
The Hunter's waking thoughts.'
W.H. Auden, 'The Dog beneath the Skin'

'Fill ev'ry glass, for wine inspires us,
And fires us
With courage, love and joy.'
  John Gay, *The Beggar's Opera*

Whether you have inspirations to hunt down your dinner yourself, or you are content to let someone else provide for you, still it must be said that game offers a marvellous range of flavours and textures to accompany fine wines. Even wines not so fine can show well against the richness of, say, a game pie made with a variety of what is in season, or even with the leftovers of a roast bird or two.

With our current enthusiasm for lean meat, the classic game birds are perfect for entertaining at dinner and although they still have the reputation of being delicacies, pheasant and partridge are no longer expensive. Cheaper still are wood pigeons, hare and rabbit, all important ingredients in fine European and British cuisine. But with all deference to the European tradition, the cooking of game is something we do very well in this country, too, and the recipes which follow reflect a British bias.

Early in the season there is no better dish than a plain roast game bird with its rather unusual classic trimmings. Later on the casseroles and pies come into their own. For some reason the simple roasts taste better with traditional wines such as good claret and red Burgundy (if these are within your budget) while composite dishes are set off by a spicy blend such as a Rhône wine, a fine Chianti or good Dão or Rioja. So the rule of thumb might be – well-established classics with a plain roast; minor (or modern) classics with a pie or casserole.

Menus with Game

MENU

Shrimp Bisque

*

Roast grouse or pheasant with trimmings

*

English cheese selection

*

Pears with ginger and brandy

*

Wines: You could serve red wine right through the meal including the cheese course if your guests are happy with this. Choose a bourgeois claret from the Médoc or Graves as St-Emilion can be much fruitier. Somehow the depth of a good Graves seems perfect with roast grouse – but try it for yourself. Offer a dry white Graves as an alternative with the first and second courses or a good Soave such as Pieropan. More claret with the cheese and perhaps you might choose another similar wine such as a good Rioja or Cabernet Sauvignon from another region, to compare and contrast with the first. Then with the pears it should be coffee and brandy – served a little early this time.

For Shrimp Bisque you need 1 pint peeled shrimps (per four people), 1 large onion, 1 tablespoon tomato puree, 3 oz butter, 1½ oz flour, 1½ pints water and a fish cube. Grate the onion and allow to simmer in the butter until soft then add shrimps, tomato puree and season. Cook together for about 10 minutes. Add flour and stir in well to cook, then lower heat to add water mixed with stock cube and stir until creamy. Simmer over very low heat for 45 minutes, then liquidise or sieve.

Grouse and duck serve from two to four according to size – a farmyard duck will certainly do four, a grouse may well need to be simply halved. To roast the game birds, put a little butter in each and season with salt and pepper. Put them on slices of buttered toast and cover with streaky bacon rashes then roast in a fairly hot oven (425°F/220°C/Gas Mark 7) for about 40 minutes, basting regularly. Pour off the fat and allow the birds to rest on a warm plate for at least five minutes before serving. Reduce the remaining juices to half the quantity and add a quarter-glass of red wine or port to make gravy. Serve with home-made bread sauce, game chips made by slicing potatoes in a food processor and crisping in the oven, browned breadcrumbs and a garnish of watercress.

Take one good dessert pear per person and peel then cut them in half and core. Use one piece of stem ginger per person and quarter. Heat an ounce of unsalted butter in a frying pan or chafing dish over moderate heat then fry the pears until golden brown – both sides need to be cooked. Warm a tablespoon then fill with brandy (three-star Cognac is ideal), light it and pour over the pears; repeat with another tablespoon for each two pears. Put the pears on plates and arrange the ginger inside the cavities. Add a little ginger syrup from the bottle of stem ginger and one tablespoon of double cream per two pears to the pan and heat very gently. Pour over and serve at once.

MENU

Melon with mint

*

Roast wild duck and orange salad

*

Sauté potatoes

*

Devils on horseback

*

Wines: With the melon, a well-chilled white Loire wine such as Vouvray, a light Mosel or an Alsace Riesling. The duck with orange is complemented by a fine northern Rhône wine such as Côte Rotie or Hermitage, or a Chianti Riserva. Serve more of the red wine with the savoury which completes the meal, or bring out a bottle of late bottled vintage port.

Buy small ripe melons such as Ogen or Charentais and halve (chill well beforehand). Sprinkle with a little caster sugar, a dash of lemon juice and some finely chopped mint before serving.

Sprinkle the wild duck with salt, cayenne pepper and a little lemon juice and add a tablespoon of water to the roasting tin before cooking. Roast in a hot oven (450°F/230°C/Gas Mark 8) for no more than about 15–20 minutes, basting with melted butter. The bird should be underdone. Add a small glass of port or madeira to the juices and heat to make gravy. Serve the breast sliced and other portions according to your skill as a carver – your tricky relationship with the bird is what gives duck its renown as a meal for two!

For the orange salad, loosen the skins of 2 oranges (per duck) by immersing them in boiling water for about five minutes, then peel and remove all pith and slice thinly. Sprinkle with a light vinaigrette (go easy on the vinegar) and with chopped parsley or chervil.

Make old-fashioned but delicious devils on horseback by wrapping a half rasher of streaky bacon around prunes or plums stuffed with Jordan almonds. Fry the almonds (remove skins) in butter and roll them in salt and a little cayenne. Insert where the plum or prune stone was, then roll in bacon and skewer. Suspend these over a small roasting tin or grill pan and grill or cook in the hot oven for about 10 minutes. Serve on small croûtes of fried bread buttered before frying, or simply on toast.

If all this savoury emphasis is too much, compensate with a few petits fours with coffee . . .

MENU

Game pie with celeriac and potato purée

*

Cheese board

*

Soufflé omelette with nectarines

*

Cobnuts with Madeira

*

Wines: This rich combination will require a prolonged digestion session after eating (with the young cobnuts and a light Madeira like Sercial to help). The pie itself looks really mouthwatering and has a very full flavour from the marinated game so choose the richest wines you know – a Priorato from Spain, a Cahors, a Vacqueyras from the southern Rhône, or an Australian Shiraz. The omelette need not have a wine at all but a bottle of Muscat de Beaumes de Venise would complement the nectarines.

For a game pie to serve six, you will need 1½ lb haunch of venison and 2 oz belly pork. Substitute pheasant or another game bird weight for weight for part of the venison if available – you can use leftovers to advantage here. Cut up the meat into cubes and trim fat. Make a marinade from 1 finely-chopped onion, 1 chopped stick of celery, a few crushed coriander and juniper berries, 2 bay leaves, a sprig of parsley, a pinch of dried marjoram, a large glass of dry red wine and a half-glass of good olive oil. Marinate the meat for at least eight hours (cover the bowl).

When the marinated meat is ready, dice the pork and fry in its own fat. Add a half-pound of sliced field mushrooms and a knob of butter, then blend in enough flour to absorb this fat. Cook together for 2 minutes. Remove the meat from the marinade then use the liquid to make the sauce, adding gradually to the pork and mushroom mixture. Add a little water if necessary. Finally add the game and bring to the boil; adjust seasoning. Simmer over low heat or in a low oven for 90 minutes.

Use bought puff pastry or make your own using 8 oz plain flour, 4 oz of butter and 1½ oz lard. Rub these together then add 2 beaten egg yolks and a little water and knead until firm. Allow to rest for an hour before using.

Put the cooked meat in its sauce into a deep pie dish and insert a pie funnel into the middle. Roll out the pastry and cover the dish, sealing edges well. Brush with beaten egg and decorate with trimmings of pastry

– make a few slits for the steam to escape while cooking. Bake in a hot oven (425°F/220°C/Gas Mark 7) for 20 minutes then reduce the heat to 375°F/190°C/Gas Mark 5 for another 30 minutes until golden brown.

Serve with celeriac and potatoes, cooked and mashed together with butter and a pinch of mace.

For the soufflé omelette you will need 2 eggs per omelette, which will probably serve two people. Cream together the egg yolks with 2 dessertspoons of caster sugar then add a dash of vanilla essence. Whisk the egg whites until stiff then fold into the rest. Meanwhile, heat an omelette pan with a knob of butter; when hot add the mixture and cook over moderate heat until the underside is golden brown. Then put briefly under a hot grill to cook the top. Lay the sliced nectarines on top (add a dash of liqueur such as Cointreau if liked) and fold over carefully. Serve at once.

SCENTED SLOPES

Typically narrow flower-decked street in Provence

The wines of the Rhône, Provence and the Midi

It is impossibly ambitious to attempt to summarise all the variety of southern France in the few paragraphs available here. But a summary is all it can be, with a few pointers to places to see and wines to try. As with all the regions mentioned in *The Wine Almanac*, the only answer is to buy the wines (not too expensive an investment for most reviewed here) and to go and see it all for yourself. What excuse do you need to visit the lavender-fragrant hills of Provence, the glorious Roman monuments of the southern Rhône or the romantic *maquis* of the arid Midi?

If wine is defined by its nose, then this is the quintessential wine area. For the most insensitive of noses could not fail to discern the pungency of the plants which grow here, warmed in the sun so that even the curious flat rocks which litter the vineyards of Châteauneuf-du-Pape seem to give off a particular aroma. Numerous poets and artists have lingered in the region, and it requires no effort to understand why they were attracted.

The south of France offers far more than just those famous Riviera beaches and the sunlit hills above the bays. There are forests, olive and orange groves, chestnuts, all set against the brilliant blue skies so poignantly captured by Van Gogh when he was living and painting near Arles. And just as the landscape merits exploration, so there are a great variety of wines to try, from the subtle red and white aristocrats of the

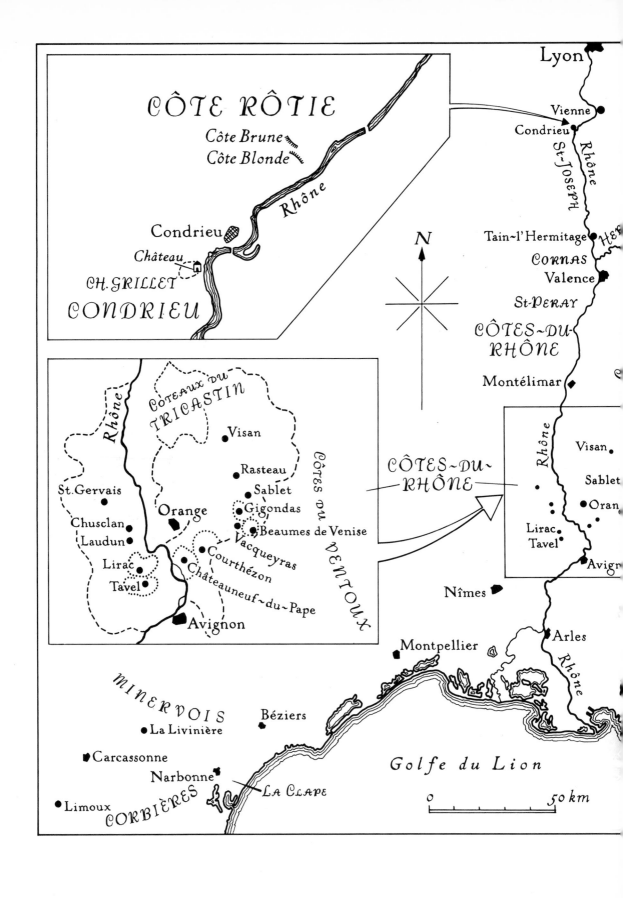

1985

**Domaine
de l'abbaye
de Valfernière**

Vin de Pays
des Côteaux de Narbonne

VIN DE TABLE

Blanc de noir

Mis en bouteilles au Domaine par Jean DEMOLOMBE
Propriétaire au Château Pech Redon 11100 Narbonne France
Produit de France

12 % alc./vol.　　75 cl e

L'ÉPERVIER®

1re mise　　　　　bouteille
9 000 bouteilles

BLANC DE NOIR

CHATEAU DU TRIGNON

03　03

MISE EN BOUTEILLE AU CHATEAU

CÔTES-DU-RHÔNE

Appellation Côtes-du-Rhône Contrôlée
CHARLES ROUX ET FILS PROPRIETAIRES A GIGONDAS
84190 · Beaumes de Venise

── PRODUCE OF FRANCE ──　75 cl e

PRODUCE　　　　　　　　　OF FRANCE

LES PONTAIX

Crozes-Hermitage

Appellation Crozes-Hermitage Contrôlée

MIS EN BOUTEILLE A LA PROPRIÉTÉ　　37,5 cl
G. A. E. C. LES GAMETS FAYOLLE FILS
PROPRIÉTAIRES · VITICULTEURS A GERVANS (DROME) FRANCE

REPRODUCTION INTERDITE　　　　　　　IMP. REYNARD - VALENCE

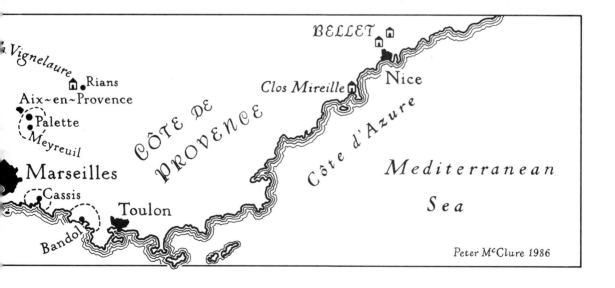

northern Rhône, like Côte Rotie and Condrieu, to the powerful and complex reds made around Avignon; from the extraordinary earthy orange-tinted rosés made at Lirac and Tavel to the exuberance of sparkling wines like St-Péray, Clairette de Die and Blanquette de Limoux. And for every expensive bottle you will find a viable and less pricey counterpart – compare a bottle of Vacqueyras with Châteauneuf-du-Pape, or a white Hermitage with the rare and *cher* Château-Grillet.

In Provence and the Midi there are other rare and expensive wines, but for the most part they represent excellent value and offer particular flavours you will not find elsewhere. The vineyards of the unfortunately-named La Clape near Narbonne, for example, yield marvellous wines made with classic varieties at a fraction of the price you will pay for a Bordeaux, and there are red wines made in Provence such as Château de Calissane which again rival those of more famous regions far to the north.

So where should a pilgrim begin? Why not start your journey in Lyon, the heartland of French gastronomy and taste your way southwards through some excellent food and drink? If the delights of the table are a priority and your credit looks good, you might begin with a meal chez Paul Bocuse who has reigned over his restaurant for some 25 years and can be found at Collonges, 9 km north of Lyons. His style is that of 'haute gastronomic' – rich and satisfying with plenty of panache in the service. Then travel on via La Pyramide in Vienne to Hiely Lucullus in Avignon. La Pyramide is no longer among the very finest restaurants of France but is a monument to fine cuisine and still rates very highly in all the guides; Mme Point rules the place at the age of 84. Again, the food is rich and classic with service by waiters who have worked here for as long as 50 years. Even the street is named for Fernand Point, the original (Mme Point is his widow). Hiely Lucullus is in Avignon and menus here are a feast of exquisite tastes, more toward 'nouvelle cuisine' although certainly copious; 'tout le soleil de la Provence' as the Gault-Millau guide poetically describes one menu. But if this is too extravagant an itinerary you should have no difficulty in eating very well at considerably less expense. Don't expect to eat nothing but garlic and tomatoes, however – this part of France may surprise you with the delicacy of its dishes, notably some marvellous seafood, some served raw with salads, some cooked in the traditional stews and soups of the south.

The official delineation of northern Rhône is from Vienne in the north to Valence in the south, the site of many impressive Roman remains including the temples of Augustus and Livia and a marvellous theatre as well as the 'pyramide' which gives its best known restaurant its name. South of the town are the vineyards of Côte Rotie, steep 'baked' slopes which yield a very fine wine made with the Syrah grape.

There are in fact two côtes – the Côte Brune and Côte Blonde, supposedly named for two daughters of a long-deceased nobleman. The grapes are usually blended in the finished wine.

Nearby is Condrieu, home to an unusual white wine made with the Viognier grape. You may taste both these wines at Georges Vernay's establishment if you make an appointment first. Château-Grillet with its tiny vineyard (the smallest *appellation* in France) is next to Condrieu.

GEORGES VERNAY,
1, rue Nationale,
69420 Condrieu.

Tain l'Hermitage is hard to miss as it is built against a distinctive rock – the home of the eponymous hermit. The chief name here is Crozes-Hermitage for good Syrah wines or Hermitage itself for exceptionally long-lived wines both red and white. The reds were formerly used to give added body to fine claret – no longer legal today. Climb the rock on a clear day for a view as far as the Alps.

The remaining names of the northern Rhône are St-Joseph and Cornas, both excellent red wines in good years, and St-Péray where a sparkling wine is made by the Champagne method from local Marsanne and Roussette grapes. Visit J.F. Chaboud to see the wine being stored and bottled (again, by appointment).

J.F. CHABOUD,
21, rue Ferdinand-Malet,
07130 St-Péray.

The Villages of the Côtes

Côtes du Rhône can be a rather confusing *appellation* as it may vary from a very simple blend made from grapes grown in various areas of the region to a fine and distinctive product of one village. Observe the label well and if it reads 'Côtes du Rhône-Villages' then you have a more original example which may cost a little more. Some of the more notable villages to look out for include Chusclan, St Gervais, Laudun, Rasteau, Sablet, Vacqueyras and Visan. All of these are south of Valence, some on the east and some the west bank of the river. An ideal place to try a good honest example of village wine is at the Cave des Vignerons de Chusclan, not far from Orange. You may taste their red and white wines without an appointment – they also make an attractive Côtes du Rhône Primeur to rival the more famous Beaujolais.

Across the river is Gigondas, where some underrated and excellent red wine is made. Visit this and other villages like Sablet from Avignon, the perfect base for a few days' touring. Be sure to go to Beaumes de Venise, one of the 'villages' but more famous for its delectable sweet wine. Other accessible villages are Lirac, where you can taste rosé as well as full reds and whites; Tavel, where some of the region's finest rosés are made; and of course Châteauneuf-du-Pape itself, where the medieval French pope spent his summers and which today is home to one of the more famous wines of France. Try contacting the Château de Beaucastel in Courthezon to taste some fine examples of this wine – but don't expect any bargains. These wines are made to be kept in the bottle for at least ten years and probably much longer than that.

Provençal not Provincial

If you think of the vineyards of Provence as essentially unsophisticated, simple plantings yielding rustic wines, then you would be wrong. It is vital to remember that the wealth and luxury of the Riviera is not far away . . . and some of the 'sons of toil' in the vineyards are actually rather wealthy jetset types themselves. Some of the more obscure *appellations* of France are to be found here, and these can command very high prices – but even a simple Côtes de Provence rosé may not be exactly cheap.

Winemaking in this area is generally practised by experts who invest time and money in their wines in order to make them pass muster with the bronzed critics of St Tropez. But of course the further you go from the coast, the more likely you are to encounter the old-fashioned family business you might expect, where wine may be bought 'en vrac' (in bulk) direct from the producer.

Taking Toulon as your centre for visits, on your first foray you might look at some of the vineyards to the west including the attractive wines of Bandol and Cassis, neither well-known in the UK. NB Be careful not to confuse the wine of Cassis with the well-known blackcurrant liqueur used to make Kir! Both are former fishing villages now more commercialised but retaining some of the charm they once held for the visitors who 'discovered' this coast in the 1920s – the Fitzgeralds, the Murphys and other luminaries of the Jazz Age.

One of the tiny *appellations* is situated near here – Palette, which is mainly produced at one small and perfect estate called Château Simone, and which was the favourite wine of Winston Churchill. Look for the name as you near the exit marked Aix-Est on autoroute A7. The lovely château is surrounded by trees which help to create a 'microclimate'; this makes it cooler than most other areas in the region and conducive to fine wine production. They make red, white and rosé wines.

Turning to the west on another day, venture as far as Nice and you will find an equally interesting 'mini-*appellation*' called Bellet. This rather smart wine is mainly produced at two châteaux – the Château de Bellet and the Château de Crémat. There are red, white and rosé varieties, all produced from a range of grape types of local origin with unpronounceable names and a few more familiar ones like Chardonnay.

While in this area there is one more estate which must be seen if possible. This is Clos Mireille, property of the Ott family and located right by a white sandy beach with twisted pines which must make painters itch for an easel. The white wine produced here tastes faintly of salt with a whiff of ozone and is marvellously invigorating. Sadly, the

Miniaturised perfection at AC Palette Château Simone; an expensive taste

CHÂTEAU SIMONE,
13590 Meyreuil.

beautiful people like it too so prices are not low. The Otts also make excellent red and rosé wines at other nearby estates. Write in advance for an appointment.

Finally it is well worth travelling into the beautiful countryside north of Aix-en-Provence and sampling the fine red wine of Château Vignelaure at Rians, a wine which is only classified as a VDQS. This wine has been poetically described as a 'Bordeaux de Lumière' because of the lovely area of production and the fact that Cabernet Sauvignon features in the wine, unusual in the south.

M Brunet of Château Vignelaure is a notable experimenter with his wines

In the Languedoc

In this extensive region, where millions of litres of table wine are produced each year, Narbonne makes an ideal point of departure and you can see the vineyards of La Clape nearby, high above the sea. Visit the Château de Pech Redon and try the very good red wine made under the guidance of Jean Demolombe, who has an enviable reputation in the region and beyond. Again, write to him first for an appointment.

JEAN DEMOLOMBE,
Château de Pech Redon,
La Clape,
11100 Narbonne.

Travelling out of Narbonne towards Carcassonne you find yourself in the Minervois hills with the steep slopes which make the area seem unsuited to any type of cultivation. Yet at La Livinière the co-operative makes exceptional wine in a very new winery, using the carbonic maceration technique and ageing the red wines in barrels.

For a change of style, sample the delicate dry sparkling wine of Limoux called Blanquette, considered by many drinkers to be as fine a wine as Champagne. Visit the Cave Co-operative to try it for yourself.

CAVE DES COTEAUX DE
    MINERVOIS,
La Livinière,
34210 Dionbac.

FLIGHT OF THE HAWK: L'EPERVIER AND THE WINES OF THE MIDI

About ten years ago Midi wines were seen as very much second-best, poor cousins to the well-known French *appellations*. Attitudes have changed a great deal since then, in no small part due to the efforts of the Wine Club and its Chairman Tony Laithwaite, who is acknowledged as being one of the first to have spotted the potential in the Midi and hence something of an authority on the subject today.

Winemakers in the Languedoc Roussillon were admittedly difficult to deal with. It was essential to find a middleman, someone they knew and trusted, to organise tastings, purchases and shipment on any sort of a regular basis. At that time wines like Minervois, Corbières and Côtes du Roussillon, now familiar on many a list, were rarely exported because it was so difficult to establish which were the best. In France, they were first popularised by the giant firm of Nicolas which was the first to offer named Midi wines in their chain of shops.

One Midi merchant who sold to Nicolas was Jean Demolombe, a forceful personality who is not only an excellent broker but now a notable winemaker as well. He sold Tony Laithwaite on the concept of Languedoc wines as reliable (the climate is of course more predictable in this area than in Bordeaux and Burgundy) and extraordinary value for money. And in the mid-1970s modern technology was alrady being introduced with cool fermentation, carbonic maceration and even wood casks (unknown until then) catching on with certain growers who aimed at quality rather than quantity.

But how to promote these wines to an audience who had never heard of them? The answer in this case was to establish a special brand, a particular label and title which would link the wines and make them easily identifiable. The name chosen was L'Epervier, the hawk which hovers above the dense aromatic scrub of the region, in search of its prey. The intention was to seek out the best wines, keen-eyed like the hawk. And this policy has continued with wines changing from year to year and no fixed allegiance to any one supplier if their wine falls down at a blind tasting. Some of the names are still tongue-twisters, like Embres et Castelmaure, a best-seller, but they are made more familiar by the labels which link them by their unusual shape and design of vines.

Jean Demolombe himself now concentrates on his vineyards at La Clape, a rocky outcrop overlooking the Mediterranean near Narbonne. His property is called the Château de Pech Redon and he creates an excellent red wine using Cabernet Sauvignon in the blend and is now starting to make a Chardonnay, as well as the traditional earthy rosé of the region.

L'Epervier is in the hands of the capable Andrée Ferrandiz, a small dynamic Frenchwoman who lets nothing escape her; her personality is in fact well suited to the name of the company. All the wines now sold under the label are estate-bottled although some may come from small farms, others from co-operatives. Once a year Madame Ferrandiz gathers together all the relevant samples and a tasting is held to select those to be offered.

The producers are definitely in favour of the scheme as their wines now sell not only in the UK through the Wine Club but also to Denmark, Germany, Belgium, Holland and even Australia. The knowledge that their efforts to improve quality are appreciated by the consumer means added effort and an upward trend from year to year.

So the Midi has come a long way from its old image as a melting pot where Algerian red met coarse French plonk. There is still plenty of simple table wine to be had from this region, of course – the endless miles of vines on the flatlands testify to that – but once you venture into the hills there are treasures to be found and enjoyed. Note that Jean Demolombe also lets out holiday gîtes in a peaceful setting high above the Mediterranean amid pines, herbs and vines.

Jean Demolombe dwarfed by the rocky outcrop called La Clape

NOVEMBER

'November's sky is chill and drear,
November's leaf is red and sear.'
Sir Walter Scott, Marmion

Red and sear perhaps, yet still impressive are the leaves of the vine as the year nears its close. After the fruit has been harvested the true beauty of the leaves becomes apparent in a mixture of tints from yellow to deep purple. In a few regions there will still be grapes on the vines, even as the leaves start to fall: if the grower wants botrytis to take its full effect, or to extract extra ripeness from the very last rays of sun they may still be there after the vines have been entirely denuded of leaves. In Germany, for example, some wines are made at Christmas from grapes previously frozen on the vine – this is the Christwein, rare and usually sweet.

But for most grapegrowers the harvest is safely in and their attention has switched to the new wine which must be carefully monitored after the first exuberance of fermentation. Many wines now begin a secondary malolactic fermentation which is usually encouraged by the winemaker to 'soften' the wine. The new wines are then racked off their lees. If the vintage has not been exceptional or if extra tannin and depth are required they may rest on the lees for longer.

Older wines may be bottled now in the cool of autumn. First they will be 'fined', using beaten egg white or a more modern concoction. The purpose of fining is to clarify the wine by encouraging particles to cling to the fining agent and thus be separated from the wine. Any tiny specks remaining will then be filtered through a very fine mesh to ensure the wine is perfectly brilliant (unless the wine is a very fine red where the tiny specks are part of the flavour itself!) Some will then rest for a year or more before release while others will be ready after just a few weeks. One wine which is rushed to market very promptly is Beaujolais Nouveau, produced by the carbonic maceration method for maximum fruit and then swiftly bottled for its November arrival on British shores and everywhere else. Its intense fruity flavour and deep colour are both typical of a new wine.

Other regions now make new wines, too, including the Rhône, the Loire (new Muscadet) and even Italy (Vino Novello). In California they toast Thanksgiving with New Zinfandel. These wines are of course sales gimmicks but they have plenty of charm and attract many inexperienced wine drinkers; the wine trade is delighted by their success.

Out in the vineyards it is not yet time to prune but a certain amount of tidying up may go on, trimming back the longest shoots and bundling them up as fuel. Winter ploughing begins if the weather is not too wet and soil is heaped around the roots of the vines as protection against frost. Some vineyards may be manured or have other fertilisers added to the soil at this stage.

FESTIVALS

With one honourable exception, the wine regions are not to be found 'en fête' at this time of year. That exception is Burgundy, of which more later (see pages 158–60), but suffice it to say that on the third weekend of November Beaune is a centre for truly Bacchanalian revelry as well as some serious business at the wine auctions. These three days (Saturday, Sunday and Monday) are known as Les Trois Glorieuses. On the first you can see an exhibition of the wines of Burgundy; on the second there is the auction at the Hospices de Beaune and the town festival with feasting, drinking and dancing; and on the third, the privileged few who are connected with the wine trade partake of La Paulée, a fabulous banquet at Meursault.

On 14 November there is a wine fair in the Beaujolais village of Juliénas in the south of the region, while on the fourth Sunday of the month there is a festival of wine and folklore at Chablis. The main presentation of the new Beaujolais takes place at Villefranche in the first week of December.

Banquet at the Clos de Vougeot during Les Trois Glorieuses

Students of wine might want to take advantage of a course on the wines of the area which coincides with Les Trois Glorieuses and covers wines of the entire Burgundy region and Chablis and Beaujolais, with tastings, lectures and visits to vineyards. Write to the Comité Inter-professionel de la Côte d'Or in Beaune.

Mid-November also sees the introduction of new wines in the Rhône – at Vaison-la-Romaine, a former spa town for the Romans where there are still many interesting remains of their luxurious villas to be seen. It is interesting to compare the Côtes du Rhône primeurs with Beaujolais of the same year.

Far to the west on the Atlantic seaboard, the town of Nantes has its Vintage Festival on the last Sunday of November. This is the centre for the production of Muscadet and its cousin Gros Plant, which for obvious reasons has less charm for the British ear but can taste just as good. While you are there, try some of the wonderful oysters which team perfectly with a bottle of the local dry white wine.

Remains of a sybaritic Roman lifestyle at Vaison-la-Romaine, Provence

ENTERTAINING

THE SEASON FOR PARTIES

Having celebrated Hallowe'en at the tail end of October, there are only a few days until Guy Fawkes Night. Then later in the month comes Thanksgiving for the Americans and all too soon December has arrived and with it the pressure of Christmas parties both obligatory and pleasurable. Dieting becomes a near-impossibility and there are a good variety of events which appear to demand ideas for very different styles of food and drink.

As the weather is cold and some of this merrymaking takes place outdoors, even the firmest of wine fanciers may consider a moderate addition of spirits to the repertoire, simply to warm fellow guests. Variants on the much-resurrected cocktail may be concocted either as the basis for a genuine 'cocktail party' or as an icebreaker to be served when guests arrive. It is amazing to see how even the stiffest upper lip can loosen after the administration of an apparently harmless hot punch or even mulled wine.

Of course you need not use spirits – there are many wine mixtures which are very attractive, including those based on port and other fortified wines. Indeed it is possible to make terrific cocktails without any alcohol at all. But most true winter mixtures tend to include a good measure of spirit together with a 'modifier' which may be fruit juice, a syrup such as grenadine, or even egg as in those rich and creamy egg nogs which taste good on Boxing Day.

For serving these drinks you may need a little more than the usual corkscrew and assorted wine glasses, but it is not vital to own a cocktail shaker, swizzle sticks or collections of paper palm trees and plastic elephants. A good-sized glass bowl looks right for punch, with an attractive ladle and simple short-stemmed wine glasses to serve the drink in. Otherwise try to use appropriately sized glasses ie, a martini glass (V-shaped with a stem) for short drinks and a tall tumbler for longer mixtures; a squared tumbler for many classics such as the Manhattan, and a wine glass or brandy goblet for any blend containing cream.

For a basic bar you will need: a bottle each of Scotch, gin, vodka and brandy (three star); a bottle each of the three styles of vermouth (sweet, bianco and dry); a bottle of Angostura bitters; a bottle of grenadine syrup; assorted fruit juices; half-bottles of one or two liqueurs such as Grand Marnier, Crème de Menthe or Maraschino; and bottles of all the mixers including tonic and soda water and ginger ale. Finally, make sure you have plenty of fresh lemons to hand and also a few eggs, although you may only need the whites to add that dense frothy look to many modern favourites such as the Daiquiri. Be sure to make enough ice for a full-blown cocktail party and you may need it on Guy Fawkes Night as well: a chilled mixed drink can taste remarkably good even standing outdoors watching fireworks, though followed perhaps by some warming coffee.

Party Particulars

THE FIFTH OF NOVEMBER   You can cater for both children and adults here by serving quite simple food and some cocktails with or without alcohol. For the kids and non-drinkers mix a St Clements which combines orange juice with lemonade (one-third juice), or for a more warming drink make real lemonade, add a dash of grenadine for colour and decorate with slices of orange or lemon. You might prepare this in advance and serve it from a vacuum flask.

For the adults, bake a few apples the day before and use them to make an apple toddy (which would of course be perfect for Hallowe'en as well): to each quarter apple (cored and not peeled and placed at the bottom of a large glass) add one measure of calvados or basic three-star brandy, then top with boiling water. Stir in a teaspoonful of icing sugar and sprinkle with nutmeg. To make for an outdoor group, just keep the hot water in a flask and mix as required – but make sure you have plenty of flares or torches to supplement the light of the bonfire!

Alternatively, serve a mulled wine made by heating each bottle of good red wine (try a Bergerac, an Italian Merlot or a Rioja) with a cinnamon stick, three cloves, a few pieces of dried orange peel (dry out in your oven when it has just been used and then turned off) and if possible some strawberry syrup (from cans of strawberries – it really does add good flavour). Add a little dark brown sugar to taste as bitter mulled wine is not good – and nor is cool mulled wine, so keep it really hot. If you are the brave outdoor type and have obedient children then you might want to try the Red Hot Poker Method. Pour the wine in multiples of bottles into a fireproof vessel (an old preserving pan would be suitable and then heat your poker in the bonfire until it glows red hot. Plunge into the wine mixture and it will sizzle in a very impressive fashion – it works for Toddy too.

The menu might include the usual baked potatoes and sausages around the bonfire but instead of ordinary bangers try something a little more spicy such as chorizos (available from delicatessens and good grocers). Or make a pot roast indoors for everyone to retreat to: take a 5 lb piece of beef such as rolled sirloin or a similar cut, rub the meat with plenty of oil, some crushed garlic and black pepper then put into a heavy casserole with a tight-fitting lid. Cook in a hot oven (450°F/230°C/Gas Mark 8) for about 15 minutes until the outside is sealed, then remove from the oven and leave in the casserole with lid on for at least another half hour and you will have a succculent pot roast for up to 20 people. Serve with salad, baked potatoes and more mulled or straightforward red wine. A giant apple or treacle tart would be just right to follow or, if you have a crowd, set out some large pieces of cheese and an autumn fruit salad (apples, pears, plums, greengages).

THANKSGIVING SUPPER (or an early Christmas family reunion)   This is a fairly informal yet generous event. Working on the assumption that your guests or family will be able to spend the night with you, this might be an opportunity to pull out the stops and serve some marvellous wines, preceded by a powerful ice-breaker. Those who frown on spirits before wine (a moot point) might offer a Kir Royale (real Champagne with a dash of Crème de Cassis) as an apéritif.

MENU

Apéritif: Almond Cocktail or Kir Royale, served with cheese gougères

*

Terrine or pâté with melba toast

*

Roast goose or guinea fowl, with assorted vegetables

*

Cheese

*

Italian Panettone (celebration cake) and new season walnuts

*

Wines: Drink a good red Burgundy with the terrine and the game, then to accompany the panettone you might choose either a Sauternes or a Late Harvest Riesling – a German Auslese, an Alsace Late Harvest wine or a California or Australian example of the same grape. If you prefer a fortified wine, Marsala would be in keeping with the Italian theme.

For the almond cocktail (to serve 6) you will need: 2 glasses (6 fl. oz. each) gin, 2 glasses inexpensive sweet white wine, 1 glass dry vermouth, 1 dessertspoonful Kirsch, 1 dessertspoonful peach brandy (or apricot), 1 teaspoonful icing sugar, 6 peeled almonds and the crushed kernel of one fresh peach (add a couple of extra almonds if not available).

Warm the gin slightly, then marinate the almonds, peach kernel and sugar and allow to cool (about half an hour or so). Then transfer to the fridge and once the liquid is quite cold add the remaining ingredients and shake or stir well, adding crushed ice to taste. Serve in martini glasses decorated with maraschino cherries.

To make the panettone you will need: 1lb strong white flour, 6oz unsalted butter, 1 tbsp dried yeast, caster sugar, ¼ pint milk, 2 eggs, 4oz each of candied peel (chopped), raisins and sultanas, and the grated rind of a lemon. (These quantities make two.)

Stir a teaspoonful of the sugar into the warmed milk, then sprinkle over the dried yeast and 4oz of the flour. Leave in a warm place for about 20 minutes until frothy. Rub the butter into the rest of the flour and add the peel, raisins, sultanas and lemon rind. Stir in 3oz sugar, the yeast liquid and 2 beaten eggs and mix to form a pliable dough (a food processor will do this rapidly). Cover with a damp cloth and leave in a warm place until doubled in size, then turn out onto a floured surface and cut in half. Knead each piece into a ball then put into two 6-inch cake tins (well greased beforehand). Cover with plastic bags and leave in a warm place until the dough is visible above the edge of the tin. Bake at 400°F/200°C/Gas Mark 6 for 25–30 minutes. Cool in the tin for 10 minutes then turn onto a wire rack. Dust with icing sugar before serving.

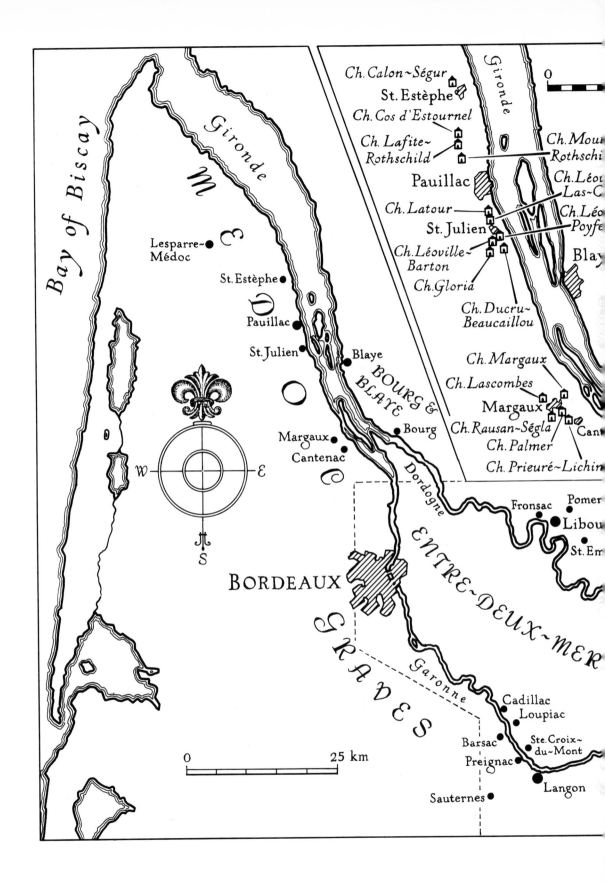

Bay of Biscay

Gironde

Gironde

Ch. Calon~Ségur

St. Estèphe

Ch. Cos d'Estournel

Ch. Lafite~ Rothschild

Ch. Mou Rothschi

Pauillac

Ch. Léo Las~C

Ch. Latour

St. Julien

Ch. Léo Poyfe

Ch. Léoville~ Barton

Bla

Ch. Gloria

Ch. Ducru~ Beaucaillou

Ch. Margaux

Ch. Lascombes

Margaux

Ch. Rausan~Ségla

Can

Ch. Palmer

Ch. Prieuré~Lichin

Lesparre~ Médoc

St. Estèphe

Pauillac

St. Julien

Blaye

BOURG & BLAYE

Bourg

Margaux

Cantenac

Dordogne

Fronsac

Pomer

Libou

St. Em

ENTRE~DEUX~MER

BORDEAUX

GRADES

Garonne

Cadillac

Loupiac

Barsac

Ste. Croix~ du~Mont

Preignac

Sauternes

Langon

W   E

S

0   25 km

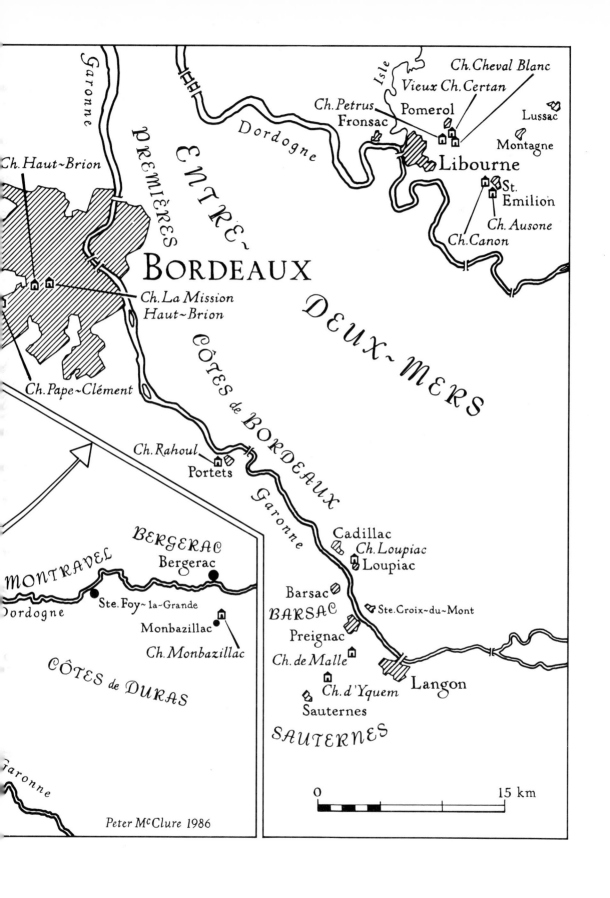

Garonne

PREMIÈRES

ENTRE-

Dordogne

Isle

Ch. Cheval Blanc
Vieux Ch. Certan
Ch. Petrus
Fronsac
Pomerol
Lussac
Montagne
Libourne
St. Emilion
Ch. Ausone
Ch. Canon

Ch. Haut~Brion

BORDEAUX

DEUX~MERS

Ch. La Mission
Haut~Brion

CÔTES de BORDEAUX

Ch. Pape~Clément

Ch. Rahoul
Portets

Garonne

Cadillac
Ch. Loupiac
Loupiac

Barsac
BARSAC
Ste. Croix~du~Mont

MONTRAVEL
BERGERAC
Bergerac

Dordogne
Ste. Foy~ la~Grande
Monbazillac
Ch. Monbazillac

Preignac
Ch. de Malle
Langon
Ch. d'Yquem
Sauternes

CÔTES de DURAS

SAUTERNES

Garonne

0   15 km

Peter McClure 1986

The Hospices de Beaune –
much-visited throughout the
year

BURGUNDIAN REVELS

In many ways Burgundy seems a far more old-fashioned region than
Bordeaux. Despite the value of many of the wines and the glamour of
the famous names most vineyards are tiny parcels of land and the
growers seem fairly simple souls. But all of this is deceptive. When
dealing with the all-important *négociants* who sell their wines these
same growers show a fierce professionalism and awareness of the value of
their creation. Similarly, if Burgundy seems at first not to be particularly
interested in its visitors, then just try going there in November when the
locals let down their hair for Les Trois Glorieuses.

The heart of this festival is a serious matter – the auction of fine
wines at the Hospices de Beaune, a dramatic medieval building dating
from 1443 which serves the sick and needy. It also owns some hundred
acres of vines which are divided between the main names of the Côte de
Beaune area. These and other wines come up for auction and the
proceeds are of course for charity. The auction is attended by members
of the wine trade and is an important indicator of how prices for the
current vintage will shape up.

For the ordinary visitor there is an exhibition of Burgundian wines to
see and various other festivities to watch or participate in – but book
your hotel early if you intend to be there. Write to the Office du
Tourisme in Beaune for information. Apart from the Hôtel-Dieu itself
where the main ward also serves as a church, there is a comprehensive
museum of the local wines at the Hôtel des Ducs de Bourgogne with
daily guided tours; these are excellent for seeing all the gadgetry
associated with winemaking.

While in this region you will find boundless opportunities for eating
well and it need not be too costly. Local dishes to try include the
delicate gougères, choux pastry puffs flavoured with cheese; jambon
persillé, a charcuterie item like a terrine made with pieces of ham and
lots of parsley and garlic; oeufs en meurette, poached eggs served in a
very rich red wine and onion sauce; pochouse, a stew of river fish such
as pike, perch, tench and eel cooked in white wine; not to mention the
famous coq au vin and boeuf à la bourguignonne both cooked in the
rich red local wine. Snails also taste good in this sauce. For the more
courageous eater there is a huge selection of sausages including the
andouillette, rather tough but said to be much more appetising than it
looks and the cervelas, which may be made with truffles. And the local
cheeses also deserve attention, particularly the Epoisses and the
Chambertin, both full-flavoured on the edge of pungent. Finally, by
way of dessert, blackcurrants are another local speciality and you will
often start a meal with Kir or finish it with a sorbet made with the fruit.

Where to eat? In Beaune itself try the Rôtisserie de la Paix (booking advisable) or, if the town is too crowded for you, move north into the Côte de Nuits and visit either the Restaurant Côte d'Or in Nuits St Georges or the smart Rôtisserie de Chambertin in Gevrey-Chambertin.

When choosing cellars to visit be aware that some do not offer very good value for the casual purchaser – think about the price in real terms before you buy. Thus the Château du Clos de Vougeot merits a visit for its visual beauty and English-speaking tours in summer but perhaps not for its wine-buying opportunities. In Beaune there are several important *négociants* who open their cellars to the wine buying public, including Bouchard Aîné et Fils, Patriarche Père et Fils, Calvet and the Reine Pédauque. Lovers of fine white Burgundy might visit the Château de Meursault where they have English tours. Note that most of the well-known names charge for tasting.

Enjoy seeking out the less famous names yourself: if you have time, venture further south beyond Santenay into the Côte Chalonnaise, the Mâconnais and the Beaujolais. Here you will find a more relaxed atmosphere and prettier countryside, especially in the hills of Beaujolais.

Drama and tension at the Hospices de Beaune wine auction as future pricing is determined

RÔTISSERIE DE LA PAIX, 47 Faubourg Madeleine, Beaune.

Restaurant Côte d'Or, 1, rue Thurot, Nuits St Georges.

BOUCHARD AÎNÉ ET FILS,
36, rue St Marguerite.

PATRIARCHE PÈRE ET FILS,
7, rue du Collège.

CALVET,
6, boulevard Perpreuil.

REINE PÉDAUQUE,
Porte St Nicolas.

Try co-operatives for the best tastings and sales opportunities. If you are fond of Pouilly-Fuissé, for instance, visit the Caveau Union des Producteurs at Solutre for the 'real thing' – but make an appointment first. In the Beaujolais follow the Route du Beaujolais – each of the villages has tasting cellars. How about the romantically-named Caveau de St Amour in the village of that name, one of the nine villages allowed to appear individually on Beaujolais labels? And, of course, the Beaujolais Nouveau will most certainly have arrived down here . . . at its very freshest and best.

View of the Clos de Vougeot in Autumn

MODERN CLASSICS: THE BURGUNDIES OF MACHARD DE GRAMONT

Burgundy has an unapproachable image for many drinkers. They may recall how their parents, uncles and aunts used to consume any amount of 'grocer's Pommard' in the good old days before EEC regulations, but somehow that opportunity seems to elude them now that prices are sky-high. If you are going to invest twice as much as usual in a bottle of wine, it is only reasonable to demand information about that bottle. So a little knowledge about Machard de Gramont will go a long way.

They are a family firm of irreproachable honesty and integrity who own vineyards in some of the plum sites on the Côte d'Or. These features are noticeably lacking in many other enterprises who have fallen prey to the temptation to overprice and skimp on quality, protected by their famous names, selling the label rather than the wine. This is the kind of situation that has given rise to such as the division between the two areas of the cellar holding wine for European and American sales, with quite different products in each. Or are they myths . . . ? In any event, the brothers Machard de Gramont certainly allow no such practices.

In the late 1970s the company expanded enormously, acquiring some quite large parcels of land (remember that one or two acres is a vast expanse in this most expensive of areas). However, the money for the expansion was coming from the rich wife of the eldest brother and when the two divorced a fair acreage went with her, as well as their rather superior cellars.

Nothing daunted, Arnaud and Bertrand Machard de Gramont moved to new premises and have managed to continue making some exceptional wines with the notable vineyards still in their care. Their holdings are scattered all over the region: at Chambolle-Musigny, Nuits St-Georges, Aloxe-Corton, Savigny-Les-Beaune, Beaune itself, Pommard and Puligny. With vineyards of this quality (each averaging less than half an acre) it is naturally vital to preserve the individual characteristics of each wine with extreme care.

This is achieved by having a row of large wooden vats for fermentation, each of which is reserved for a certain wine. After the harvest the weather can be quite cool, so it is often necessary to heat the cellars to keep the fermentation going and to encourage the wine to undergo the secondary fermentation – the malolactic – for added smoothness which is a feature of any fine Burgundy.

The Machard de Gramont cellars are hardly the Clos de Vougeot; instead of the romantic wooden beams and ancient stone, slide-shows and souvenirs, there is a simple concrete structure of minimal charm dedicated to serious winemaking. Just taste any of their 1983 wines if you want to test for yourself the success of their venture.

At the cellars of Machard de Gramont wine is constantly monitored for quality

DOMAINES MACHARD DE
   GRAMONT,
rue Gassendi,
21700 Nuits St-Georges.

DECEMBER

December – season of frosts, of new activity in the vineyards as pruning begins, and of tasting in the cellars of both the new and the older wines. At home, it is a month for thinking about stocking up the cellar for the Christmas season and beyond. And then of course there are parties, gatherings of all kinds from the office inevitable to the home original (see *November* for ideas on home entertaining).

Apart from a few very late pickings of grapes for *Eiswein* or late harvest styles, the vines will now be bare and looking very bleak and straggly; in most areas pruning begins in the second half of the month. The groups of pruners clad in overalls working away with secateurs powered by compressed air make a curious sight – the compressor roaring away next to them as if they were about to repair a road. Although dull, the weather in the grapegrowing areas of Europe is rarely at its bitterest in December and so pruning is relatively agreeable.

Every region has its own distinctive style of pruning, usually related to the grape variety grown as certain grapes respond to being cut hard back to one fruiting shoot only, while others do better with two or more. Very abbreviated pruning is known as spur pruning – this is used in the Beaujolais region to form the 'gobelet' shape of the vine and in other areas where the vines are not grown against wires or poles. Spur pruning is also used for vines grown against walls at home.

Cane pruning allows the vine to grow fairly high against a support of wires or poles with one or two long spurs for next year's fruit. In France the single shoot is the single Guyot and the double, the double Guyot. The canes may be trained horizontally along a wire or bent down to make loops as you will see if you visit the Mosel, where long runs of wire are often impracticable on the steep terrain.

Speaking of practicalities brings us to the question of planting the vines. The traditional gap between vines used to be about four feet, with five feet between the rows, but these distances are being increased to cope with machine ploughing, spraying and even harvesting. For machine harvesting the vines must also be allowed to grow taller. In some areas you will see ingenious tractors rather like mechanical insects which are able to plough or treat traditional plantings by straddling two rows at once. Vineyards are usually ploughed in December to break up the ground before the frosts come in earnest; some growers also apply fertilisers at this time but if the winter brings severe rain and snow these may be leached away before spring.

Regions which specialise in very light, fruity wines will prepare some bottlings by Christmas to keep the intensity of flavour – Beaujolais is the obvious example, but the Mosel, Alsace and the Loire also make some wines which repay very early drinking. But remember that all wine should rest for a short while after bottling and before despatch so these wines don't actually appear on our wine lists until the New Year.

STARTING A CELLAR

You do need a certain passion for wine to begin a real cellar, and a fair amount of money as well. But there's nothing to prevent you from beginning to build a modest collection of bottles and building up from there. Similarly, the cellar itself need not be a subterranean vault all cobweb-hung; a cool spare room, closet or odd corner will do, though the romance of it all will be lacking. One Californian collector spent literally all he earned on fine German wines, which were kept in the spare room of his modest flat – suitably air-conditioned and insulated for the purpose.

Thus does a wine cellar get hold of its owner. If you are among those likely to feel this passion, then buy a cellar book and do like George Saintsbury by recording in faithful detail each wine you sample, each occasion it was savoured. Then the cellar becomes a marvellous asset over the years and a source of fascinating comparisons and memories. The rest of us, more practical souls, might follow the 'grid system' I describe (page 164) and keep simple notes to accompany it.

How to Store Your Wine
There are a few simple criteria for keeping wine healthy. Seek out a dark or dimly-lit spot, cool and free of vibration. Passing trains or the shuddering of a boiler igniting are not plus factors and some famous institutions even put their wine cellars *upstairs* to keep the wine away from the traffic vibrations! Your wine store need not be very cold as wine survives well between 50 and 70°F but the temperature should be consistent year-round and there should be no threat of frost. So avoid the garage, attic and garden shed unless you have made them frostproof.

'I have been in love, and in debt, and in drink,
This many and many a year.'
   ALEXANDER BROME, *The Mad Lover* I,i

An ideal cellar is slightly damp: this humidity keeps the corks from drying out and enables the wine to 'breathe' freely and age gradually. The humidity is not essential but very dry conditions are not good as the corks might dry and even disintigrate into the bottles over time. Even the finest cellars cannot keep wine forever without some attention and rare long-lived vintages are commonly recorked and even topped up during their lives in bottle.

Bright light can harm the chemical composition of the wine, hence the green glass for most wines apart from those like Sauternes which cannot resist showing off their golden hue and those like Mateus Rosé which are not meant to be kept anyway.

Keeping a Record

The easiest way to store your wine is in a metal and wood rack – the traditional grid. If you buy really large quantities then you may prefer to lay them down in a 'bin', a container like a box with one side missing. The bottles are stacked horizontally on wooden slats; in fact, all bottles should be kept on their sides so that the wine is in contact with the cork. If you buy château-bottled French wines, these may be sold in wooden cases which are fine for storage.

Using the grid of your rack, draw up an identical grid on graph paper or a piece you square off yourself. Enter each wine in pencil as it arrives and delete as it goes. For extra help use coloured pencils to 'code' the wine – a green for white wines and a pink for rosé perhaps? For a more permanent record you will also need a ledger-type book to mark quantities of each wine, when purchased and, most important, how it tasted. Buy a case of wine to sample over a year or more and see if it improves.

Logically, the wines you plan to drink soon should be stored near the entrance to your treasure trove, long-term investments further away. Keep spirits, vermouth and fortified wines in the same place so that you can see at a glance how your 'stock' stands. Enter them on your grid as well. If you prefer not to erase the grid entries you could keep the dated sheets in a folder for reference.

The choice of Wines

Personal taste plays a substantial role in your choice of wines but there are certain basics it is sensible to begin with. Try to taste before you buy by testing a variety of samples, then opt for a case or two of those you prefer. Despite your own preferences keep a balance between red and white, still and sparkling to cover all eventualities.

Apart from these obvious differences of style, wines also come in different weights. Your favourites may tend to the substantial (such as Burgundy and Rhône wines) or to the delicate (Mosels and Muscadets)

but a cellar needs balance just as wines do. The odd bottle of Champagne
or sherry may seem a little unnecessary but think of your pleasure when
you can celebrate a sudden announcement of happy news with a friend,
or delight an elderly caller with your offer of 'medium' sherry. So start
with an assortment of such oddments – a couple of bottles of Champagne,
or more if your budget will run to it; half a case of less distinguished
sparkling wine to be mixed with Crème de Cassis for Kir Royale or with
orange juice for Bucks Fizz; two bottles each of fino and amontillado
sherry; two bottles of Late Bottled Vintage port; a bottle of Madeira
(not the sweetest style) which will do for sauces as well as morning
tippling with the vicar; and a basic selection of spirits and mixers as
outlined in the *November* section.

As for table wines, go for a balance as follows:

1 case very light dry white wine (cases may of course be mixed) such as
    Vinho Verde, Muscadet, Mosel or Chablis.
1 case fruity white wine such as Vouvray, Hock (any QbA from the
    Rhine qualifies), or Riesling from another area of the world such as
    Alsace or Australia.
1 case fruity red wine such as Beaujolais, Valpolicella, Bardolino, Loire
    Gamay or a Gamay from another wine region.
1 case full red wine to include claret or another Cabernet Sauvignon; or
    Burgundy; and other full-bodied wines such as Chianti, Rioja, Dão,
    Rhône reds, Bergerac, Midi reds, and those from California and
    Australia.
1 case a mixture of sweeter wines and rosés, balanced as you prefer.

Adjust the cases in stock according to the logic of the season. In
summer you will tend to go heavy on the light white wines, the
sparkling wines and perhaps fruitier reds, while in deepest winter you
will want the fullest reds to warm you. The wines you may choose to 'lay
down' will normally fall into this last category or into the rather
specialised category of rich yet dry white wines such as white Burgundy
and California Chardonnay. The full reds need not be expensive: wines
high in alcohol which also have a good fruit taste when young are an
excellent choice and these may just as soon come from Bulgaria as
Burgundy. Buy enough to enable you to taste and compare as the
months or years pass and keep notes in your cellar book. But as soon as
the tinges of brown become noticeable and the alcohol seems to
predominate over the fruit flavours, you should drink the rest before it
fades into a not-too-graceful old age.

Inspired by these notes, you may feel the only answer for you is to install
a purpose-built cellar at home. Look at the new 'spiral' designs which
cleverly use the space around a spiral stairway for storage, and also at

the rather pricey but undoubtedly effective cooled cabinets you can buy like those you see in elegant restaurants which lack real cellars.

If these options seem too expensive, it may seem preferable to dig your own storage space: if there is plenty of room in your back garden and you have a tolerant family, you might set to and literally burrow into the earth to make a wine pit. Line this with waterproofing and then with brick to give an excellent private cellar – but beware of frost.

ENTERTAINING

'Dis-moi ce que tu manges, je te dirai ce que tu es.'
('Tell me what you eat, I will tell you what you are.')
ANTHELME BRILLAT-SAVARIN,
Physiologie du Gout

The wily French gastronome, Brillat-Savarin, certainly knew a great deal about human nature but his reference to food could just as well be applied to drink, and particularly wine. We choose wines for a variety of complex reasons, not always related to logic. We may want to impress a guest, to sample a famous name mentioned in conversation, or to dazzle with our originality. Similarly, the way we serve wine and food at home tells much about us and our aspirations.

Of course there are fashions in wine as in every other aspect of modern life. One year Sancerre Rouge may be the most popular; the next, Muscat de Beaumes de Venise seems indispensable at every dinner party. But in recent years it has become much more acceptable to offer 'house' wines on your table: a bottle of supermarket Champagne or a Club claret are no longer viewed with suspicion but talked about during the meal and considered 'good buys'. Wine journalists concentrate on pointing their readers towards the 'wine of the week', be it first growth or (more usually) a wine you have never tried before.

Over the Christmas period you are likely to entertain more than usual and perhaps to make more effort than you might do over the course of the rest of the year. You may want to choose special wines to accompany the food you offer and so the following notes on serving wines are intended as a guide, of particular value during the festive season perhaps but useful throughout the year.

The Choice of Glasses

Wine snobs can be very expansive on the subject of glasses and you could be made to feel very inadequate indeed if you believed all you heard about size and shape. In reality, however, a wine glass need only have a stem (to keep the wine away from the warmth of your hand) and be made of clear glass (to ensure you see the wine accurately). All the further niceties are just that. Of course an attractive wine glass looks

The classic taster's glass may be used for any wine, including Champagne

very well on an elegant table, and there is an undeniable pleasure in handling a glass made with very thin crystal or a massive antique glass. There are also glasses associated with certain traditions which serve their regional wines well.

For your basic selection of wines you will therefore need a fair quantity of plain stemmed glasses which may either be the simple Paris goblets as used in pubs nationwide, or something a little smarter – if you choose a tulip shape the incurving bowl will help to concentrate the aroma and bouquet and allow room to swirl and savour your share.

Size is important. An enormous balloon is not only wasteful of wine (and means inebriated guests) but the bouquet will be lost too fast. Red wine should be served in a slightly larger glass as it is important for a white wine to be consumed while cool.

For Champagne and sparkling wines the tall slim flute is perfect to display its beauty and keep the bubbles flowing as you sip. You might consider indulging yourself by buying special flutes which have a tiny etching in the base of the bowl; this 'irritates' the bubbles and creates a stream within the glass. If you have no flutes use a small tulip glass. This would be quite acceptable in France.

The copita is the traditional glass for sherry – an exaggerated tulip which is certainly more attractive than the schooners used in pubs. Again a small tulip-shaped glass is fine, and for port as well. For spirits such as brandy avoid the balloons and use the same short-stemmed version of the basic wine glass.

Some Like It Hot – A Temperature Guide
In the USA they like their whites almost icy and their reds almost bubbling with heat; in France you may be served white wines which seem warm and reds alarmingly cool. The respective hosts would no doubt defend their style of service with vigour but the way the wine tastes is radically different. Keep to the middle ground and you should get the best from your wine. Remember that few wines benefit from being served cooler than 5°C (approximately the temperature of your fridge) or warmer than 20°C (a centrally-heated room).

The exceptions to this rule are sparkling wines and very sweet wines such as Sauternes which can tolerate very low temperatures. Transfer the bottle from the fridge into a bucket filled with a mixture of ice and water or, if your wine is not of the best quality, risk a brief stay in the freezer.

The 10°C mark is the perfect cellar temperature and is perfect for light red wines such as Beaujolais and Chianti. All white wines should be served just above fridge temperature – take the bottle out of the fridge about a quarter of an hour before serving to lessen the chill. Full red wines may go up to 20°C but warmer than this they will give off fumes of alcohol which obscure the flavour and taste 'flabby', as wine tasters say.

PUNCH OLD AND NEW   On Christmas Day or thereabouts thoughts turn to Dickensian milk punch, to toddies and other warming blends. Sadly these can be less than delightful unless made with care and without too many strong ingredients. Try one of the following as a winter warmer – sweet enough to give a tiny sedative sip to the children as well . . .

For a *Milk Punch* take one glass of hot milk per person, a tablespoonful of icing sugar and a measure of your chosen spirit – rum, whisky or brandy. Stir together and serve topped with grated nutmeg in a glass, or bowl.

To make a *Breakfast Egg Nog* take one egg per person, ¼ pint of milk, a measure of brandy and a dash of Curaçao or Grand Marnier. Mix in a blender or whisk by hand. Warm gently if liked and serve with grated nutmeg again.

A really Hogarthian touch could be added to your festivities with a glass of *hot gin* – mix the juice of a lemon, 2 pieces of preserving sugar and a measure of gin and fill up a tall glass with hot water. Serve with a long spoon.

For *Patrick's Punch* you need the freshly-squeezed juice of an orange per person. Warm this gently with a measure of brandy plus a teaspoonful of icing sugar and a half-measure of Benedictine (or use the ready-blended B & B). Serve warm or make a cold version instead by adding sparkling mineral water to taste and decorating with orange and lemon slices.

Finally, a *Temperance Punch* from the good ol' days of American Prohibition, served cool and refreshing. This one is *entirely* suitable for the children and tastes pretty good even without alcohol, but be sure to buy the best red grape juice you can find. For each litre of grape juice add ¼ lb icing sugar, ¼ pint lemon juice and a litre of sparkling mineral water. Pour this over a large block of ice in a punch bowl (make this in your freezer in advance) and add plenty of sliced citrus fruit and apples to taste.

CHRISTMAS COCKTAILS   There is bound to be at least one occasion when you will entertain informally over the Christmas period: you may be in the habit of holding an Open House for friends and neighbours on Boxing Day or inviting a few friends to spend an evening with you before Christmas. Instead of the basic sherry, whisky and wine combination consider a version of the traditional cocktail party, but supplemented with plenty to nibble at and a good range of drinks including the strong and the not so emphatic.

Cocktails might include the Eton Blazer, the Blue Blazer, the Sidecar, Champagne Julep, Mimosa and Virgin Mary.

For the *Eton Blazer* you need the juice of half a lemon, ½ tablespoon icing sugar, one measure of gin and a dash of Kirsch. Shake the ingredients with crushed ice or ice cubes *or* simply pour over crushed ice after stirring in a tall glass or jug. NB Plymouth Gin is traditional for this drink – the variety normally used to make nautical Pink Gin (gin with Angostura bitters).

For the *Blue Blazer* a chief requisite is a fairly sober bartender as this is quite a spectacular concoction – it is a *flambé* version of the whisky toddy. You also need two silver or pewter mugs (glasses will not do for reasons which will become obvious). Take one small wine glass of warm Scotch and one of boiling water and put the Scotch into one mug, the water into the other. Ignite the spirit and create the mix by pouring them four or five times from one mug to the other, blazing all the while so that the whole operation looks like the pouring of liquid fire. Add a teaspoonful of icing sugar and a twist of lemon peel as you serve.

The *Sidecar* is a classic based on brandy: this need not be a Cognac but it tastes better with the real thing. An alternative can give the drink a strong flavour of caramel as producers use this to smooth a young brandy. Take one measure of brandy, a half measure of Cointreau and a half measure of lemon juice and stir together with ice cubes. Strain into a cocktail glass and serve.

Champagne Julep is a little unseasonal as it needs fresh mint but these days this can be purchased in supermarkets most of the year round; alternatively keep a root growing in a pot in the kitchen over the autumn and winter. Take one cube of white sugar and two sprigs of mint and put these in a Champagne glass – fill with Champagne or dry sparkling wine. Decorate with a slice of kiwi fruit.

A *Mimosa* is simply another name for Bucks Fizz – half and half orange juice and sparkling wine. Use freshly-squeezed juice if possible and serve well-chilled.

A *Virgin Mary* is the non-alcoholic version of a Bloody Mary, a flavourful drink for those who have had enough alcohol or don't want any at all. Take a good measure of tomato juice and add a sprinkle of celery salt, a couple of celery seeds, a dash of Tabasco and a generous helping of Worcester Sauce, plus black pepper to taste. Serve adorned with a celery stick and a slice of lemon.

Food to accompany this array of cocktails might include small quiches made with mushrooms or smoked salmon (see *June* for recipe); warm cocktail sausages served with tomato dip spiced like the Virgin Mary (use tomato purée for this); anchovy straws made by wrapping canned anchovies with anchovy purée in strips of bought puff pastry brushed with egg; cherry tomatoes stuffed with tuna mayonnaise or cream cheese with walnuts; and other spreadable cheeses such as roulé with herbs, dolcelatte and garlic cheese served with melba toast and various crackers. Later in the evening you might offer a savoury such as Devils on Horseback (see *October* for recipe).

Sweeter snacks could be grapes dipped in egg white and coated with orange halves filled with caster sugar; orange jellies made with fresh orange juice; home-made cookies or petits fours; and the inevitable but delicious mince pies. Try making your own mincemeat using green tomatoes (which substitute well for the apple mentioned in most recipes), or add a little brandy to any jar you buy.

Decanters and Corkscrews

Of course you need a corkscrew but ignore anything which pumps air or uses electricity and go for the very simplest of technology – a 'waiter's friend', which looks like a penknife, or the infallible Screwpull. Another good investment is the two-pronged corkscrew which will extract corks starting to crumble. Fancier models are fascinating for collectors of corkscrews but they are not strictly *necessary*.

If you are offering white or rosé wine, remove the corkscrew just as it is served. For sparkling wine the same is true but more effort is required. Have a dazzling white cloth draped over your arm and glasses ready. Remove the foil and untwist the wire; hold the cork down with your thumb and push gently upwards with your other hand. Then hold the cork and twist it, keeping the bottle steady. It should 'hiss' out rather than exploding, in best motor-racing style!

For red wines you may want to use a carafe or decanter. The former disguises a large bottle of relatively humble wine rather well and allows air to mingle with the wine and let it 'breathe'. If the wine is young and quite heavy you might allow this breathing to continue for about four hours before serving. If it is rarer and finer then your carafe becomes a decanter and you may have to cope with some sediment. Let the wine stand upright for a day before decanting if possible, then pour very slowly and steadily; expect to waste a little at the end. This may be filtered through muslin or a filter paper as a 'butler's treat'. If you doubt your pouring ability use a funnel, either basic plastic or elegant silver. Some silver funnels incorporate sensible strainers.

Other silver paraphernalia you may acquire includes neck labels or cork holders which are really for show; coasters to keep your table ring-free; or the Heath Robinson decanting machine, which despite its appearance really does work. The wine is held in its metal cradle and the handle cranked to lower the neck towards a glass. It is intended for very delicate old wines such as Burgundy and vintage port and is certainly eye-catching, especially if your budget runs to the gold-plated version (rumoured to be exported in secret to Arab palaces).

A Wine Table

For a dinner or lunch where you intend to show off various good wines, remember to arrange appropriate glasses. These should include a large tulip-shaped glass for red wine; a smaller version for dry white; and perhaps a short-stemmed tulip for sweet Muscat or Sauternes, or a glass of port afterwards. Don't forget the water glass: a stemmed goblet looks attractive. And finally you will need flutes or similar for sparkling wine, otherwise how can it be a special meal? Arrange all these glasses directly in front of each place-setting in the French style as the British way of placing them to the right can confuse when several glasses are involved.

Your generosity may be boundless but if you want your guests to appreciate several wines during a meal you will have to exert a discreet form of rationing. If Champagne is your apéritif, replenish while glasses are still half-full and serve the first course fairly promptly. Allow five glasses per bottle although the tradition in the trade is to count six – home hosts are more generous than pubs as a rule.

Light white wine with the first course or courses may be served liberally and there may be some unfortunates who cannot or will not be partaking of the red to follow, so have enough to allow for them. Make sure there is plenty of cool tap water on offer, or serve bottles of lightly-sparkling mineral water from the fridge. Only half-fill the red wine glasses and explain this is not due to parsimony but to taste – encourage your guests to savour the aroma and bouquet of the wine without being too pedantic about it. And one glass of the sweet dessert wine is almost always enough for most drinkers!

SUN AT CHRISTMAS: The wine traveller in Australia and New Zealand

If you choose these distant Antipodean parts for a winter holiday, the familiar ingredients of a British Christmas will still be reassuringly present, but the sleet, frost and chill are magically banished by a benevolent Australian sun and the opportunity to go to the beach even on Christmas Day. All this *and* a wealth of wines to sample!

If you want to indulge in some wine-tasting, choose Adelaide, Melbourne or Sydney: the greatest concentration of vinous activity is in South Australia but the other areas also have plenty to attract the visitor.

First-time visitors are liable to be startled at the contrast to Australia's beer-swilling image so often portrayed in Europe. In fact it is a country of serious winemakers and drinkers at every level of quality from the drinkable basic 'cask' wines which offer wine on tap for outdoor life to the very fine and rare bottles often labelled individually by bin number. Grape varieties will be fairly familiar although the intensity of flavour may surprise those accustomed to the delicacy of European wine.

The traditional success stories in Australia have been the Riesling (often described as the Rhine Riesling); the Sémillon, used in the making of Sauternes and dry white Bordeaux in France; and the Shiraz, another spelling for the Syrah grape of the Rhône Valley. Formerly these varieties were used both for table and dessert wines, with some areas (near Sydney, for example) seen as impossible for light wines. Modern technology has been responsible for a change of direction and so now the lighter wines have taken over and the so-called 'sweaty saddle' aroma of an alcoholic red Shiraz is almost extinct. Dessert wines *are* still made of course and some Australian port is excellent – the Shiraz grape plays a part here too.

The famous duo of 'noble' grape varieties which must be among the most popular in the world of wine also make their mark in Australia. Cabernet Sauvignon has been planted for some time and is now frequently blended with Merlot for added complexity, with considerable success. Chardonnay, too, is becoming a force in the Australian wine world and indeed Australian wines have actually beaten the French in various 'blind' tastings. Sometimes it is blended with Sémillon which gives an unusual and distinctive dry style. Other more unusual white varieties include Traminer or Gewürztraminer, some examples of which can be very spicy indeed, and Sauvignon Blanc which is doing well in Australia as in California. Again, as in California, winemakers have grappled with the problems of growing Pinot Noir, the Burgundy grape, and only lately have some really attractive wines of this type begun to appear.

Although Australian winemakers are capable of high seriousness about their wines, they are also given to some amazing tricks of the wine trade, varying from the 'Kanga Rouge' which once swamped British shelves to Cab Mac, made by harvesting grapes straight into plastic bags which are then tightly sealed. In three weeks 'voilà!' – you have an instant version of Beaujolais Nouveau. They are also quite unscrupulous about borrowing names so you will spot lots of 'Champagne' (likely to be inexpensive and very drinkable) as well as 'claret', 'Burgundy' and 'Chablis'.

The most famous area within South Australia is the Barossa Valley where a vast amount of wine is produced in large wineries such as Seppelt. There are plenty of wine tours available and it is certainly an attractive area with its German-influenced architecture and wine festivals – emphasis on food as well as wine.

Smaller wineries may be seen in the Southern Vales, very close to

The dramatic landscape of the
Barossa Valley, South Australia

Adelaide and even running into the outskirts of the city itself. This was
once the home of full-bodied and very earthy red wines but today is
renowned for the fine port made by the Hardy and Reynella wineries as
well as excellent Chardonnay and most of the other top varieties.

Another essential stop on your South Australian tour is Coonawarra, an
area which has been making wine since the 1890s and is now very
highly regarded for good red wines made with Shiraz and Cabernet
Sauvignon (first planted in the early 1960s). There are some vast
operations here such as Wynn's, which owns no less than a third of the
total area of 4500 acres; they make every style from light Rhine Riesling
to four-year-old Cabernet Sauvignon, all sold at very competitive
prices.

Sydney has many attractions apart from wine and would make an
excellent choice as a holiday destination. The Hunter Valley is the
most famous wine area here in spite of its unlikely climate: it suffers
from excessive rain and humidity as well as hailstorms and intense heat.
Tyrrells is one of the most important wineries around, traditionally

THE HUNTER TOURIST
    ASSOCIATION,
Ground Floor,
City Hall,
King Street,
Newcastle 2300.

producers of wines made with white Sémillon and red Shiraz although now Chardonnay is becoming a winner. Other notable wineries are Saxonvale, Rosemount and the Rothbury Estate, as well as Lindeman's whose wines include the top-selling medium-dry white wine called Ben Ean and a selection of much older vintages dating back to the 1960s.

You can reach the Hunter Valley by car (in about two and a half hours) and there are hotels and motels in the area including chalets at the Rothbury Estate. Get more information from the Hunter Tourist Association.

Winemaking in the Coonawarra is on a massive scale but this does not mean a scarifice of quality

MAGAZINE ART LTD,
35 Willis Street,
Hampton 3188.

The scenery around Melbourne is extremely attractive with the Grampians and the old gold rush country, and this is close enough to Sydney for you to be able to manage both regions in one visit. You will eat well in Melbourne as this is where the gastronomes of Australia reputedly linger; write to Magazine Art Ltd in Hampton for a copy of their brochure. 'Dining Adventures in Victoria', and whet your appetite.

Some of the smaller wineries are in the Yarra area close to the city. Other areas to see include Bendigo, where the red wines are said to taste of peppermint; the Pyrenees area and then Great Western where bulk wines are often made into local 'Champagne'. In the nearby Goulburn Valley visit Chateau Tahbilk which has a history dating back more than a hundred years and is renowned for its red wines, especially some classic Shiraz. The winery is very decorative as well as interesting and is open daily for visits and picnics amid the vines.

New Zealand wines are impressing the most hardened of experts and gaining acceptance even in supermarkets in Britain. A great many founding fathers of the wine industry in New Zealand came from the Dalmatian coast of Yugoslavia to find an ideal grapegrowing climate, cool enough to rival the finest in Europe with time and experience.

Historic Château Tahbilk dates back a century

A plethora of signposts in the Hunter Valley

That moment seems to be arriving for New Zealand now and production has spread from a concentration around Auckland to the Gisborne and Hawke's Bay areas on the opposite side of the North Island and to the Marlborough area on the northern coast of South Island. The Germanic style has been predominant with a third of the land being planted with Müller-Thurgau. Cabernet Sauvignon is the principal red grape with the Palomino of Spanish origin, a blending grape, grown for 'box' wines. Chardonnay is a more recent success and Chenin Blanc and Gewürztraminer are also important. The cool climate favours white wines, a favourable commercial coincidence in this age of the dry white wine drinker.

Major producers include Cooks, who have their vineyards at Te Kauwhata near Auckland, home of the Viticultural Research Station; McWilliams, who are renowned for Cabernet Sauvignon; Montana, a Dalmatian firm by origin and now owned by the huge Seagram Corporation, producers of every New Zealand style and known for good value; and Hunters from the South Island who make extraordinary Chardonnay and Fumé Blanc (Sauvignon Blanc) somewhat like that produced in Alsace.

There are wine routes in all the major areas and many producers are well-geared to receive visitors. For more information write to the Wine Institute of New Zealand in Auckland West or the New Zealand Tourist Office in London.

THE SMITHS OF SOUTH AUSTRALIA

It is true to say that it has been an uphill struggle for Australian wine over the past twenty years. Since the unfortunate days of rough Australian red the image has been fixed and the quality level determined as somewhere below that of Algeria. As Michael Hill-Smith has said, 'Most Britons expect Australian wine to taste like a blend of methylated spirits and boot polish – but only half as palatable!' This was unfair even twenty years ago and today is downright unjust but prejudices die hard and the Australians themselves have not until recently exerted themselves enough to correct the false impression.

The Smiths of South Australia or, to be more precise, the Hill-Smiths of Angaston are among those in the forefront of the 'quality revival'. In typically Australian style their marketing methods are cheeky, with descriptions like 'South of France vineyard' peppering the copy (they go on to explain that the vineyard in question lies some 13,841 miles south of France). But the family have been making wine in this far-flung spot for nearly 140 years now, ever since a certain

Samuel Smith, a brewer from Dorset, set sail with his wife and four children, bound for Australia on the barque *China*. He began colonial life in Adelaide but soon took up a position as a gardener in the Barossa Valley, working for one George Angas (hence Angaston). Somehow he overcame the natural inhibitions of a brewer and perceived the potential of the country as future vineyard.

In 1849 he acquired thirty acres of land which he planted with vines: cuttings were fairly freely available as many settlers at that time were German or Swiss and brought vines as well as their grapegrowing expertise with them. This was a notable 'golden' year in Australia as in the USA and many sought to make fortunes from the rush for ore. Sam Smith had no qualms in joining the throng in the hope of increasing his acreage back home – after a singular lack of success at first he finally struck lucky in Victoria and was able to add another eighty acres, a horse and a plough to his domain. This new estate he called 'Yalumba', an Aboriginal word meaning 'the land of all around'.

YALUMBA VINEYARDS,
ANGASTON,
South Australia 5353.
Open: 9am weekdays,
10.30am weekends.

The rich earth of the Barossa Valley

Sam's son Sydney later took over the now flourishing business and built the winery which still stands today, described by one writer as 'rather like a solid Dorset railway station'. The current chairman of the company is Wyndham Hill-Smith, grandson of Sydney, who acquired the 'Hill' while at school. (Such was the proliferation of Smiths in the classroom that an extra name tag was needed.) Apart from wine his passion is for horses and he has interests in a Barossa stud farm on land once owned by George Angas.

Rob Hill-Smith (Wyndham's son) is now the company's marketing manager and cousins Michael and Matthew also play a part. Vineyard holdings are impressive: they own some 1000 acres themselves and buy in more grape from outside, quite a common practice in Australia. The family were pioneers in the Pewsey Vale region, a hilly area above the Barossa Valley floor which has proved ideal for Rhine Riesling. Their next venture was the Heggies vineyard, again in the hills on land which was formerly wooded and with its own lake, thus following the European tradition that 'the vine must see the water' for true quality. Their range encompasses all styles and prices from table wines such as Carte d'Or Rhine Riesling to fortified wines, notably some excellent port. Pewsey Vale has proved cool enough for the production of spicy Cabernet Sauvignon as well as Riesling and they also make woody Shiraz which deserves keeping.

A more recent venture is the separately run Hill-Smith Estate, specialising in premium wines from family vineyards in the eastern Barossa, currently some 200 acres. The company only dates from 1981 but already the wines have won more than their fair share of gold awards in the very serious Australian wine fairs. Varieties include all the classics: Rhine Riesling, described by one taster as 'definitive of Australian Rieslings'; a Sémillon aged in wood; and a Cabernet Sauvignon of notable complexity. The more obscure varieties include the Viognier of the Rhône Valley and the Malbec of Bordeaux. The facilities for visitors at the Hill-Smith Estate are less sophisticated than at Yalumba but wines are available for sale at Eden Valley Road, Angaston.

For general information about visiting Australia's vineyards write to the Australia Tourist Commission in Folkestone and they will send you a copy of their leaflet 'Discover the Wines of Australia', a wine map and a copy of their 'Australia Traveller's Guide'. Alternatively visit Australia House in London.

APPENDIX

A FEW NOTES ON WINE LAW

FRANCE

The Institut National des Appellations d'Origine was founded in 1932 to regulate the quality wine part of the French production. At the same time an Office National Interprofessionel des Vins de Table was organised to keep up standards on ordinary *vin de table*.

The various levels of quality now in operation are:

Appellation d'Origine Controlée (AC or AOC) – this is to ensure that the wine is exactly what it claims to be on the label. Precise quality control of each bottle (as in Germany) is not usual. The rules govern the grape varieties used, winemaking methods, alcoholic strength and the quantity produced from each vineyard. Pruning plays an important part in controlling the 'rendement' – the number of hectolitres per hectare permitted to be made into a named AC wine. An AC may apply either to a whole area eg Côtes du Rhône; to a village eg Fleurie; or to an individual vineyard eg Château Latour. The emphasis is on tradition and keeping to the zones and winemaking styles used over the centuries to make a certain distinctive quality wine. Inspectors are used to keeping winegrowers up to the mark and as a rule they do their difficult job with great rectitude; imagine having to distinguish between, say, the nine different Beaujolais villages in particular vats in a négociant's cellar.

Vin Délimité de Qualité Supérieure (VDQS)
This is the next quality level down from AC and many wines such as Cahors and Corbieres have been 'promoted' from this status to the AC. Again the emphasis is on tradition and preserving important wines which are not quite as fine as those awarded the AC.

Vin de Pays
This category has only existed since 1973 and covers all the simple *vins de table* which also have a regional origin rather than being bulk blends made from grapes grown over a wide area. Vin de Pays is something of a marketing term to make vin de table more attractive, especially abroad, and there is no guarantee of quality. Many are labelled according to the principal grape variety which is useful.

Vin de Consommation Courante
This is the proper name for everyday 'plonk', which may be blended with some wine from other EEC countries. The price is fixed according to the alcohol level.

GERMANY

German Wine Law
In truly Germanic style, the laws here are labyrinthine and very rigid, laid down for the most part in 1971 with some revisions since. Very roughly speaking, quality wines are categorised according to sweetness and in this northern clime sugar levels are of paramount importance. The following is an outline guide, sufficient to help your choice of wine without covering every technicality:

Qualitätswein mit Prädikat (QmP) is the top quality level and the wines are judged according to their sugar levels at the time of the harvest. An average wine made with ripe grapes is a *Kabinett* (the term historically means 'grower's reserve'). Grapes picked later are *Spätlese* ('late-picked') and these wines are slightly sweeter without being noticeably sugary in the mouth, except in rare hot summers like 1976.

Auslese wines are also made with late-picked grapes some of which may have been affected by botrytis (Edelfaule in German). A grower may choose either to leave some residual sweetness in Spätlese and Auslese wine by stopping the fermentation with sulphur, or to ferment out dry and have a high alcohol content. Hence you may see the term *trocken* on any of these wines, meaning there is very little residual sugar in the finished wine.

The fashion for dry wines is fairly new and seems to contradict the traditional image of German wines as sweet. Be sure to check the label carefully for mention of trocken if you are seeking a sweeter wine. Quality wines which are truly sweet are the rare *Beerenauslese*, made with selected very late-picked grapes, and *Trockenbeerenauslese*, which is only made with nobly rotted grapes (Edelfaule), each individually selected. Naturally these two wines are extremely rare and expensive. Finally, *Eiswein* is made with grapes literally frozen onto the vine; the freezing has the effect of concentrating the sugars and the resulting wine is high in acidity yet also very rich in sugars.

Reading a QmP Label
The first name is the town or village eg. Bernkastel. Add on 'er' for the possessive, hence Bernkasteler. The next name is that of the vineyard eg Doktor; Bernkasteler Doktor. The grape is often mentioned but if not you may assume it is made of Riesling in any QmP area. Finally comes the category eg Kabinett, Spätlese, Auslese.

The *second* name may not be a single vineyard but an official grouping known as a Grosslage eg Piesporter Michelsberg. There is no way to know if a single or collective vineyard is involved except by experience! In practice, this is not all that important for quality but do take good advice when choosing fine German wine from someone who does have experience.

Qualitätswein bestimmter Anbaugebiete (QbA): the essential difference between this and the higher category is that QbA wines are made with grape juice which has sugar added to raise the alcohol level artificially. QmP wines are entirely 'natural'. Adding sugar like this is quite legal but the wines are never of such flavour and style as the better category. A typical QbA style of wine is Liebfraumilch or those eminently drinkable wines often simply called house Mosel or house Hock.

Tafelwein Simple Tafelwein is rarely exported. A good deal is red, a watery wine not to British tastes at all. It may be made with wines imported from other European countries eg Italy.

Deutscher Tafelwein must be made with all-German grapes. Similarly *Sekt* may use imported grapes unless it is labelled *Deutscher* Sekt which must use only German grapes. It may also have a 'bA' added to the label which means that like the wine so labelled this sparkling wine comes from a specified region.

The *number* which appears on the neck label of German wine is the Prufungsnummer which proves the wine has been tasted by an official panel and analysed before bottling to ensure authenticity.

The 11 *principal wine areas* in Germany are the Rheingau, Rheinpfalz (or Palatinate); Rheinhessen; Nahe; Mittelheim; Ahr (chiefly for red wine;) Mosel-Saar-Ruwer; Baden; Franconia or Franken; and Wurttemberg in the south.

ITALY

The DOC Laws

These laws came into effect in 1963 in imitation of the French version. About 10 to 12% of Italian wine production is permitted to carry the DOC (Denominazione di Origine Controllata) and these wines must conform to minimum standards concerning growing area, grape types, cropping, alcohol level and ageing – similar controls to the French AC. As in France, the regulations tend to preserve the traditional and often ignore new developments such as the growing of unusual grape varieties in certain regions (eg Cabernet Sauvignon in the Veneto). So some fine wines are only allowed to be described as simple *vino da tavola* (the wines of Venegazzu, for instance).

There is a top-notch category for the very finest wines which has only recently been put into action. This is the DOCG – the G means Garantita – and the first four wines to be awarded this distinction are all red: Barbaresco, Barolo, Brunello di Montalcino and Vino Nobile di Montepulciano.

Addresses to note

FRANCE
FOOD AND WINE FROM FRANCE
Nuffield House, 41/46 Piccadilly
London W1V 9AJ
(Tel: 01-439 8371)

Champagne
THE CHAMPAGNE BUREAU
c/o Malcolm McIntyre & Partners
Crusader House
14 Pall Mall
London SW1Y 5LV
(Tel: 01-839 1461)

Cognac
THE COGNAC BUREAU
25 Westbourne Grove, London W2
(Tel: 01-221 2519)

GERMANY
WINES FROM GERMANY INFORMATION
    CENTRE
121 Gloucester Place
London W1H 3PJ (Tel: 01-935 8164)

ITALY
ITALIAN INSTITUTE FOR FOREIGN TRADE
37 Sackville Street
London W1X 2DQ (Tel: 01-734 2412)

SPAIN
VINOS DE ESPANA
22 Manchester Square
London W1M 5AP
(Tel: 01-935 6140)
(includes Rioja Wine Information
    Centre)

SHERRY INSTITUTE OF SPAIN
23 Manchester Square
London W1M 5AP (Tel: 01-487 5826)

PORTUGAL
PORTUGUESE GOVERNMENT TRADE
    OFFICE
1/5 New Bond Street
London W1Y 9PE (Tel: 01-493 0212)

AUSTRIA
AUSTRIAN WINE BOARD
11 Childs Place, London SW5
(Tel: 01-373 2552)

AUSTRALIA
SOUTH AUSTRALIA HOUSE
50 The Strand, London WC2
(Tel: 01-930 7471)

VICTORIA HOUSE
Melbourne Place, The Strand
London WC2B 4LG
(Tel: 01-836 2656)

AUSTRALIAN TRADE COMMISSION
Chatsworth House, Lever Street
Manchester M1 2DL (Tel: 061-236 9815)

CYPRUS
CYPRUS TRADE CENTRE
213 Regent Street, London W1
(Tel: 01-734 4791)

ENGLAND
ENGLISH VINEYARDS ASSOCIATION
    INFORMATION SERVICE
English Wine Centre
Drusilla's Corner, Alfriston
East Sussex BN26 5QS
(send an SAE for a leaflet about visiting
    English vineyards)

WINE DEVELOPMENT BOARD LTD
Five Kings House, Kennet Wharf Lane
Upper Thames Street
London EC4V 3BH (Tel: 01-248 5835)
(For general information about wines,
    leaflets and pictures)

WINE AUCTION HOUSES
CHRISTIE MANSON & WOODS LTD
8 King Street, St James's
London SW1Y 6QT (Tel: 01-839 9060)

PHILLIPS
7 Blenheim Street, London W1
(Tel: 01-629 6602)

SOTHEBY'S
34 New Bond Street, London W1
(Tel: 01-493 8080)

GRANDS CRUS CLASSÉS OF ST EMILION
(This classification is currently being revised)

Premiers Grands Crus Classés

Ausone	H. Dubois-Challon – H^tiers Vauthier
Cheval-Blanc	Fourcaud-Laussac
Beauséjour	Bécot
Beauséjour	Duffau Lagarrosse
Belair	Dubois-Challon
Canon	Fournier
Clos Fourtet	Lurton
Figeac	Manoncourt
La Gaffelière	De Malet-Roquefort
Magdelaine	J. P. Moueix
Pavie	Valette
Trottevieille	Borie Manoux

Grands Crus Classés

L'Angélus	De Bouard
L'Arrosée	Rodhain
Balestard la Tonnelle	J. Capdemourlin
Bellevue	Société Civile
Bergat	J. Bertin
Cadet-Bon	Gratadour
Cadet-Piola	Jabiol
Canon-la-Gaffelière	De Neipperg
Cap de Mourlin	J. Capdemourlin
Cap de Mourlin	J. Capdemourlin
Chapelle-Madeleine	H. Dubois-Challon – H^tiers Vauthier
Chauvin	Ondet
Corbin	Giraud
Corbin-Michotte	Boidron
Côte Baleau	Société Civile
Coutet	David-Beaulieu
Couvent des Jacobins	Joinaud Borde
Croque-Michotte	Géoffrion-Rigal
Curé-Bon	Landé
Dassault	Dassault
Faurie-de-Souchard	Jabiol
Fonplegade	Moueix
Fonroque	Moueix
Franc-Mayne	Theillassoubre
Gd-Barrail-Lamarzelle-Figeac	Carrère
Gd-Corbin-Despagne	Despagne
Grand-Corbin	Giraud

Grand Crus Classés

Grand-Mayne	Nony
Grand-Pontet	Barton-Guestier
Grandes-Murailles	Société Civile
Guadet-St-Julien	R. Lignac
Haut-Corbin	Guinaudie
Haut-Sarpe	Janoueix
Jean-Faure	M. Amart
Clos des Jacobins	Cordier
Clos la Madeleine	H. Pistouley
Clos St-Martin	Société Civile
La Carte	Bécot-Berjal
La Clotte	Chaillot
La Clusière	Valette
La Couspaude	E. Aubert
La Dominique	Fayat
Laniote	Freymont Roujat

Larcis-Ducasse	H. Gratiot
Lamarzelle	Carrère
Larmande	Meneret
Laroze	Melin-Gurchy
La Serre	L. d'Arfeuille
La Tour-du-Pin-Figeac	Giraud-Bélivier
La Tour-du-Pin-Figeac	Moueix
La Tour Figeac	Société Civile
Le Chatelet	Berjal
Le Couvent	Galhaud
Le Prieuré	Guichard
Matras	Bernard-Lefèbvre
Mauvezin	P. Cassat
Moulin-du-Cadet	Fagouet-Moueix
L'oratoire	Société Civile
Pavie-Decesse	Valette
Pavie-Macquin	F. Corre
Pavillon-Cadet	Le Morvan
P^t-Faurie-de-Soutard	Capdemourlin-Aberlen
Ripeau	M. Janoueix
Sansonnet	Robin
St-Georges-Côte-Pavie	Masson-Charoulet
Soutard	De Ligneris
Tertre-Daugay	De Malet-Roquefort
Trimoulet	P. Jean
Trois-Moulins	Gauthier
Troplong-Mondot	Valette
Villemaurine	Giraud
Yon-Figeac	Lussiez

The Graves Classifications of 1959

The vineyards of the Graves district were officially classified in 1953 and in 1959. Château Haut-Brion, is also officially classified with the great Médocs.

Classified red wines of Graves	COMMUNE	TONNEAUX
Château Haut-Brion	Pessac	150
Château Bouscaut	Cadaujac	120
Château Carbonnieux	Léognan	90
Domaine de Chevalier	Léognan	40
Château Fieuzal	Léognan	60
Château Haut-Bailly	Léognan	55
Château La Mission-Haut-Brion	Pessac	70
Château La Tour-Haut-Brion	Talence	18
Château La Tour-Martillac (Kressmann La Tour)	Martillac	50
Château Malartic-Lagravière	Léognan	45
Château Olivier	Léognan	10
Château Pape-Clément	Pessac	100
Château Smith-Haut-Lafitte	Martillac	140

Classified white wines of Graves	COMMUNE	TONNEAUX
Château Bouscaut	Cadaujac	18
Château Carbonnieux	Léognan	150
Domaine de Chevalier	Léognan	10
Château Couhins	Villenave-d'Ornon	40
Château La Tour-Martillac (Kressmann La Tour)	Martillac	6
Château Laville-Haut-Brion	Talence	20
Château Malartic-Lagravière	Léognan	6
Château Olivier	Léognan	80
Château Haut-Brion *	Pessac	16

* Added to the list in 1960.

The Sauternes and Barsac classification of 1855

As in the Médoc, the Sauternes vineyards were officially classified in 1855. This classification is known as the Official Classification of the Great Growths of the Gironde.

The total production from these vineyards represents approximately 25 per cent of the total Sauternes production, amounting roughly to 150,000 cases per year.

The following figures of production are approximate, and indicate average annual output, as given by the communes and taken from their Déclarations de Récoltes records.

	TONNEAUX
Premier Grand Cru (First Great Growth)	
Château d'Yquem	80
Premier Crus (First Growths)	
Château Guiraud	120
Château La Tour-Blanche	50
Château Lafaurie-Peyraguey	50
Château de Rayne-Vigneau	120
Château Sigalas-Rabaud	35
Château Rabaud-Promis	75

	TONNEAUX
Clos Haut-Peyraguey	25
Château Coutet	75
Château Climens	65
Château Suduiraut	110
Château Rieussec	90
Deuxieme Crus (Second Growths)	
Château d'Arche	80
Château Filhot	50
Château Lamothe	25

	TONNEAUX
Château Myrat	50
Château Doisy-Védrines	60
Château Doisy-Daëne	20
Château Suau	15
Château Broustet	30
Château Caillou	40
Château Nairac	25
Château de Malle	40
Château Romer	15

The Medoc Classification of 1985

	COMMUNE	HECTARES	TONNEAUX
Premiers Crus (First Growths)			
Château Lafite	Pauillac	88	300
Château Latour	Pauillac	59	200
Château Mouton-Rothschild*	Pauillac	70	250
Château Margaux	Margaux	42	200
Château Haut-Brion	Pessac. Graves	66	160
*Decreed a first growth in 1973			
Deuxièmes Crus (Second Growths)			
Château Rausan-Ségla	Margaux	37	130
Château Rauzan-Gassies	Margaux	21	50
Château Léoville-Las-Cases	St Julien	62	330
Château Léoville-Poyferré	St Julien	45	200
Château Léoville-Barton	St Julien	46	200
Château Durfort-Viviens	Margaux	35	90
Château Lascombes	Margaux	100	375
Château Gruaud-Larose	St Julien	76	330
Château Brane-Cantenac	Cantenac-Margaux	115	375
Château Pichon-Longueville-Baron	Pauillac	27	90
Château Pichon-Lalande	Pauillac	49	200
Château Ducru-Beaucaillou	St Julien	57	300
Château Cos-d'Estournel	St Estèphe	60	275
Château Montrose	St Estèphe	49	200
Troisièmes Crus (Third Growths)			
Château Giscours	Labarde-Margaux	75	300
Château Kirwan	Cantenac-Margaux	23	100
Château d'Issan	Cantenac-Margaux	35	130
Château Lagrange	St Julien	39	190
Château Langoa-Barton	St Julien	17	50
Château Malescot-Saint-Exupéry	Margaux	26	80
Château Cantenac-Brown	Cantenac-Margaux	32	150
Château Palmer	Cantenac-Margaux	40	140
Château La Lagune	Ludon	55	220
Château Desmirail	Margaux	0	0
Château Calon-Ségur	St Estèphe	70	260
Château Ferrière	Margaux	–	10
Château Marquis-d'Alesme	Margaux	12	45
Château Boyd-Cantenac	Margaux	18	60

	COMMUNE	HECTARES	TONNEAUX
Quatrièmes Crus (Fourth Growths)			
Château Saint-Pierre-Sevaistre	St Julien	17	60
Château Branaire	St Julien	43	160
Château Talbot	St Julien	76	340
Château Duhart-Milon-Rothschild	Pauillac	46	80
Château Pouget	Cantenac-Margaux	7	25
Château La Tour-Carnet	St Laurent	30	60
Château Lafon-Rochet	St Estèphe	40	160
Château Beychevelle	St Julien	53	275
Château Prieuré-Lichine	Cantenac-Margaux	57	260
Château Marquis-de-Terme	Margaux	29	170
Cinquièmes Crus (Fifth Growths)			
Château Pontet-Canet	Pauillac	65	280
Château Batailley	Pauillac	40	100
Château Grand-Puy-Lacoste	Pauillac	30	125
Château Grand-Puy-Ducasse	Pauillac	26	100
Château Haut-Batailley	Pauillac	22	80
Château Lynch-Bages	Pauillac	59	250
Château Lynch-Moussas	Pauillac	16	18
Château Dauzac-Lynch	Labarde-Margaux	40	160
Château Mouton-Baronne-Phillippe (formerly known as Mouton Baron Phillippe)	Pauillac	50	200
Château de Terte	Arsac-Margaux	50	200
Château Haut-Bages-Libéral	Pauillac	19	80
Château Pédesclaux	Pauillac	15	50
Château Belgrave	St Laurent	35	100
Château Camensac	St Laurent	13	50
Château Cos Labory	St Estèphe	15	50
Château Clerc-Milon	Pauillac	27	100
Château Croizet-Bages	Pauillac	22	90
Château Cantemerle	Macau	25	100

INDEX

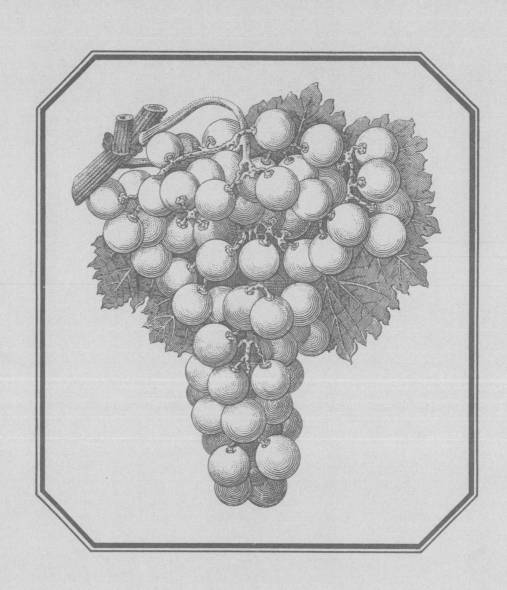